DE SOTO
and the Conquistadores

LONGMANS, GREEN AND CO.
55 FIFTH AVENUE, NEW YORK
221 EAST 20TH STREET, CHICAGO
TREMONT TEMPLE, BOSTON
128 UNIVERSITY AVENUE, TORONTO

LONGMANS, GREEN AND CO. LTD.
39 PATERNOSTER ROW, E C 4, LONDON
53 NICOL ROAD, BOMBAY
6 OLD COURT HOUSE STREET, CALCUTTA
167 MOUNT ROAD, MADRAS

HERNANDO DE SOTO
[From the 1728 edition of Herrera]

DE SOTO
and the Conquistadores

BY

THEODORE MAYNARD

Author of *Exile and Other Poems, Our Best Poets*, etc.

LONGMANS, GREEN AND CO.

LONDON · NEW YORK · TORONTO

1930

MAYNARD

DE SOTO

To *Michael*
Because he *Always* Wanted to Know who Won

"At the taking of *Atabalipa*, Lord of *Peru*, as at the assault of the city of *Cusco*, and in all other places where they found resistance, wheresoeuer hee was present, hee passed all other Captaines and principall persons."

From *Virginia Richly valued*, written by a Portugall gentleman of Eluas, emploied in all the action, and translated out of Portuguese by Richard Hakluyt.

PREFACE

I AM aware that from the aspect of artistic effectiveness it would have been well if I could have omitted from this book the early chapters dealing with the complicated affairs of Castilla del Oro and Nicaragua. In them De Soto [1] played a minor part, though one that steadily increased in importance. These matters, however, are essential to his story because it was under Pedrarias that he acquired as a young man his power of command and developed his soldiership. In the conquest of Peru he was subordinated to Pizarro, but without attempting to detract from the glory of that great man I have attempted to show that De Soto has never received the credit due to him for his share in that astonishing achievement. It was precisely the prestige he enjoyed because of this among his contemporaries that brought so large a body of enthusiastic recruits to his banner when his intention to invade Florida became known. For the first time a Spanish conqueror found himself with more volunteers than he needed, and was obliged to reject many

[1] The name should be Soto, except when written out in full, but I lack the hardihood of a thorough precisian and so follow the accepted mode.

[vii]

of them. Throughout the disasters of the expedition he was much more than the central figure: his was the single will sustaining the whole army.

The range of his conquests was perhaps greater than that of any other commander. From Central America to Cuzco, from the Carolinas to beyond the Mississippi takes in a block of the world five thousand miles long by three thousand wide; and these far-flung territories were traversed by him within ten years. Yet he died overwhelmed with a sense of his own failure.

There have been only three biographies of De Soto covering the whole of his career, for Theodore Irving, Grace King, and Cunninghame Graham confine themselves to the last three years of their hero's life. Lambert A. Wilmer published his book in 1858. In his preface he reproves Prescott and Irving for having made, as he says, so poor a use of the Spanish archives. Nevertheless, he does not, I think, cite a single authority with which these authors were unacquainted, or had failed to quote. But he does make a number of statements, giving no reference whatever in their support, which are mainly mythical. He seems to have worked upon the principle that if Prescott and Irving said no worse things than they did of the *Conquistadores* it must have been because they were suppressing the truth, which he might therefore with impunity guess at. He also freely added for the glorification of De Soto thick slices of romance. A large

PREFACE

part of his biography was apparently made up by Wilmer as he went along. Afterwards John Abbott rehashed Wilmer, and Frederick Ober rehashed Abbott.

I have to acknowledge the kindness of Professor Herbert I. Priestley, Mr. Irving B. Richman, and Dr. James A. Robertson for their reading of my manuscript. Each made valuable suggestions concerning details of this book. Most of these have been gratefully adopted; but I am not less grateful for those few which I could not use. Professor Josef Solterer, one of my colleagues, has been of great help in the correction of the proof.

T. M.

Georgetown University
Washington, D. C.

CONTENTS

LIST OF ILLUSTRATIONS

[xiii]

DE SOTO

and the Conquistadores

DE SOTO
and the Conquistadores

INTRODUCTION

I

PRESCOTT, in the introduction to *Ferdinand and
Isabella,* the earliest of his works, remarks that the
reign of these sovereigns is the proper basis for the
study of the history of Spain. It is true — especially as
applying to the hundred glorious years then begun, during which occurred that explosion of Spanish energy
which is perhaps the most brilliant chapter in all history.
In a single year, 1492, Granada was wrested from the
Moors, America was discovered, and the Jews were ex-
pelled. Twelve years previously occurred an event in-
timately, though obscurely, connected with the others
of the *annus mirabilis:* the Inquisition began to operate
in Spain with a peculiar thoroughness.

Ferdinand and Isabella may be taken as the two lobes
of the Spanish brain directing everything. The King
was by no means lacking in piety, but in the main he
represented political sagacity and practical ability; the

[1]

Queen was not lacking in these qualities, but her distinguishing contribution was an exalted religious passion. Ferdinand, left to himself, would in all probability not have initiated the furious drive of the Holy Office, though he certainly approved of the extirpation of heresy: that needed the mysticism or (if the word be preferred) the bigotry of Isabella the Catholic. But when the Inquisition had begun its work the King was glad to see the confiscated property of the condemned pass into the royal treasury. And this proceeding, Isabella, though she, unlike her husband, was untainted with a mercenary motive, felt to be eminently just.

In all the great happenings of the reign the virtuous Queen who made all her husband's shirts must be allowed to have been the moving spirit. It is true that she might not, indeed that she could not, have brought them all to success without the co-operation of the very able man who was her consort; but she was the inspirer where he was only the agent. She was a genius; he was merely capable.

It is this combination in the Spanish character of the qualities we see in collaboration in the two sovereigns which has been so confusing to historical commentators. The exploits of the *Conquistadores* have been accounted for, with too smug a facility, on the ground of their thirst for gold. It has even been suggested that the Inquisition was mainly a device for filling the coffers of the King. That in each case there was an eagerness to gain material profit cannot be denied; but it was not a chief motive. Avarice is always sterile of achievement. The man who becomes inordinately rich never exhibits any other capacity. He has a certain gift — it is his only gift, and is not to be acquired: any coin thrown in his direction sticks to him. An aged American multimillionaire recently confessed in a moment of candor that the basis of all immense fortunes is "pure green greed." It is the basis of nothing else.

Greed assuredly cannot explain Spain, by natural character the least avaricious of countries. George Santayana, in two magnificent odes offers us the right key. He tells us how Spain became "cursed with barren gold" by sending Columbus out to the New World. In that rocky country all men forgot their gain: the Tyrian, the Greek, the Roman, and the Arab. There even "the Semite became noble unawares." Why could not Columbus, he asks, have gone to Genoa, Venice, or "some shrewd princeling by the marshy mouth of Scheldt," or to England ?

These should have been thy mates, Columbus, these
Patrons and partners of thy enterprise,
Sad lovers of immeasurable seas,
Bound to no hallowed earth, no peopled skies.

Columbus did not go to other countries because none of them would have had the imagination to let him test his vision. If Aragon and Castile supported him, it was for one reason:

Those thoughts, to Spain's fresh deeds allied,
Painted new Christian conquests, and her hand
Itched for that sword, now dangling at her side,

DE SOTO AND THE CONQUISTADORES

Which drove the Moslem forth and purged the land.
And then she dreamed a dream her heart could under-
stand.

These lines reveal the inner truth about the Spanish adventurers. Their mainspring was religion. But, while the missionary enthusiasm was never lost, it became confused with something which blended with it, yet was different and inimical. That the heathen were to be converted meant in practice that the heathen were to be conquered: that the heathen were to be conquered meant that the heathen were to be despoiled. The fantasticality of Spanish chivalry is the theme of one of the world's greatest books. In it the eyes of Cervantes are fastened upon the antique ideal, which they see to be at once adorable and absurd. Transferred to America that chivalry became, all the more easily because of its naïveté, burnished and tarnished with gold.

Circumstances made this inevitable: the temptation was too extreme for frail humanity. To the everlasting credit of her rulers it must be remembered that they always held steadily before them a noble policy and did their utmost to restrain the rapacity of their own colonial administrators.

The active self-discipline has been too often forgotten, the rapacity too often remembered. And now that Spain has receded from conquest — even if the recession, like the conquest, was to some extent forced upon her — she is pointed out by the fat merchant nations as an instance of the doubtful law of inevitable ethnic decadence. Really she has returned to the orbit of her native genius,

[4]

exhausted, as well she might be, by her expenditure of
energy; and in repose is renewing her spiritual force.

And now within her sea-girt walls withdrawn
She waits in silence for the healing years.   *✓ rud. ` comp .*

II

THE reign of Ferdinand and Isabella has been taken as
the starting point of this book. The Inquisition offers
the necessary clue.

In 1480 the Holy Office, which had existed since the
thirteenth century, began to operate in Spain without
qualification, with a ruthlessness it exhibited nowhere
else. The Pope in fact considered its zeal excessive, and
tried in vain to restrain it.

The Spaniards thought they knew what they were
about. The Inquisition was not, in their case, directed
primarily against Protestants — for there were none in
their country then, and few later. Indeed it perhaps was
unfortunate, as Hilaire Belloc suggests, that the nation
during the Reformation, which was so near at hand,
never had to bend its strength against and subdue the
grim theology of Calvin. The Spanish Inquisition was
faced with a different and a unique problem.

Upon the rugged peninsula only gradually and with
infinite pain — "inch by inch, each step counting a century" — says Hubert Howe Bancroft, the Christian people had been able to push back the Moslem conquerors.
It was a campaign lasting eight hundred years and including three thousand battles that was brought to its

triumphant close under the generalship of Gonsalvo de Córdoba, the Great Captain.

Upon the establishment of the Inquisition, though the end was already in sight, much remained to be done. The country was still full of Mohammedans and of Jews, the allies of Islam — many of them in very high places — who found it to their interest to pretend an acceptance of the Faith. Seville is said to have contained a hundred thousand of these "New Christians." It was this class of *Moriscos* and *Marraños* that constituted the greatest danger to the Christian state. The now united kingdoms had no intention of allowing what they had won by their heroic struggle to be undermined by the insidious burrowing of treachery. Accordingly, the "New Christians" were watched and, when detected in the clandestine practice of their religion, were apprehended and put to death. Those who openly professed the law of Israel or Islam were not at first molested — and never by the Inquisition — though they were under grave disabilities.

All European societies at that time accepted the principle that heresy — logically a crime worse than murder, since it destroys the soul — was a capital offence. Its extirpation was regarded as a surgical operation, to which pain, however grievous, was only incidental. Strange as it may seem, Torquemada was a notably compassionate man.

Protestants, a little later, concurred quite as fully as Catholics in the theory of the righteousness and necessity of religious persecution. But Spain, because of the special problems presented by the presence in the community of a large number of concealed Jews and Moslems, practised it with a thoroughness which has appalled the conscience of all other races.

Let us not fall into the common mistake of calling the chorus of horror hypocritical. England, under the half-Spanish Mary Tudor, was shocked at the burning of Protestants, though the people were at that time overwhelmingly Catholic in sentiment. The reason is that burning was a form of execution which violently twisted some nerve in the national character. Englishmen objected to the Spanish technique, not at all to the Spanish principle. They themselves used torture freely: it was the accepted judicial procedure of the time. And they had no objection to persons whom they considered heretics being killed. But burning affected their imagination in quite another way. During the reign of Elizabeth, huge crowds went out in holiday mood to see innocent priests dragged on hurdles to Tyburn, hanged, cut down while still alive, disembowelled, and quartered. And nobody seemed to mind it in the least, unless those who suffered felt a faint distaste. As for the "crop-headed Irish kerns" slaughtered by the thousand, who was ever so sentimental as to dream of raising any protest on their account ?

The fierce religious temper of Spain (where, it must be remembered, the Inquisition was immensely popular) carried the nation on to the decision of expelling all the Jews in the kingdom. So drastic an act was attended with inevitable cruelty. This we must deplore. We may regard it also as an error in statecraft. But we must not forget the idea that prompted it: that Spain could not be

fully herself while secret Jews were within her borders.
The Moslems also went; but as they were known to be
a simple military race they were not regarded as so dangerous once they had been decisively crushed.

In the same year that this happened, and that the Great
Captain reduced the last stronghold of Islam, Spain,
swept and upborne by a wave of religious enthusiasm,
sent Columbus westward to discover the Indies.

The famous explorer had the red hair and blue eyes
that so often indicate the mystic or the twin-brother of
the mystic, the practical mystic, the man of action. He
was, it must be admitted, something of a charlatan, with
his eloquence and braggadocio; but he was profoundly
devout, and like all mystics he had patience. If he
made extravagant demands upon his royal patrons it was
in order to use the profits of his expedition for the redemption of the holy places from the infidels. He was
buried, as were Michelangelo and Dante, in the habit of
the third order of St. Francis.

III

WITH a fortitude developed in the long wars against the
Arabs, and fired by the example of the Inquisition, the
Spaniards went out to conquer the New World. They
regarded themselves as crusaders, and were convinced of
their divine mission to win to the cross the heathen in
the Indies lately discovered. It was this conviction, not
their supposititious greed, that enabled them to endure all
that awaited them.

The *Conquistadores* were not always admirable or edifying men; but they were absolutely sincere, and, in their soldierly fashion, very devout. Among all the conquerors, there is only one recorded example of irreligion — that of the picturesque ruffian Francisco de Carbajal, who at the age of eighty-four was executed by the Pacificator Gasca. He jested all the way to the scaffold, as though he were a saint like Sir Thomas More and, when urged by the attendant priests to say at least the Our Father and the Hail Mary as a sign of penitence, snarled, silencing them by shocking them at his obduracy, "Our Father, Hail Mary — there !" With this solitary exception the Spanish adventurers were not only pious but apostolical in spirit.

The trouble is that, being so confident that they were conferring an inestimable benefit upon the aborigines by converting them, they had no patience with any failure to recognize that benefit. All resistance was considered to be wickedness prompted by the Devil, and was drastically dealt with. Spaniards had preserved the Faith at home by the use of arms; they could not be expected to have much compunction at extending it in their provinces by the same means. They did not look upon this as cruelty, but as the truest form of kindness.

All the same their severity has been grossly exaggerated. It must be granted that many terrible things were done by them; but these were not merely unauthorized, they were condemned by the Council of the Indies. Las Casas was by no means the only man who denounced the crimes of the administrators; and the Crown always appointed a priest as Protector of the Indians. Señor Salvador de Madariaga has well summed up the matter:

"Taken as a whole, the exploration and colonization of America by the Spaniards is perhaps the most inhuman, but also the most human, of its kind. Spaniards were, no doubt, the men who committed the abuses and ill-treatments so often exposed since; but the Spaniards also, were those who laid down the standards of humanity by which the inhuman acts of their countrymen were condemned. And while the former, the brutal and unscrupulous colonizers, found imitators, and do to this day, the latter were far in advance of their time, and even of ours."

It is a just claim. Exactly forty years after the momentous voyage of Columbus, Francisco de Vitoria, a Dominican theologian, delivered a series of lectures in the University of Salamanca which has made that eminent authority, James Brown Scott, call him the father of international law. In this the Dominican amplified the teaching of St. Isidore of Seville and St. Thomas Aquinas; but, by going back to them for his principles, he ran counter to the conscienceless political theories of the Renaissance, and propounded a system superior in several respects to the colonial policy of the present day. It is Vitoria and not Grotius who is the first international lawyer. The Dutch writer confesses time and time again his indebtedness to his Spanish predecessor.

It is true that the Spanish government would have strongly dissented from Vitoria's argument that the Pope, having no jurisdiction over the Barbarians, can give none; but it is significant that, although the Inquisition was operating in Spain, Vitoria was never called to account:

his theological position was recognized as being too sound.

Indeed, though the court of Spain was ready enough to avail itself of Alexander VI's dubious partition of the Americas between the kingdoms of the peninsula, it also accepted, even before Vitoria propounded them, that friar's main conclusions and exercised its powers in a humane temper. Machiavelli admiringly sneers at Ferdinand, saying that he never preached anything else but peace and good faith and to both was most hostile, therefore rising from being an insignificant prince to the position of the foremost king in Christendom. In this he is unfair. Ferdinand, like Isabella and their grandson Charles V, did all he could to see that the Indians were fairly treated.

To what extent the *Conquistadores* carried out the instructions of the King's Requisition will appear in the pages of this book, where the worst that can be said of them is faithfully set down, as well as the best. It is notorious that the infamous Pedrarias often ignored his orders; but he was removed from office in consequence. Most of the colonial officials, however, tried to follow the general lines of Spanish policy, though it sometimes happened that in an altogether unforeseen emergency they had to act in contradiction to it.

We must never forget the difficulties of their position, nor that if they inflicted severe punishment upon recalcitrant and treacherous savages, they were prepared to bear, and did bear, at least an equal amount of suffering themselves. It is a little smug for us, living our comfortable sheltered lives, to reprove men in a desperate extremity for their harshness.

Let us also compare the Spanish eagerness to convert and educate the Indians, the readiness for assimilation on both sides, with the icy aloofness of the Puritan or Virginian colonist. The advantage is, at every point, with the Castilian. It was the Spaniards who built the first cities in the New World, who founded the first churches, hospitals and universities, who printed the first books, and who made in the seventeenth century the first rudimentary newspaper.

Let us not press the *tu quoque* argument to the point of making it embarrassing to our illustrious selves. A decent veil must be drawn over the nigger-snatching of Hawkins, of the slavery of the West Indies and the Southern States, of Lord Amherst's ingenious method of clearing away inconvenient Indians by distributing among them blankets infected with small-pox, of the systematic extermination of the Irish — fellow Christians — under Elizabeth and Cromwell, of the perfidy of Drogheda, or (to come a little closer to our own time) of the British savagery at Badajoz, or of the cannon from whose mouths mutinous sepoys were blown to fragments, or of the Amritzar massacre, within the memory of our own school-children, or of a recent lynching when a pregnant woman was jeered at for her figure as she was being hanged. If there can be any ground for excusing such enormities, the Spanish conquerors, acting under greater provocation, have a still better defence. Their method of administering a few terrible blows was — judged as pol-

THE SIXTEENTH-CENTURY CONCEPTION OF THE INDIANS

[From De Bry]

icy — successful, and in its result, though possibly not in its intention, ultimately merciful.

It may be argued that, though they were few in numbers, the armor and firearms of the Spaniards gave them advantages so overpowering as to take from them most of the glory of their conquests. This is not the case. The moral effect of firearms was, doubtless, considerable; and without armor they would soon have been wiped out by arrows tipped with bone or by swords of obsidian. But the Spanish arquebuses were crude, laboriously loaded, and short-ranged; and they possessed exceedingly few of them. The sole signal advantage of the *Conquistadores* lay in their possession of horses. These gave them a decisive mobility.

What really made them unconquerable, however, was not their equipment but their unexampled military aptitude and valor. That valor reposed upon and was animated by their faith. The early history of America is the story of a crusade.

CHAPTER I

DARIEN IS FOUNDED

AT THE beginning of the sixteenth century the centre of Spanish exploration was Darien, in what is now known as the isthmus of Panama. Thither, to fabulous Asia as they supposed — for not until the return of Magellan's expedition was America ascertained to be a distinct continent — sailed adventurers on fire for the discovery and conquest of the Golden Chersonese. "Upon the imagination of such," says Washington Irving, "the very idea of an unknown sea and splendid empire broke with the vague wonders of an Arabian tale."

To the colonies came, as usually happens in such cases, the best and the worst of men: dreaming youths, valiant gentlemen, and greedy old scoundrels who were sure that they could make their fortunes in these newly discovered lands where gold was in every river and where pearls abounded in the ocean. And many a cavalier who had sold or mortgaged the whole of his possessions to buy the fine horse and armor needed for following the Great Captain to Italy, and was in want of occupation since the campaign had been cancelled, thought to find in the Indies a profitable use for his rusting equipment. In

Darien the *hidalgo* formed part of a very mixed crowd of knights-errant and cut-throats. There were, it is true, many of his own class there, young, ardent, brilliant—such men as Coronado, Bernal Díaz, the historian of Cortés, Oviedo, a still more famous historian afterwards, Almagro, and Pascual de Andagoya — but he and they came into close contact with others of a totally different stamp, rough, boorish, down on their luck, some of them just out of jail minus their ears, making a fresh and ruffianly start in the new world.

Many of these men became planters, for they had been given lands by a government at home that wished to get the colonies quickly settled and Spain freed from undesirables. But every planter had a sword within reach and sometimes found, as did Pizarro, who had been a *ranchero,* a quicker way to get rich than by digging the soil.

There was also a sprinkling of government officials — for the most part elderly men — and of priests, who were generally young enthusiasts eager for the conversion of the heathen, but with here and there among them a middle-aged cleric now *in partibus infidelium* because his bishop thought he would do less harm abroad.

Those who went to the new colony had had their imaginations fired by accounts of La Española, and expected to find a bright-blossomed, palm-shaded paradise, basking by a halcyon sea. Instead Darien was a patch of low-lying land in an isthmus that was an unbroken range of all but impassable mountains which concentrated the heat upon the settlement. It was situated upon a pestilential swamp, infested with cohorts of the most ferocious species of mosquitos. For dragons there were alligators, and for vampires large bats, whose bite was frequently fatal. [1] In the waters were the jagged-toothed shark and, far more hideous, the octopus with its soft, quivering, monstrous arms. Miasma and a burning sky, desolation, hunger, drouth, death: all except the last were the universal portion: the ultimate evil came to many.

The hardier ones got inured to the rigors of colonial life, but became, like the men who had preceded them, "all pale and yelowe, like unto them that have the yelowe jaundice." Peter Martyr writes of them to Julius II: "These olde souldiers of Dariena were hardened to abide all sorrowes, and exceedingly tollerable of labour, heate, hunger and watching, in so much that merrily they make their boast that they have observed a longer and sharper Lent than ever your holiness enjoyned: for they say that for the space of foure whole yeere they eate none other than hearbes and fruits, except now and then perhappes fysshe, and very seldom fleshe; yea, and that sometime for the lack of all these, they have not abhorred from mangie dogs and filthie toads."

Pedrarias, who was seventy-four when he went out as Governor, felt this was altogether too much for a man of his years to endure. He had no single day free from the pain of his ailments; and shortly before leaving Spain had actually died, to all appearance. In the nick of time, while his body was lying in church awaiting burial, he

---

[1] On the other hand, Peter Martyr tells an "amusing story" to the Pope of a servant to the friars who was sick and who appeared to be dying, the surgeon having tried vainly several times to draw blood from his veins. While abandoned to his death, he was saved by a bat settling upon him and gorging itself with blood, leaving the vein open.

THE DRAGONS OF DARIEN
[From Montanus' *America*, Amsterdam 1671]

AMERICAN INDIANS
[From a print in the British Museum, made at Augsberg *circa* 1500]

revived. Catalepsy, he surmised, would have less chance in Darien.

He was, therefore, all in favor of abandoning the colony and would have done so had his council permitted it. Reluctantly, under pressure, he stayed, but built a house upon a neighboring mountain where the air was better than in the town, and reserved for himself the best food available. His care of his health was rewarded by sixteen more years of life.

It was this man who was the patron of Hernando de Soto, having paid for his education at the University of Salamanca, provided his equipment and passage to the New World, and obtained for him the commission of a captain of dragoons; it was this man, too, who was the personal mentor of his protégé as well as the responsible director of the administrative policy of Darien.

Pedro Arias de Avila, Count of Puño en Rostro, or Pedrarias, as he is generally called, was an interesting and detestable figure. He had been a good soldier in his time and a famous rider in the tilting-yard, but impaired health had soured his temper, and made him suspicious and irritable. With him had come to the colony his wife, a niece of Beatrice de Babadilla, the renowned Marchioness of Moya, the bosom friend of Isabella the Catholic. Their eight children had been left behind in Spain.

Bancroft has called the dark, grizzled governor "the swarthy-souled." The Spanish colonists had a still harder name for him: to them he was *Furor Domini.* Every historian damns him.

All the same we must very heavily discount many of

the charges that have been brought against him and others of the *Conquistadores*. The good Las Casas, for example, brings all his accusations under suspicion because of what are obvious and fantastic exaggerations. He tells of pregnant women thrown into pits full of stakes upon which they were impaled; of a gallows just high enough to allow those who were hanged upon it — in batches of thirteen "in honour and reverence of our Redeemer and the twelve Apostles" — to have their feet burned as they died; of a victim who was being slowly roasted to death over a trestle being gagged so as not to disturb with his groanings the siesta of his executioner; of Montejo in Yucatan feeding his dogs on Indian babies. And while all these things might be just possible, he snaps our straining credulity when he writes of Alvarado, the hero of the famous leap of the *Noche Triste,* acting in the following fashion in Guatemala: "It was his custom when he went to make war on some town or province, to take with him as many of the Indians as he could, to fight against the others; and as he had ten or twenty thousand and gave them nothing to eat, he allowed them to eat the Indians they captured. And so a solemn butchery of human flesh took place in his army where, in his presence, children were killed and roasted; and they would kill a man only to eat his hands and feet, which were esteemed the best bits." [2]

It is the same thing with his figures. He puts the

---

[2] See the print facing this page. It is taken from the German translation of Las Casas published in 1599. The English edition of 1656 reproduces some of the German illustrations (badly) but improves upon them to the extent of changing, when possible, the sex of the sufferer, so as to make the point more effective by increasing the horror.

A GERMAN ILLUSTRATION TO LAS CASAS, 1599

number of those exterminated by his countrymen at from twelve to fifteen millions, or, if we take his computations province by province, at twenty millions. The computations are self-evidently preposterous. There were nothing like that number of aboriginal inhabitants in Central and South America at the beginning of the sixteenth century and had there been it would have been physically impossible for a handful of Spaniards to have slaughtered so many people.

But it was an age when propaganda[3] to be effective had to pass far beyond the bounds of reason. To be believed at all Las Casas had to allow a heavy margin for disbelief.

The accuser of the Conquerors wildly exaggerated, but had nevertheless, some grounds for his charges. The conditions of colonial life, its rigors, its precariousness, its remoteness from civilization, coupled with the insidious workings of the climate, told to some extent even upon men naturally kindly. They came too easily to justify to themselves the terrorism which had grown to be a system, on the ground that these Indians were children who had to be taught their lesson by whipping. Once docility had been achieved by these means a fatherly gentleness, that gentleness so strictly enjoined by the court should follow. In the meanwhile the only true form of kindness was severity.

Then, too, there were spasms of panic. "When the Spanish looked out to the mountains and the plains," as

[3] The propaganda of the *Brevissima Relación* could be, and very promptly was, turned against Spain, who was hated because of her ascendency by all the other European nations. De Bry even tries to show that the Spaniards were cowards — which is going a little too far.

Herrera puts it, "the boughs and the very grass which grew high in the savannahs appeared to their excited imaginations to be armed with Indians, and when they turned their eyes towards the sea they fancied it was covered with the canoes of their exasperated foemen." The rigidity of the Spanish mind made it incapable of understanding the savages, who could pass at a moment's notice from abject docility to insane fury. If the Indians were attacking, they could be killed in fair fight; if they were quiet, it was a sign that they were hatching mischief — so they were hanged to be on the safe side.

Gradually the conscience became calloused from habit. And there were convenient devices in Darien, as elsewhere, for stilling its inconvenient movement. Queen Isabella had been appalled, for example, that Columbus — her Columbus! — had brought slaves to Spain. The Crown accordingly forbade the enslavement of the Indians unless (here was the fatal loop-hole!) they were prisoners captured in just war. Very well, since that was how matters stood, ways should be devised — it was not a difficult matter — of provoking war. The justice of it was a problematical question that monks could settle at their leisure.

There was another loop-hole in the humane instructions given to the officials. Cannibals might be seized and sent to distant provinces "in order that, being in the service of Christians, they might the more readily be converted and brought to our Holy Catholic Faith." It was soon unhappily (or happily, according to the taste) discovered that the Indies swarmed with cannibals. Again the policy was distorted by the administrator.

It was all very well for the learned members of the Council to lay down the law as to what should or should not be done. The man on the spot needed slaves and *repartimientos*. If they were going to throw themselves away tanned and tattered on this blighted soil, gold would have to sweeten their sacrifice. So if a *cacique* was coy about handing over the trinkets of his village, a little torture was applied. If he was still obdurate, the bloodhounds made an end of him.

With gold coming suddenly into the hands of men unaccustomed to it, an orgy of reckless gambling began. It was the only amusement available, and it led to murderous quarrels and a frenzied waste of time. The King, understanding this, had prohibited the sending of playing-cards to the colonies; but packs were bootlegged, and there were ways of gambling that did not necessitate the use of cards. The Council of the Indies then legislated on the matter. A twenty-four hours' loss at play was to be limited to ten *castellaños*. Ten *castellaños*! A man scorned to have a stake less than a gold piece; and a slave was a common wager. What hope was there of enforcing the law when Pedrarias himself, the members of his council and all his officers were forever at the table? The first instance of prohibition in the New World has a history similar to that of a more recent noble experiment.

The Governor was known to play away a hundred slaves at a sitting. He could replace them upon his next excursion into the interior. The hunting of the Indians for their labor and their gold became a method of relieving boredom. It provided occupation and a means of paying gambling debts. If the rough trooper of Spain, or his officers, felt any compunction in the matter, they could easily resolve it with the reflection that all men in that lost land were desperate and doomed.

It will be seen that Darien when Hernando de Soto went out there in 1519 at the age of nineteen was an acid test for any man's morale. He took out, as Hakluyt's translation of the *Relation* of the Gentleman of Elvas puts it, nothing of his own save his sword and his target. He went back to Spain sixteen years afterwards with an enormous fortune. But he had to wait the first thirteen years of that time without notable advancement. He owed everything to a gambler's throw in Peru — for he too was a gambler, though a careful one, playing only for high stakes and when gain seemed certain. He was destined later to lose everything he had won upon another cast of the dice; and to find in his ruin undying fame.

He supposed, as did the other adventurers to the western shores, that gold was as common there as stones in the streets of Xerez, his birthplace. But, unlike so many, he did not become impatient with fortune's delays, for he had at his command — as he was to show in Florida — almost unlimited staying-power.

A handsome, curly-haired, swarthy boy, he arrived fresh from the university, more deeply read in horses and in arms than in books; proud, like all the Spaniards, but engaging, eager, and extraordinarily level-headed for one of his years. We early hear of him entering into a partnership with Hernán Ponce de León and Francisco Campañón, brother-officers, by which they pooled their possessions. It was the basis of his subsequent success. For when Pizarro sought him out to help in the conquest of Peru, he went to him because De Soto was not only an excellent soldier, but a man of substance.

Though De Soto was shrewd, however, he was not supple-minded. He exhibited in Florida an obstinacy that was absolute. He formed, it is true, his conclusions after reviewing all the available facts in a given case and listening to all possible arguments against it; but the conclusions, once formed, were irremovable.

With this stubbornness of will and fixity of judgment went a quality that appeared to be opposed to them: too great a trust, too sanguine a temperament. In part this came from the frankness of the man, his most charming characteristic. But part of it was due to the narrower as well as the more generous elements in his being. His confidence in his own judgment was excessive, and he would never admit a mistake or seem to admit weakness by a retreat, however strategic that retreat might be.

To say that he was a Spaniard is to say that he was brave. But even among Spaniards he was marked for his impetuous courage. He was at his best in spontaneous actions, not in those that were carefully considered. As a cavalry leader under the command of a man like Pizarro, he was unexcelled. In supreme command he displayed — along with very great qualities, such as promptness in emergency, resourcefulness in ruse, and an intrepid leadership that endeared him to his men — a rashness in attack, and a carelessness in making proper dispositions for defence, that time and time again brought his army to the verge of complete disaster. He counted too much upon his ability to extricate himself by some brilliant exploit.

The tutelage of his kinsman and patron (afterwards father-in-law) Pedrarias was in many ways unfortunate. We do not know positively what part De Soto had in the harrying of the savages; though Oviedo, who knew him in Darien, describes him as being much given to the sport of hunting Indians. His name does not, at all events, figure in any of the recorded atrocities; but he was probably obliged to do, under the direct orders of the Governor, pieces of sufficiently dirty work. And he is not likely to have been squeamish about it. What we do know positively is that on several occasions — notably in his vigorous protest against the trial and execution of Atahualpa — he showed himself to be a man conspicuously honorable and humane. No single act of cruelty stained his name in Peru. And when he was *Adelantado* in Florida his severities were never wanton, but were called for by military necessity.

We have one glimpse of him in action soon after he had arrived in Darien, in one of those few military operations against the Indians that may be dignified with the name of battle. He was still hardly more than a boy, just twenty-one, but he has already learned the art of command. On two successive days he charges at the head of his dragoons, and each time saves a Spanish army from destruction. A remarkable feat on the part of so young an officer.

In 1521, Urraca, a chieftain of considerable ability and persistence, ruling in the district of the river Nata, began a formidable rebellion. It was never quelled; for, when defeated, he took to the mountains, where with varying success he resisted the advance of the white man until his own death in 1530. The danger of his offensive was crushed at the outset of the nine years' sporadic war.

Upon the first gesture of his defiance, two small columns were sent against him, one of two hundred men under the command of Francisco Pizarro and the other of a hundred men under that of the *Alcalde Mayor,* Gaspar de Espinosa. This lawyer had discovered in himself military talents worth cultivating, but amused his soldiers by riding out to battle upon an ass. That mild and stubborn beast he felt, perhaps, to be better suited than a horse to a person of his sedentary habits.

Espinosa went to the seat of the rising by sea, while Pizarro, with De Soto, who captained thirty dragoons, followed by land.

Urraca, upon the disembarkation of Espinosa's force, went boldly out against it. A group of Indian auxiliaries had been sent forward as scouts by the Spaniards. These were surrounded and wiped out. Encouraged by this success, Urraca immediately attacked the main body of the army, using the poisoned arrows so dreaded by all who had to face them. These were weapons against which armor was but slight protection, since a wound made between the joints of the mail or on the hand or face was sufficient to cause death. Such arrows or darts could be aimed accurately and rapidly, and made the use of bloodhounds ineffective. Espinosa's men began to fall back before an onslaught conducted with the determination and skill Urraca showed.

Things would have gone badly that day for the gallant lawyer had not De Soto arrived at the moment of extremity. The young captain had been sent forward by Pizarro, who was himself hard beset, to find a pass through which the two divisions of the Spanish forces could affect a juncture. He found it, but found, too, that Espinosa was in full flight for the refuge of his ships, with the yelling warriors of Urraca in hot pursuit.

The intervening ground was broken with rocks and gulleys — a most difficult place for cavalry operations. De Soto's eye took in at a glance that he would waste time by attempting to ride directly towards Espinosa. He would have had to cut his way through, under a handicap, to the distressed commander; for there was no clear space for a charge. He wheeled, therefore, to the left instead, and unmolested gained the open stretch sloping towards the beach. Then the thirty dragoons, having now ample room for a charge, with flashing sabres and the battle-cry of "Santiago!" crashed down upon the Indians who were already closing in to intercept Espinosa's flight. In all directions they scattered as the steel did its deadly work, making little attempt to stand before the impact of mounted men.

Espinosa, reinforced by De Soto, and seeing Pizarro's contingent moving through the pass, insisted upon advancing again, with the result that he became cut off from the sea in a place where there was no chance for De Soto to use his cavalry effectively. There was only one thing to do now; wait for the arrival of Pizarro.

That officer understood much better than did Espinosa the jeopardy in which they all stood and, taking charge of the situation, made an effort to regain the open plain under cover of the darkness. The wily Urraca allowed his enemies to go just so far as to get themselves securely bottled up in a narrow defile. The whole army was now in the gravest danger of annhilation. They represented the largest effective force that the Spaniards could put into the field in Darien. Their decisive defeat would have been the signal for a general rising; and possibly the expulsion of the Christians from the isthmus.

Pizarro was always at his best in a crisis of this sort, and he had at hand the very man he needed for the emergency. At the first glimmer of dawn, before the exultant hosts of Urraca had the opportunity to come again to the attack, De Soto banged through the opening of the defile. Coming behind the hurling momentum of the weight of his metal, followed the steady footmen of Pizarro. They suffered heavily, being vastly outnumbered, but succeeded in bursting open the bottle-neck and in gaining the beach, where, under the protection of the dragoons, the army took refuge in the ships.

Espinosa, whose life had been saved, had a good reason for having a high opinion of Pizarro's generalship. It was he who afterwards secretly financed the Peruvian expedition. And Pizarro, for his part, had an equally good reason for wishing to enlist for his great enterprise the impetuous valor of De Soto.

CHAPTER II

CONFLICT AND INTRIGUE

FROM the beginning the régime of Pedrarias was one of internal conflict. He was sent out in 1514 to supersede Vasco Nuñez de Balboa, whose discovery of the Pacific on the 25th of September of the previous year was not known in Spain — most unfortunately for the discoverer — until after the new Governor had been appointed.

A clash between the two men was inevitable. The Court, when it heard of Balboa's having penetrated to the farther ocean, gave him his reward — not the Governorship of Castilla del Oro, to which no doubt he considered himself entitled by right of exploration, but the titles of a provincial Governor and *Adelantado* of the South Sea. The signing of that commission was also the signing of his death warrant.

The appointment left Balboa humiliatingly subordinate to Pedrarias. It also made Pedrarias believe that Balboa intended to consolidate his office into independence — an intolerable position to both men.

To make matters worse, Balboa, smarting under what he conceived to be a wrong done him, lost no opportunity of writing to the Court complaining of the cruelties committed by Pedrarias, or of complacently comparing, for the benefit of the older colonists, the peaceful condition of Darien during his own administration with the later troubled state of affairs.

The Franciscan Juan de Quevedo, Bishop of Darien, tried to patch up the quarrel — in which he was aided by Doña Isabella, the Governor's wife — by arranging a marriage between the *Adelantado* and Pedrarias' eldest daughter, María. She was still at her convent school in Spain, but was solemnly betrothed to Balboa by proxy — the father answering for the bride.

Peace was not maintained for long. Pedrarias was incensed by hearing — what was quite true — that his son-in-law continued to live with his Indian mistress, the daughter of the chief Careta. It so happened, too, that Garabito, one of the *Adelantado's* friends and followers, became infatuated with this beautiful Indian girl, and, maddened by hopeless desire, determined to destroy Balboa. He therefore informed the Governor that his son-in-law was on the point of striking for independence. He was planning to sail away in the ships which had been carried piece by piece, with infinite sorrow to the native porters, over the mountains from the waters of the Atlantic to the Pacific.

Balboa was summoned to Acla and, though warned not to go, foolishly trusted himself to Pedrarias. He was promptly arrested for treason by Pizarro, his second-in-command at the time of the discovery of the Pacific,[1] and thrown into prison.

[1] It is not quite clear why Pizarro should be sneered at as "the ever dutiful one, the model subordinate" because of this. The arrest merely happened to fall to his duty.

The trial, presided over by Gaspar de Espinosa, the *Alcalde Mayor,* was grotesquely unfair. Things that had occurred long before Pedrarias took office, things such as the expulsion of Nicuesa and the deprivation of Enciso, things which had been tacitly condoned by Balboa's appointment as *Adelantado,* were now brought up against him. In fact, as Arthur Strawn says in *Sails and Swords,* "The only charge which was not clearly defined and exactly stated was the very charge on which he had been arrested for treason."

He was led out in chains and beheaded, Pedrarias looking on gloatingly from behind a palisade twelve feet away while his son-in-law and four of his followers were executed. The sun was dropping behind the mountains as the last of the condemned walked to the block, and the spectators, sickened by bloodshed, appealed to the Governor to let the approaching darkness be the signal for clemency. He roared, "I would rather die myself than that one of them should escape!" Well was he named the Wrath of God.

Hernando de Soto, who arrived in the colony about this time might have found in the career of Balboa valuable instruction. The two men were born in the same town, rocky Xerez. Both attended the same university. Both married daughters of Pedrarias.

Codro, the Venetian astrologer, one of the cosmopolitan group of settlers in Darien, is said to have seen a parallel between the lives of the two men, and to have prophesied for De Soto the same number of years to which Balboa attained, forty-two. His predictions enjoyed considerable prestige in the colony. He had once pointed out a star to Balboa, warning him that when it appeared in a certain point in the sky the crisis of his fate would be at hand. "Your fortune will then be in jeopardy, and your life in peril. But if you escape that danger, wealth and renown such as have fallen to the lot of no captain in the Indies will be yours." The prophecy was forgotten till towards the end of 1518, five years later, when, walking the beach one evening at the Pearl Islands, Balboa saw the star of his destiny burning in the fateful quarter. He pointed it out to his companions and jested about it. And jested too soon.

Even after death, however, Balboa continued to affect the fortunes of the peninsula. He had long advocated the transference of the seat of government from the Atlantic to the Pacific. On the 15th of August 1519, the city of Panama was formally founded. The site was quite as unhealthy as that of Darien, but it was on the narrowest neck of land, and permitted the building of a road between it and Nombre de Dios that has been described by Peter Martyr. It was wide enough to permit two carts to go upon it side by side to search the secrets of either spacious sea, "through mountains overgrown with woods never touched from all eternity."

The founding of Panama opened up the Pacific and made possible the conquest of Peru. But this enterprise, though it had always been Balboa's fondest ambition, was not at all to the mind of Pedrarias. He foresaw that his execution of the *Adelantado* would be condemned in Spain, and was preparing to extend his operations to

[31]

the north, not the south, after his expected ejection had occurred. For his plans Panama would be an excellent *point d'appui*.

At the same time, in anticipation of the customary *residencia*, that is an inquiry into the official acts of a deposed functionary, he put his affairs in order, arranged for exculpatory testimony, and — most prudent stroke of all — sent his wife home with the whole of his treasure-trove of gold and pearls.

These elaborate precautions proved unnecessary. A new governor, Lope de Sosa, was, indeed, duly appointed and arrived in May 1520. Pedrarias was preparing to receive with proper ceremony the man who was to oust him, and De Sosa was in his cabin dressing for the occasion. But that same hour he was suddenly stricken and died.

Cloaking under a decent parade of sorrow whatever internal satisfaction he may have felt over his astonishing luck, Pedrarias had De Sosa's body conveyed to the church with befitting pomp, and there interred it before the high altar. The son of De Sosa, his chief officers, and the new *Alcalde Mayor,* before whom the inquiry into the official past of Pedrarias was to have been conducted, were treated with the highest and most ironic deference. In the circumstances the *residencia* was a farce.

But the districts to the north, towards which Pedrarias was now turning his eyes, were, especially in view of his doubtful status, to be regarded as a no-man's-land, open to the exploitation of anyone who chose to go there. Such, at least, was the view of Gil González Dávila, who arrived as Captain-General of an expedition to find the mythical straits leading to the Spice Islands. He was a man of good family and of first-rate ability, and had been *Contador* of La Española — just the sort of adventurous spirit to which the Spanish Court was always willing to allow a certain amount of independent action, even at the risk of annoying a duly appointed Governor by seeming to permit poaching upon his preserves.

Pedrarias dared not actively oppose an officer coming armed with the Emperor's warrant, but he did all he could to hinder him. On one pretext or another Balboa's old ships, which had been ordered to be delivered to the expedition, were refused.

But González was a man of great determination. As he could not have Balboa's ships, he would do what Balboa had done before him. Accordingly he dismantled his own caravels and carried them, piece by piece, across the mountains to the South Sea. When they foundered upon being launched, he built new ones.

Three of these were made unseaworthy by worms, the plague of Pacific timber; but undismayed by disaster, he marched north with a hundred men, only four of whom were mounted, leaving his pilot to follow with the ships.

There was, of course, no sign of a strait; so González struck inland, thereby, in the eyes of Pedrarias, exceeding his commission.

By the Indians he was well received; and he showed a remarkable faculty for making friends of the savages and for converting them to Christianity. His exordium to Chief Nicaragua [2] has been preserved for us by Peter

---

[2] Here, as elsewhere, the Spaniards were indifferent about giving the name of the district to the chief, or the name of the chief to the district.

Martyr. "Embrace the cross, bathed by Christ, the God-man, with His blood for the salvation of the lost human race, and you will live happily and gain for your souls an eternity of bliss. The Creator of the universe also loves not war, for He prefers peace among neighbours, since He commanded us to love our neighbours as ourselves." His march became a missionary tour, during which the exhortations of the Captain-General and his priests resulted in the baptism (according to González' own estimate, which we may receive with due reserve) of over thirty-two thousand souls. It also resulted in the acquisition of a hundred and twelve thousand *pesos* of gold.

Reports of this treasure aroused the animosity of Pedrarias. It was just as he knew it would be: give one of these free-lances the right to explore and he shouldered the authority of an administrator! The Governor, therefore, marched to Nombre de Dios to arrest the Captain-General.

González sailed from that port, taking with him his gold, a few hours before the incensed Pedrarias arrived. The authorities at Santo Domingo listened to his story and applauded his exploits. Bancroft summarizes them aptly: "No other Spaniard ever before covered so many leagues on foot with so few men so poorly equipped; no other man ever converted so many souls to Christ in so short a time; no discoverer as yet had brought in so much gold; and, finally, no one before him had ever returned from a voyage of discovery without having lost to the adventurers the cost of the outfit." The opinion of the Santo Domingo officials was shared by the Emperor. González was instructed he might go on with his explorations.

The Captain-General, however, without waiting for the royal reply to his representations, anticipated it, and sailed again in March 1524. His intention was to reach Lake Nicaragua, the freshwater sea, by way of the San Juan river, its turbulent outlet into the Atlantic.[3] He miscalculated his course and landed instead on the northern shore of Honduras, from which point he marched in a southwesterly direction.

Some time before this Hernández de Córdoba had been dispatched from Panama, with De Soto, Compañón, and Gabriel de Rojas as his lieutenants, to occupy Nicaragua, and so forestall González. They founded a settlement at Bruselas, and another — one destined to be far more important — at Granada, on the shores of the lake. Again, and for the third time, the incredible feat of carrying a ship piece-meal overland was accomplished, and the freshwater sea had its brigantine. To the Spaniards such a miracle of energy was all in the day's work and was only casually noted by the chroniclers, exciting no special comment.

While Córdoba was founding Granada, and, farther to the north, the city of León, De Soto marched to intercept the advance of González. In the centre of that knee of land which constitutes Honduras and Nicaragua, the two bodies of soldiers encountered each other. The place was Toreba.

With two rival claimants to the jurisdiction of the dis-

[3] Only now is it about to be made navigable by the construction of canals at the necessary places.

trict, there was only one method of settling their dispute: that of fighting it out. Just before dawn González surprised the camp of De Soto. But the young captain, though decidedly at a disadvantage, was always prompt in such an emergency. As the trumpets rang out in the camp to waken the dragoons from their all but fatal sleep, De Soto and those who had hastily donned their armor and saddled their horses flung themselves upon the cautiously advancing line of the Captain-General. It broke under their impact and fell back, giving the rest of De Soto's men time to come up; and González, seeing the battle beginning to go against him, cried out, "Peace! Peace! Señor Capitán, in the Emperor's name!" Neither he nor De Soto had much stomach for fratricidal war. A truce was arranged.

But González, thinking the matter over at leisure, felt that he could not allow his great plans to be thwarted by the opposition of a boy. Yet if he attempted to advance into the country he would have to fight this fiery cavalier and his hard-riding dragoons — not a very pleasant prospect for any man, still less for one who loved peace better than war.

He had observed that De Soto was a young man without subtlety. The open brow and candid eyes indicated a trustful nature. This fact should be made to serve the Captain-General's purpose. As De Soto had the advantage of youthful vigor, it was only fair that González should use his own advantage, the wisdom of middle-age. While he parleyed, prolonging the discussions as much as possible, he brought up the main body of his army, consisting of a hundred soldiers with two hundred Indian allies.

He now outnumbered De Soto by more than six to one, and was able to surround him and to take the whole of the little force opposed to him prisoners. The good-natured but crafty Captain-General had gained his point, and did not wish to press his advantage too far. His prisoners were given back their arms and released upon parole. The understanding was that they were to retire. As for González, he had heard from De Soto of the establishment of Granada and León. His way being blocked in that direction, he agreed to confine his activities to Honduras.

De Soto rode off with his dragoons technically defeated, but by no means disgraced. In fact, his services at To-reba merited the gratitude of the Governor, for he had at least turned González back.

Arriving in León, he found a much more serious threat to the authority of Pedrarias than that which he had just succeeded in averting. Córdoba had strongly fortified Granada and León, and was bent upon making himself independent of his superior.

"After all," he argued, "I, and not Pedrarias, have conquered this province. It is geographically distinct from Castilla del Oro. It can be much more effectively administered from Granada than from Panama. The Crown therefore would be well served by my taking over the command." He succeeded in inducing the settlers in the two cities to petition the Emperor for his appointment as an independent governor; and to strengthen his position he wrote to Cortés seeking an alliance.

He approached De Soto on the matter, only to have his advances indignantly rejected. It is very much to the

young officer's credit that at that time of general intrigue
and devious treachery he saw his duty clearly. Whatever might be said against Pedrarias, De Soto knew that
loyalty, to say nothing of gratitude, demanded that the
Governor should be supported. His reward did not come
to him until many years afterward. It was that he, alone
among the early Spanish administrators, never encountered insubordination against his command.

It was too late for Córdoba to withdraw now. Had
he done so at this stage, when his intention of treason
was patent, he would have invited the contempt due to
pusillanimity as well as the punishment due to his offence. He therefore arrested De Soto and locked him
up in the block-house in Granada. There at least he
would be safe, and perhaps, by having an opportunity of
considering the situation, he might come to change his
mind.

Córdoba made a mistake. There were others in Granada who were not enthusiastic supporters of his ambition, but who so far had not dared openly to oppose it.
The clapping of De Soto in jail fired their anger. Compañón refused to allow his friend to be treated in this
fashion. He gathered a group of loyalist soldiers, broke
open the block-house, and set the prisoner free.

They numbered less than a dozen men all told; but
they were well armed and mounted, and shouted defiance to Córdoba as they galloped to the country beyond.

Córdoba set out instantly in pursuit and overtook them
not far from the city. Brought to bay, the fugitives
wheeled round their horses. "You outnumber us, Cór-

doba," De Soto sabre in hand called to him, "but be very certain of this, unless you leave us alone each one of us will single you out to kill you. Be warned and go back."

The rebellious lieutenant of Pedrarias hesitated. He knew De Soto to be the best horseman and swordsman in the army, and that Francisco Compañón was a cavalier almost as dashing. To fight with these furious men would be to risk too much upon a single throw. It would be safer to let the little band of loyalists go. Pedrarias would sooner or later have to hear about what had happened in Nicaragua. De Soto and his dragoons would not augment the army of the Governor to any great extent. The soundest policy would be to consolidate quietly his own forces in Granada and León. He therefore ruefully returned, hearing to his chagrin the mocking laughter of the unmolested fugitives. He was to hear something still less to his liking before long.

De Soto's journey to Panama was attended with enormous difficulties. The stony mountains, broken with innumerable gulleys and ravines, were succeeded by swamps and forests. Frequently the Spaniards were attacked by hostile Indians, who would have been afraid of a larger body of their enemies. When their horses had worn their shoes through, and had cut their hoofs to shreds upon the flints, and so had to be abandoned, it seemed unlikely that any of the group would live to tell their story to Pedrarias. Yet on foot they reached Punta de Burica on the Gulf of Fonseca. Half starved and in tatters they staggered in.

Here the commander, Benito Hurtado, supplied them with a canoe, in which they might finish the journey to Panama. The coast was rugged, with headland after headland; being in a canoe they had to hug the shore, even so contending with treacherous currents and a choppy sea. The journey, upon the water alone, must have been one of at least two hundred miles.

At the town of Nata — it was the spot, De Soto remembered so well, where he had rescued Espinosa and his army from destruction at the hands of Urraca — they beached their frail craft. There, through the pass by which he had come more than four years ago, the trail went that led to the capital. They were too tired to go any further, but while they rested, a horseman from Nata dashed off carrying a letter from De Soto to the Governor telling of Córdoba's insurrection.

Pedrarias was now eighty-five; but his spirit was indomitable. He at once decided to march in person against his insubordinate lieutenant. One cannot but admire the thunderous energy of the old scoundrel. With him it was not merely a question of punishing Hernández Córdoba, but of making Nicaragua safe against the encroachments of both Cortés and González.

It was difficult to obtain men, for Panama had been heavily drained because of the expedition to Peru under Pizarro. However, Nombre de Dios and Acla sent their levies, and Pedrarias sailed for the northern province in January 1526.

Córdoba had already begun to slip from his brief eminence. The settlers who had formerly supported him had seen his weakness before the challenge of De Soto. The jeers of the loyalists who had been allowed to go on their way unmolested had been hard to bear on that day; they proved still more damaging afterwards. The citizens of Granada and León were now trembling for their own skins.

Being far outnumbered, and consequently disheartened, they had just one chance: it was to go humbly, cap in hand, before the Governor when he arrived and ask his forgiveness. When, therefore, a messenger from Pedrarias reached León, ordering Córdoba and his council to appear beyond him to give an account of themselves, they very meekly obeyed. Outside, in the square, the Governor's soldiers stood stiffly in their ranks, and the settlers shifted uneasily from foot to foot waiting for the outcome of the interview. The harsh high voice of the Governor came to them through the windows, ominous, threatening.

After ten minutes that seemed ten years a halberdier came out bearing the head of Córdoba upon a pike. It was the termination of a twelve years' duel between Pedrarias and his enemies.

De Soto had done much towards saving Nicaragua for Pedrarias. Which was well for the old man because, though he had one foot in the grave, he needed to place the other firmly upon an undisputed province of his own. He had been superseded at last in Darien by Pedro de los Rios, but Nicaragua was safely his, so without many regrets he surrendered the isthmus to his supplanter. With all his faults and crimes, he is reputed to have been generous with money. And we may be sure that De Soto did not go unrewarded.

As the years had gone by De Soto had become prosperous, not fabulously but still substantially wealthy.

Many years before, as has been said already, he had entered into a partnership with Francisco Compañón and Hernán Ponce de León. Compañón died soon after the treason of Córdoba, and his share, according to the terms of the contract, had been divided between his associates. We find these two men owning a couple of ships, and engaged in what was no doubt a lucrative slave trade.

They arrived in the spring of 1530 at the port of Panama, having carried their human cargoes from Nicaragua to be sold at auction. And there they encountered Pizarro. He had just returned from Spain with his brothers, who were having one of their many violent disagreements with their partner, Diego Almagro. Owing to this the Peruvian project had met with what seemed to be an insuperable obstacle. Pedro Pizarro tells the story in some detail. Almagro had been insulted by Hernando Pizarro, and had taken himself and all his money off, leaving the expedition stranded. The men who had been collected for the conquest were deserting; those who remained faithful were sick or starving. They had no means of transportation to Peru, and no funds for purchasing supplies. The deadlock was heart-breaking.

The arrival of De Soto[4] and his friend seemed to be a gift from heaven. Here were the ships that Pizarro wanted so badly; and here were the men. Hernán Ponce de León would seem to have done the bargaining, and made an agreement by which he himself was to receive one of the best *repartimientos* in the province they

---

[4] It is not certain whether De Soto joined the expedition then, or came on a little later.

proposed conquering, while De Soto was to be in command of the ships on the voyage and to be appointed lieutenant-governor. Ponce, with the inflexible De Soto in the background, was a hard bargainer.

But they saved the Peruvian expedition. As soon as the sulking Almagro heard what had been done, he swallowed his wrath. For he knew that if he stayed out now, he would lose all the money he had contributed during the past five years, as well as his share of the spoils.

On the 27th of December 1530, the feast of St. John, Evangelist and Apostle — he who saw in apocalyptic vision a new heaven and a new earth — the banners of Pizarro were blessed in the Cathedral of Panama. Mass was sung, every soldier communicating; and the Dominican Father Juan de Vargas preached. With the turn of the year the invading army of two hundred men sailed.

CHAPTER III

PIZARRO PERSISTS

TO BEGIN the story of the conquest of Peru at the point at which De Soto comes into it would be unfair to Francisco Pizarro and to the story itself. For though the time from when his army marched inland until Atahualpa was in his hands was very short — only a few weeks — all this was made possible by the dogged persistence of six years. And while it is true that De Soto's ships and the reinforcements he brought made the final advance possible, these came only at the last moment. De Soto may be regarded as the spearhead of the conquest; the shaft which directed the thrust was grasped firmly in the hand of Pizarro.

That great man was born in 1471 or 1475 at Truxillo, in the province of Estremadura from which so many of the *Conquistadores* came. He was an illegitimate son of a Colonel Gonzalo Pizarro who sired a string of stalwart men, of whom only Hernando, the eldest, was born in wedlock. The colonel never did anything for his bastard progeny. The future conqueror of Peru was left as a foundling upon the doorstep of a church and grew up in Truxillo as a swine-herd. His acquaintance with pigs — according to the pleasant apocryphal story — was

FRANCISCO PISARRO

FRANCISCO PIZARRO

[From Ogilby's *America*, London 1671]

still earlier and more intimate: he outdid Romulus and Remus by being suckled by a sow.

A man in his position has nothing to lose. While young he migrated to La Española, to become a *ranchero;* and from the island went with Balboa to Darien, where he developed those talents of military decision and dependability which led him in the end to so illustrious a career.

After much difficulty Pizarro obtained backers for his hazardous undertaking, Father de Luque, Vicar of Panama, acting as the agent of Gaspar de Espinosa, once *Alcalde Mayor* but now Captain-General of the South Sea, and Diego de Almagro putting up the money. Pedrarias was at first a partner. He did nothing towards financing the undertaking. But he demanded a fourth share as the price of his official consent. In November 1524 a hundred men sailed in search of Peru.[1]

They found nothing but vast swamps and clouds of mosquitos and, upon going farther, equatorial forests, tangled, humid, dismal. The men cursed their leader for bringing them to such a place, and, threatening mutiny, demanded to be taken back to Panama. From that point and for five more years, Pizarro had, almost literally, to carry his men forward upon his own back.

At the moment, the only way of going on was to stand still. They needed food, but if they went to Panama to get it, Pizarro knew they would never leave Panama again. For this reason he remained with half of his company upon the desolate shore, while one of his officers was dispatched to the North for supplies. The

[1] Or, according to Herrera, eighty.

energy of the captain extended to the smallest needs of his men. His own store of provisions he shared with those who lacked; he nursed the sick with his own hands, and built shelters for them. Above all, he imparted something of his serene courage to them.

They needed it. There was nothing to eat except berries and roots, some of which proved poisonous, and seaweed. Xerez says that in their hunger they even boiled and devoured a tanned cow-hide which had been used to cover the pump. Twenty-five of the fifty who had remained perished. In the sardonic humor of soldiers the survivors called the spot the Port of Famine.

Upon the return of the ships they sailed on for Peru, not by the open sea, for Pizarro dared not put the shore out of sight; but from headland to headland he went forward like a man groping in the dark.

Again he landed, in densely wooded country, and found a village from which the savages fled upon their approach. Such was their haste that they had left roasting upon their fires human flesh. The horrified Spaniards called this place *Pueblo Quemado,* the burnt village.

At a still lower point down the coast they were attacked by hordes of Indians, and lost several men before beating off their enemies. Pizarro barely escaped with his life. He was wounded seven times — each time seriously — and as he retreated with his men towards their palisades, he stumbled, weak with loss of blood. Instantly the savages, who had recognized the leader, were upon him, eager to make an end. But he staggered to his feet, rallied his strength, slew two of his yelling assailants and held off the others until he was rescued.

It was a warning that reinforcements were needed. So, entrenching himself at Chicama, he sent Nicholás de Ribera back in the ships to Panama. That officer carried with him the trinkets of gold collected on the trip, in the hope that they would be an inducement to prospective volunteers.

It was a most inopportune moment to ask the Governor to allow anybody to leave the colony on what he had always believed to be a wild goose chase. He was preparing to march to Nicaragua to execute his wrath upon the insubordinate Córdoba. But Father Luque possessed a persuasive tongue; and he had a powerful weapon available, ready cash. Pedrarias, chuckling at his own shrewdness, sold out his share in the expedition for a thousand *pesos de oro*. In doing so he was jockeyed into sanctioning a continuation of the enterprise.

On March 10, 1526, Pizarro having come to Panama for the purpose, a new contract was made. Father Luque administered holy communion to the partners, breaking the Host into three pieces, one for himself, one for Almagro, one for Pizarro. In this manner they solemnly sealed their pact.

For the voyage they engaged the services of the Andalusian pilot, Bartolomé Ruiz. But they found it almost impossible to obtain recruits. The better class of colonists shared the skepticism of Pedrarias about the wealth of Peru; and fifty men who had gone on the previous voyage now deserted — their loud complaints about their privations disheartening Panama.

Eventually, after much trouble, a company of a hundred and sixty, mostly desperadoes and the dregs of the colony, consented to go. They were all soon appalled by the terrors inspired by the wild country. There seemed to be no end to the forests with their pulpy floors, where glowered broad, beautiful, and poisonous flowers; where overhead monkeys and parrots chattered at the disturbers of their solitudes, and death coiled silent in the sleek strength of the boas wrapped round the cyclopean branches, or watched hour by hour from the black, all but submerged heads of the alligators in the gloomy swamps. The Indians, too, were hostile; and one band of fourteen men, whose canoe had become stranded on a mud bank in a river, was wiped out.

Farther south the country improved. Instead of the jungles of mangrove trees coming down to the very edge of the sea, clumps of ebony, sandalwood, and mahogany were seen. And, better still, patches of cultivated land and clusters of huts became more frequent.

But again they were attacked by a large army of natives. The General, upon seeing them coming, had landed with a few of his men for a parley. The savages were in no mood for peace. They charged forward howling for blood, and the career of Pizarro would have come to a close there, had not the yells of the Indians startled his horse. It reared and he was thrown. They had never seen before any creature that a man could ride, and took rider and horse to be one animal. But while ready to fight and kill these centaurs, they did not know that a centaur could come in two. As they recoiled in astonishment, Pizarro had a moment in which to clamber hurriedly into a boat, and so regained his ship.

The incident emphasized the necessity for reinforcements. They retreated to Gallo Island, where Pizarro determined to remain with his men, holding it as a garrison while Almagro tried once more for recruits. Those who were compelled to stay behind, wishing to let their friends know how they were being sacrificed to the ambition of their officers, but knowing that Almagro would deliver no complaining letters, concealed in a ball of cotton, which ostensibly was a specimen of the products of Peru, the following scrap of doggerel:

> *Look out, Señor Governor,*
> *For the drover while he's near;*
> *Since he goes home to get the sheep*
> *For the butcher, who stays here.*[2]

It fell into the hands of the wife of the new Governor, who passed it on to her husband. Pedro de los Rios had hitherto shown himself favorable to the projects of Pizarro, but now he was very indignant, and all the bluff eloquence of Almagro and the suave diplomacy of Luque could not move him. The men were being murdered to no purpose. He dispatched Tafur with two ships to Gallo Island with strict orders to bring back with him the whole company of Christians upon it.

His arrival was wildly acclaimed. Pizarro's men embraced each other as though they had been raised from the dead and blessed De los Rios as their father and liberator.

But if Pizarro turned back now he knew that it would

[2] Prescott's translation.

[49]

mean the end of everything. He listened quietly to Tafur and read the Governor's letter. Then he made a characteristic gesture. With his sword he drew upon the sand a line going east and west. Still standing upon the north side he addressed his men.

"Friends and comrades!" he said, "On that side are toil, hunger, nakedness, and the drenching storm; on this side, ease. But there also lies Peru with its riches; here, Panama and its poverty. Choose, each man. For my part, I go to the South."

With the last words he crossed the line. Thirteen men followed him out of two hundred. It is a pleasure to write their names down here. They are Bartolomé Ruiz, Cristóbal de Peralta, Pedro de Candia, Domingo de Soria Luce, Nicholás de Ribera, Francisco de Cuellar, Alonso de Molina, Pedro Alcón, García de Xerez, Anton de Carrión, Alonzo Briceño, Martín de Paz, Juan de la Torre.

They were not to be turned aside from their decision even when Tafur, who regarded the whole affair in the light of insubordination against the Governor, refused to leave them one of the ships. If they chose to maroon themselves on a rock in the Pacific, it was on their own responsibility. He gave them a little food and sailed away.

Pizarro and his faithful men did not suffer as much this time as before. It occurred to them that the island of Gorgona, forty miles to the north, would offer, could they reach it, a better refuge than Gallo. It was uninhabited, high above the sea, wooded in part, and — best of all — well stocked with small game, pheasants and hares. At Gallo they had nothing but the shellfish they had come so strongly to loathe.

The difficulty of getting there was great, but not, as it turned out, insurmountable. They made a raft — probably with a sail, such as the native *balsas* carried — and succeeded in crossing the stretch of sea between the two islands.

Nothing could be more admirable than the conduct of this resolute band. And their courage was sustained by their piety. Pizarro said morning and evening prayers for his men, and the rosary; and one of their number who possessed a Book of the Hours led them in that part of the divine office. All carefully observed the festivals and fasts of the Church. Herrera specially mentions their devotion to the *Salve Regina*. The touching words took on in that lonely island, during the seven months they watched for a sail, a unique poignancy: "To thee do we cry, poor banished children of Eve. To thee do we send up our sighs, mourning and weeping in this vale of tears."

With the cooling of his anger De los Rios relented. A small ship was sent in search of the marooned men. But his orders to Pizarro were explicit: he must, in any event, return within six months with a report of his doings.

As Pizarro had been given six months, he would use the time in exploration before going back to Panama.

They went now further south than anyone had gone before — though Ruiz the previous year had crossed the equator for the first time in this direction. All the way along the coast rose, range behind range, the awe-inspiring and magnificent crests of the Cordilleras, austere rock and snow. Tumbez was reached, and the local *cacique* was entertained at dinner in the floating Spanish castle. To him Pizarro professed the most amicable intentions, but added that he was the officer of a great king, the greatest in the world, and that he had come to assert his lawful supremacy over the country and to bring to Peru the knowledge of the one true God. The Spaniards were always perfectly candid about their mission.

When Pizarro upon returning to Panama displayed to Pedro de los Rios the llamas and the beautiful garments of vicuña wool he had brought back, the Governor refused to be impressed. Their story was admittedly interesting; but it was as much as he could do, with the means at his disposal, to administer his province. He had no intention of sacrificing valuable lives in order to gather a menagerie of exotic animals.

There was only one thing to do in view of the Governor's attitude: an appeal must be made directly to the Court of Spain. And Pizarro determined to go himself.

But before he got to the imperial presence, a misadventure befell him of the sort most calculated to be damaging to his reputation. Upon his landing in Spain, Enciso had him arrested for an old debt.

The Emperor, however, heard of his plight, ordered his release, and summoned him to court. The unlettered swine-herd of Truxillo rose to the occasion. He was by nature taciturn, but when the occasion called for it he could be movingly eloquent. Out of his heart came what he had to say, out of a heart that had hoped, dared, and suffered much. Charles wept to hear it and promised his support.

But the Council of the Indies proceeded, as do all such bodies, at a leisurely pace. Not until July 26, 1529, was the *Capitulación* signed, Isabella in the absence of her husband writing, "I the Queen," Pizarro putting beside her signature his mark.

The business with the Crown being settled, Pizarro set himself to secure the required number of two hundred and fifty recruits. The chief of these were his four brothers, Hernando, Gonzalo, Martín, and Juan, each destined to play a striking, though not always a fortunate part in the conquest. They soon showed that they formed a closed corporation.[3]

The one who looms largest in history is Hernando. Like the other Pizarros, he was valiant and skilled with sabre and lance. But above all the brothers he was punctilious in pride; and his extravagant view of knighthood was strongly tinged with quixoticism. Tall, gaunt, ungainly, with a red bulbous nose and heavy pendulant lips, a conspicuous figure, he used to ride out to battle wearing over his breastplate a surcoat of yellow or scarlet damask and flaunting an enormous white plume. As he had personal enemies, he intended to give them no excuse to pass him by if they wished to measure swords with him. "Whatever sudden event might happen," says Quintana, "however unforeseen, he saw with the glance of an eagle how it might be met, and with equal rapidity put his thought in action." He was devoted to his

[3] Mention must also be made of their cousin, Pedro Pizarro, one of the most important historians of the Conquest.

brother, but served him badly. For the fatal quarrel with Almagro he must be held mainly responsible. He paid the penalty by twenty years of imprisonment in the fortress of Medina del Campo; but, though old and broken in spirit when released, was so tough-fibred as to live to be a hundred. He died in the odor of sanctity.

Other recruits were not easy to find. The very eloquence which had made the Emperor weep made prospective volunteers wonder if they had a vocation to endure the hardships of Peru. When word came that the Council of the Indies was about to look into the lack of the stipulated numbers, Francisco Pizarro with one of his three ships slipped out of the harbor of San Lucar on January 19, 1530, leaving Hernando to explain to the Emperor's officers, when they came to make their inspection, that the remainder of the necessary complement of men had gone on ahead with his brother. The officers pretended to believe him, and he was allowed to proceed.

In Panama, difficulties arose with Almagro, who felt that he had not been fairly treated in the distribution of territory and honors. He had been made subordinate instead of equal to Pizarro; and withdrew in disgust. Many of those who had come out from Spain heard from the colonists in Panama, some of them former voyagers with the Captain-General, of what they might expect, and repented of their adventurous ardor. It was at this moment, when the force gathered for Peru was dwindling and disheartened and without funds, that the enlistment of De Soto to the cause gave it men, money, and the means of transportation.

CHAPTER IV

PERU OF THE INCAS

PIZARRO had intended to disembark at Tumbez, where previously he had been so well received, but, being carried out of his way by adverse winds, found himself at Coaque in the bay of San Mateo, nearly five degrees to the north. The misadventure was fortunate, because there they came upon emeralds, coronets of gold, and other jewelry which amounted to more than two hundred thousand *castellaños* in value.[1] Strict orders were given that all the treasure taken should be put in one heap for the Governor to distribute according to each man's deserts. It was a provision directed to the maintenance of discipline. From the time they reached Coaque until they came to Caxamarca no more gold — at least in any large quantity — was seen, the Indians, no doubt, having taken the precaution of hiding it.

As they marched down the coast the soldiers suffered intensely from the glaring sun and the sand blown into their eyes. Moreover an epidemic of ulcers broke out from which many died. And the Indians were openly

---

[1] It would seem from Pedro Pizarro that it was the shipment of some of this gold to Nicaragua from Coaque that brought De Soto post-haste out to Peru. He says that it was at the island of Puna that De Soto joined the expedition with a hundred men.

[55]

hostile. The invaders, therefore, crossed over to the island of Puna, to the north of Tumbez, to rest and to perfect their plans.

Here the *caciques* came out with protestations of friendship, but the Spaniards' interpreters, who were natives of this place, warned their masters to be on guard. Pizarro took the hint and promptly arrested the chiefs, charging them with plotting treachery.

At this point occurred an incident which throws a curious light upon the affairs of Peru. As soon as the Indians of the mainland heard that the chiefs of the island were prisoners, they came over asking that they might have the pleasure of killing them. Somewhat reluctantly, and only because of his former reception in Tumbez, Pizarro handed them over, and they were beheaded. The chief *cacique,* however, the Governor refused to deliver for execution, keeping him as a hostage until the Spaniards were ready to leave.

The animosity of the Indians of Tumbez towards the *caciques* did not imply, as the Spaniards rashly believed, any friendliness toward themselves. For during the journey to the mainland, which was made on the native *balsas,* three men were treacherously slain, and Pedro and Martín Pizarro, among others, came within an inch of suffering the same fate. All those who had entrusted their baggage to Indian keeping — one of whom was De Soto — were very dexterously robbed, and left with nothing but the clothes they wore.

The Governor, not knowing for certain what had happened to the missing men, sent a message to the *Cacique* of Tumbez demanding their release. He got no reply, but he observed that the Indians on the side of the river opposite to that upon which he was encamped were building forts. Eventually they tauntingly invited the Spaniards to cross, boasting that they should be served in the same way as their three comrades.

A great raft of wood was hastily made, and upon this a band of horsemen was carried, who quickly dispersed the savages. Their orders, however, were these: "To make war upon the Indians, because they were rebels and had slain the Christians; and, after they had suffered such punishment as their offence deserved, they were to be received peacefully in accordance with the commands of his Majesty."

The policy of Pizarro is indicated here. Just severity was to be used when necessary; but, whenever it was possible, friendly relations were to be established with the natives. When the *Cacique* of Tumbez sent word to say that he would come before the Governor were it not for his fear of being killed, Pizarro's answer was that no harm would be done to anyone who came in peace, even though he had formerly been in rebellion.

To those Indians who showed signs of goodwill crosses were distributed for them to place on their houses; and, with that sign there, no Spaniard dared to molest them. This, according to Pedro Sancho, was done wherever the Spaniards went in Peru, until Pedro de Alvarado arrived with his contingent from Guatemala.

De Soto, whom we shall notice throughout the history of Peru as always being chosen for difficult scouting operations, was sent to investigate the state of affairs in the city of Tumbez, and to take Chile Masa, the *cacique* of the district, into his custody. He found the town burnt; but he managed to bring Chile Masa back with him to camp.

From this chief they discovered, through their interpreters, why the city had been destroyed. A civil war was raging. Huayna Capac had divided his kingdom by will between Huascar (who in compliance with Peruvian custom should have been sole war-lord) and Atahualpa, a son by a favorite concubine. The two brothers were engaged in fighting out their rival claims.

This was a good piece of news. A civil war was an excellent opportunity for invaders. The attention of the country would be diverted from the foreigner. And as no doubt the Spaniards shrewdly surmised, they would be able to utilize one of the factions to their own advantage. Moreover (though this they did not know), Incan civilization was a spent force. It had long ago reached its peak; it showed no power of going beyond the point already gained; its stagnation was the first stage of its decline. The invaders had come at just the right moment.

From this chief, Pizarro heard something else that pleased him still more than did the news of civil conflict: it was that Cuzco, the capital, was full of vessels of gold and silver and things inlaid with gold. But the soldiers were so downcast because of the bare condition of the district in which they were, that they did not believe it. This was a strategem on the part of the Governor, a method devised for raising the drooping spirits of his army. They saw through it all and laughed bitterly. Coaque was cursed because of the misleading idea it had given them of the wealth of the country, and some of the men went back to Panama, the greatest number of defections being among De Soto's contingent. Among those who returned was Hernán Ponce de León.

De Soto himself felt very much dissatisfied. He had abandoned the prosperity which he, unlike so many, had found in Nicaragua, to come out to this wilderness. It was not in his nature ever to let go of a project he had once taken up; but he proceeded without enthusiasm, and felt ashamed at the conduct of his half-hearted followers.

Moreover, he had a personal grievance of a more definate sort. He had arranged to come out on the distinct understanding that he was to be the Lieutenant-governor, but he found that position occupied by Hernando Pizarro. His character, however, was magnanimous, and he accepted the existing order of things with a good grace. There was some consolation in the fact that, as Quintana says, the army considered him the second person there. Quintana goes on: "De Soto dissembled his sense of this indignity, with the temperance and presence of mind that characterised him, and his address, capacity, and valour, conspicuous on every occasion of importance, quickly won for him the distinguished place, which he ever possessed in the esteem of both Indians and Spaniards."

He would, however, have been less (or more) than human had he not given some indications of his disgust. And the Pizarros, who had a bad conscience over this breach of faith, suspected that he was intending to separate himself from the main body of the army with the object of conducting a little conquest of his own. For this reason the two younger brothers, Juan and Gonzalo, were told off to accompany him in his expeditions and to watch his movements.

This does not fit in with what we know of De Soto's character, in which loyalty was the distinguishing mark. And in any event so very level-headed a man would have understood that to have divided an army, which even when united was meagre in numbers, would have been to invite the destruction of the whole force. One suspects here Hernando Pizarro, whose suspicious nature and sharp tongue were always a fruitful cause of trouble.

After garrisons had been established at several points along the coast — the chief of these being at San Miguel — on the 24th of September the decisive stage of the campaign was begun. Within six weeks, Peru for all practical purposes had been conquered.

There was, however, discontent rumbling in the army of sixty-seven horsemen and a hundred and ten foot-soldiers, "three of them with guns, and some with cross-bows," that marched out of San Miguel. Aware of the danger of this, Pizarro now made one of those bold strokes so characteristic of him, a stroke comparable with that played upon the sea-shore at Gallo. He drew up the whole body in squadrons and addressed them. Those who wished to go back to San Miguel might do so. The garrison there was too small in any event. This saved those who chose to remain behind from the imputation of cowardice. The Governor was careful to add that the garrisons on the coast would share equally in the spoils with the men who accompanied him. Five dragoons and four halberdiers took him at his word. This left only a hundred and sixty-eight soldiers; but disaffection had been scotched. Nobody, after so tactful and generous an offer, would have the right to complain.

At Zaran, where the foot-hills began, the army halted. The Governor decided to ride southwestwards to explore the Sechura desert, while De Soto went into the mountains to look for the passes. Xerez gives a full account of what was a very brilliant piece of reconnoitring.

So far the Spaniards had seen nothing but wilderness and a few clusters of squalid huts. Tumbez, the only considerable town they had reached, was in ruins. It was De Soto, therefore, who got the first glimpse of the wonders of Peru.

As he approached Caxas, crossing the Andes on the Marañon watershed, he came to an Indian road. It was not the great highway that stretched from Quito to Cusco, a distance of fifteen hundred miles, but a road connecting with it. In some parts it was little more than a trail, but as it neared the Inca's fortress it was solidly built of great blocks of stone, covered with a bituminous substance almost as hard. No cart went upon it, for the wheel, like the arch, was unknown in Peru. And it was trodden only by the bare feet of the Indians and the light hoofs of the llamas. He saw many of these animals being driven along, each with a not too heavy load reposing in a nest of the thick soft hair on its back.

De Soto, too, was the first white man to cross one of the osier bridges. They have been described for us by all the chroniclers, for nothing in Peru seized their imaginations more powerfully. From towers of stone on

[61]

either side of dizzy canyons these frail structures were suspended, an intricate network of vines, steadied by stones attached underneath. When the Spaniards first came to them we may be sure they did not venture to cross until they had seen a herd of llamas and their Indian drivers go over in safety. Then gingerly, on foot, not yet trusting the bridges to support the weight of their horses, and grasping the balustrades fitted to the sides, they dared the abyss. As they proceeded towards the centre the osiers sagged alarmingly, and from that point they had to climb upwards on a steep incline to the opposite bank, the whole thing swaying and quivering at each step. Xerez admits that "it is a nervous thing to pass over it for the first time," and Sancho that "it goes to the head of him who is not accustomed to it." Upon similar bridges, still in use in Peru, the traveller is often blindfolded and tied to his litter when being carried across. There was really no danger to De Soto, who got his men and horses across without mishap, but we need not wonder if he was more frightened than he had ever been before in his life.

In Caxas he found a small town in which the people lived in wretched adobe hovels, but, as this was a small garrison of the Incas, he saw also buildings of a very different type. They were made of enormous blocks of stone, some of them ten feet long by six feet wide, so closely fitted together that a knife could not be inserted at the point of juncture. But they were all thatched. Stout walls were wanted for the repelling of attack; but Incan ingenuity did not extend to the problem of constructing a solid roof. Here was a symbol of the Incan dominion — stone and straw: the strongest and the weakest of things !

The official levier of taxes came out to meet De Soto, carrying in his hand the *quipus*. Through the interpreter he learned the use of these bundles of threads of various colors, in which he observed many knots. This was the Peruvian adding machine; it was also the nearest approach the country had to a system of writing. It might be made to stand occasionally for certain tangible things: white could be silver, yellow gold; or for simple abstract ideas, when white could indicate peace, and red war.

In Caxas there was one of the granaries maintained by the Incas in all military stations for the use of their armies when upon the march. The whole civilization of the country was founded upon and maintained by war.

In the centre of the town was a large adobe house. Through the gateway De Soto caught a glimpse of a number of girls sitting spinning *vicuña* wool in the courtyard within. Outside there hung the naked bodies of another girl and several older women and of a man.

De Soto summoned the chief of the place to inquire about the meaning of this. He gathered, by means of his interpreter, that this was a house of the Virgins of the Sun.

"Oh, yes, I understand," said the Captain, "a convent ?" It was the nearest he could get to it. In the same way he and all the Conquerors always spoke of the heathen temples as "mosques," and of their high-priests as "bishops."

"But what about those people who have been hanged? Who are they ?"

The local chief explained that the man was the violator of the chastity of the dead girl, and the elderly executed women were some of the portresses of the house who had given the man entrance.[2]

The chief now grew confidential and spoke bitterly of the Inca. Atahualpa took any of their daughters that he wanted and kept them in this and other similar houses. He put them here shortly before adolescence and kept them usefully employed in weaving garments for his household and, when they had reached a marriageable age, summoned such as he needed to replenish his seraglio.

There were many keys here to the so-called Peruvian civilization. But De Soto did not understand, at this stage, the significance of all that he saw.

The famous Incas — who included at once something like a royal house and a superior caste — were the tribe which from its fortress valley of Cuzco had been able to impose itself, by reason of its superior valor and martial aptitude, over the other tribes of Peru. They had begun their career of conquest by barricading themselves in their valley, the passes of which could be held securely against all aggression. Growing strong through their strategic position and the fruitfulness of the soil in their district, they were able afterwards to raid their neighbors. This they could do successfully not only because they had grown to be the most powerful by far of

---

[2] Garcilasso says that it was a capital offence to violate one of the Virgins of the Sun; but the law had never been put into execution, because their chastity had always been immaculate. Even without the evidence of De Soto's eyes, we could not believe this.

the Peruvian tribes but because they raised large herds of llamas, the sole beast of burden in South American at that time. By means of these animals they carried a supply of food with them in their campaigns. The other tribes, who were of a much lower grade of mentality and of softer fibre, found it convenient, one by one, to buy off the harassing Incas with a yearly tribute. Garrisons and fortresses were built for the protection of the officials who levied tribute, and caravanserais and granaries for their armies when they had to take the field. For the most part the original tribal life went on undisturbed. The minor *caciques* paid their "Dane-geld" as the price for being left to their own devices.

As for Peruvian religion, there was a good deal of fetich-worship, which hardly rose to the dignity of the adoration of idols, among the tributary tribes, but the Incas themselves deified the sun.[3] It is sometimes said that they were monotheists. The truth would seem to be that they were — like almost every heathen race — polytheists in practice, with vestiges of monotheistic theory. It is usual for anthropologists to regard monotheism as a mark of civilization, the culmination of a long process of intellectual development. There is more justification for the view that it is a relic of an older conception of the universe, corrupted, confused, overlaid, and all but lost in the process of time. It proves little concerning the civilization of a people.

We need not suppose, however, that these people neces-

[3] The historian Balboa gives an amusing account of the origin of this worship, or rather of the identifiction of the Inca with the sun. It originated, according to him, as a pious hoax.

sarily physically identified the sun with God. It was rather, as it always is with sun-worshippers, a poetic identification, a simple and very natural instance of symbolism.

The Inca was styled the Child of the Sun. Again, the Peruvians probably did not believe that the first Inca was literally born from the marriage of the Sun and his sister-wife, the Moon. Court flattery — of which an example may be seen in the perfunctory deification of the Roman Emperors — called for something of the sort. Everybody admitted it — and nobody for an instant believed in it. But a government reposing upon religious sanction was securely entrenched; and this was a way of blending together the terrors of the secular sword with the tenderness and passion of religious adoration.[4]

But we may be sure that De Soto did not bother his head with the intricacies of Incan theology. His attitude, and that of all of the *Conquisatadores,* was expressed in in the soldierly doctrine of the *Song of Roland:*

Paien unt tort e chrestiens unt dreit

Behind the horrible figures of stone and wood, the heathen idols, lurked the Devil, the inspirer of these abominations. The Spaniards had come to rescue these souls from perdition, to bring to them the inestimable gift of the Catholic Faith. They could not comprehend how the Indians could fail to appreciate their benevolence, which was absolutely sincere, or refuse to accept

---

[4] That the Peruvians did not take this tradition too seriously may be seen by the fact that Atahualpa, the son of Huayna Capac and a concubine, could oust the legitimate Inca, Huascar, who was the son of his father's only true wife, the Inca's full sister, and was therefore the real Child of the Sun.

the jurisdiction of the Pope who had consigned these lands to the keeping of their kingdom.[5]

After gazing with astonished interest at the things he had seen in Caxas, and reassuring the terrified natives as to the pacific intentions of the Spaniards, De Soto rode on to Huanca-pampa, on the river of the same name, which flows into the Marañon. As he proceeded, the road broadened, so that six horsemen were able to ride abreast without being crowded.

At Huanca-pampa a messenger met De Soto, sent from Atahualpa. He conveyed the Inca's greetings, and an invitation to the Christians to go to Caxamarca, where he was staying. His porters carried presents of the fine *vicuña* cloth, more like silk than wool, with patterns and figures upon it of beaten gold, and two fountains of carved stone, fashioned in the form of fortresses. It

[5] Dr. James Brown Scott, in his monograph *The Spanish Origins of International Law*, brilliantly expounds the doctrine of Francisco de Vitoria, who, in the very year of the invasion of Peru, was lecturing in the University of Salamanca. Vitoria, of course, was only expounding the principles of his fellow-countryman, Isidore of Seville, and of his fellow-Dominican, St. Thomas Aquinas, and applying them to the new conditions in the lately discovered Indies. He is exceedingly bold in denying the right of the Pope to parcel the Americas between Spain and Portugal; and affirms that the aborigines might not be dispossessed of private property. He even inclines to the view that their civil rights are violated by invasion, and this on the ground that they possess civil dominion. But he is doubtful about this point, as he well might be, and allows that a claim for annexation may be advanced on the ground that they are "unfit to found or administer a lawful state up to the standard required by human and civil claims." Yet he adds that, though "in their own interest the sovereigns of Spain might undertake the administration of their country . . . such interposition should be for the welfare and in the interests of the Indians and not merely for the profit of the Spaniards." No doubt many of the *Conquistadores* were more concerned with their own profit than with the interests of the Indians; but it should never be forgotten that the principles of Vitoria, taken generally, animated the policy of the Court, however much that policy was deflected by its human instruments. But naturally the Court did not agree with the Dominican in his view of the invalidity of the papal partition of the New World.

should be noted that the Inca sent no solid gold. The most curious of his somewhat niggardly presents was a couple of loads of dried and powdered goose-flesh, much valued, according to the strange taste of the country, for fumigation.

De Soto's absence, which had been well over a week, had begun to alarm his comrades in Zaran, when he arrived bringing with him the messenger and the gifts of Atahualpa. The ambassador seems to have been a most indiscreet man, for he went from one Spaniard to another "trying their strength in such a manner that they laughed at him," says Pedro Pizarro, and asking them to show him their swords. All this was considered amusing, though it should have been regarded as ominous, but when he ventured to put his hand upon a soldier's beard he was promptly knocked down.

What this ambassador was trying to do was better understood by an Indian chief of the plains who arrived about this time. He had been sent to Caxamarca by the Spaniards, and had not been well received. The city was deserted and everywhere he perceived hostile preparations. When he went out to the Inca's camp, he was refused speech with Atahualpa; and, his life being threatened, he had escaped only by warning the warriors that if he were killed, the Christians would certainly execute the Inca's ambassador by way of reprisal.

As soon as this man saw the Indian chief whom De Soto had brought back with him from Huanca-pampa he rushed savagely at him, catching him by the ears and calling him a rogue and a liar. Here, he insisted, was a spy, sent to find out the Spanish strength.

Pizarro quieted his own furious Indian supporter, and apologized to Atahualpa's emissary for the rough handling he had received. He affected to attach no importance to the charge of spying, and sent him back to his master with a shirt of Seville and a cap and a number of compliments. But he added, to quote Xerez, the significant remark, "If he wishes for war, I will make war, as I have done against the chief of the island of Santiago,[6] and against the chief of Tumbez, and against all others who have wished to make war against me. I make war upon no one, nor do I molest anyone, unless war is made upon me."

[6] The name the Spaniards had given to Puna.

CHAPTER V

THE CHILD OF THE SUN

CONFIRMATION of this warning came almost at once after they began their march to the Inca's camp. They extracted, under torture, from a chief they captured, information that Atahualpa had mustered his army and was allowing the Spaniards to advance merely because, once they were in the valley of Caxamarca, they could be trapped and destroyed at leisure. The passes were left open for them — in itself a highly suspicious circumstance. But they dared not retreat, nor show any sign of fear. It was to see the Inca that they had come to Peru.

They rode in narrow file up into the Andes. Everywhere was silence, beauty, and desolation. Their path was in many places cut into the living rock, at any point of which they could easily have been stopped. Overhead the obscene condor, which must have seemed an emblem of what was waiting for them, winged his way in the azure sky, or, watching from a crag, waited for a foot to slip to provide him with a carcass. The air was cold, and in many places the men saw snow.

At the hour of vespers on Friday the 15th of November

1532, the Christians, riding three deep, entered the deserted town of Caxamarca. The crisis of their fate was at hand.

From the walls of the town they could see on the slope of the opposite side of the valley "a white cloud of pavilions covering the ground as thick as snowflakes." It was the camp of the Inca.

Noon had passed. A storm brooded in the sky. Rain mingled with hail was already beginning to fall. But Pizarro determined to act at once. The day should not be allowed to close without his having learned a little more about Atahualpa.

He therefore ordered De Soto to take fifteen horsemen with him and to go at once to the camp. He was instructed to get speech with the Inca and to invite him to have supper with the officers. And he was to find out in which of the buildings of the town it was Atahualpa's pleasure that they should lodge. Pizarro wanted to lose no time in making a courteous gesture, in order to show that the Spaniards came as friends.

The fifteen dragoons had hardly left — they were still in sight, thundering along the paved road across the valley — when Hernando Pizarro went, as he himself tells us, to the General. He pointed out that the army possessed only sixty cavalrymen in all; that of these De Soto had taken the pick; and that while fifteen were far more than they could afford to lose, they were too few to put up an effective resistance if attacked. He asked to be allowed to follow, to bring De Soto and his men off in case any violence was offered them. The General recognized the force of the argument and dispatched a company of twenty more men under the command of his brother.

A small river had to be crossed, on the further side of which lay the tents of the Indian army. De Soto ordered his men to accompany him no further. He would encounter Atahualpa alone, except for his interpreter. Allowing this native to go over by a frail wooden bridge, which looked as if it could not bear the weight of his horse, he took the twenty-foot breadth of the stream at a bound, for he had a pride in his horse, and, no doubt, in his own horsemanship. It was a gallant sight, and one new to every Indian there, a bearded young athlete in steel, upon a white horse. A white horse and he that sat on him went forth conquering and to conquer.

We are told that from thirty to fifty thousand warriors were encamped about.[1] They lounged outside their tents, their spears stuck upright in the ground, and stared at the strange light-skinned man, clad in iron, astride a ferocious monster. But they were expecting him and pointed out the way to the Inca's apartments.

This was one of Atahualpa's bathing places. He had constructed here a tank fed with hot and cold water brought from distant springs, and had behind it his pavilion, which De Soto noted as being covered with a shining plaster. Around it were pleasant gardens.

The Inca was sitting upon a low stool, waiting to receive his visitor. The chiefs and women of his household were grouped around him, the chiefs standing, the women sprawling at his feet. As De Soto drew near,

---

[1] The figures given by the chroniclers are always to be received with reserve. It is more than doubtful if Atahualpa could have mustered fifty thousand men.

DE SOTO'S FIRST MEETING WITH THE INCA

[From De Bry]

two girls brought a thin veil which they held up to ob-
scure the dazzling vision of sacred majesty from profane
eyes. This, however, was lowered as soon as the officer
began to speak, with Martinello interpreting.

It was all very embarrassing. Atahualpa never condescended to raise his eyes from the ground or in any way
to notice the presence of his visitor. De Soto did not
then know that this impassivity was carefully cultivated
as the Peruvian fashion of sustaining dignity. He later
came to see the greatest chiefs of the land treated in
exactly the same way, with this addition: they were not
admitted to the Presence unless they carried upon their
backs a slight load to denote their servile status.

De Soto, without dismounting, addressed the Inca,
saying that he was a captain sent by the Governor to bear
his compliments and to ask for an interview. The Inca
still disdained to look at the speaker and offered no reply.
Even though the officer's horse was so close to Atahualpa
that the animal's neck was arched over the imperial head,
the war-lord of Peru bore himself as though unaware
that anyone was there. This serene disdain is astonishing
when we remember that the Inca had never in all his
life seen any beast larger than the mild llama. Horses
were to the Peruvians as terrifying as dragons.
Our familiarity with them prevents us from realizing
how strange these creatures must be to a man seeing them
for the first time: the strong thick neck, terminating in
a thin small face terrifying in its mouth and nostrils, the
bristling ridge of the mane, the hoofs of horn and iron
that clang upon the ground and strike fire from the flint.
Yet Atahualpa never stirred.

At this moment Hernando Pizarro arrived at the outskirts of the camp. He at once hurried on to join De Soto, leaving all his men, except two, on the farther side of the stream, ordering them to charge at the first hostile sign.

Encouraged by his support De Soto spoke again: "This, he said, "is a brother of the Governor who comes to see you." Then at last the Inca raised his eyes and looked the Spaniards in the face. They saw before them a young man of about thirty, handsome in a heavy, loose-lipped style, but melancholy and apathetic in expression, and with blood-shot eyes. He was wearing around his head plaits of colored wool, with a fringe of fine crimson threads enlaced with gold falling over his forehead. This was the *borla,* which without being exactly the emblem of sovereignty was the nearest approach to one in vogue among the Peruvians. The head-dress, as Xerez remarks, made Atahualpa look graver than he really was. They did not quail as he expected, though his first words were threatening: "Malçabilica, a captain that I have on the river Turica, sent to say that you ill-treat the *caciques* and put them in chains, in proof of which he sent me a collar of iron. However, I am told that he killed three Christians and one of your horses." He added, however, in a different tone, "But I intend to go to-morrow to see the Governor, and to be a friend to the Christians." Somehow the assurance was not very comforting.

This was too much for the plain-spoken Hernando Pizarro. He bristled at once and blurted out, "Malçabilica is a scoundrel; and as for killing Christians, he and all the Indians of that river together could not kill one. How could they kill a Christian — or a horse — seeing that they are mere chickens ? We do not ill-treat the *caciques* unless they are hostile. Those who are friendly we treat well. But those who attack us we destroy."

The atmosphere was growing warm. De Soto whispered to the truculent man by his side, who continued more graciously, "I want to tell you that the Governor has a great regard for you. If you have any enemies say so, and we will conquer them for you."

Atahualpa probably thought, and with reason, in view of his recent triumph over Huascar, that any conquering that needed to be done he could undertake himself. But he answered mildly, "In a place distant a four days' march there are some rebellious Indians, and I should be glad if the Christian army would go there to help my troops."

At this the fiery-tempered officer laughed contemptuously. "Ten of our horsemen, would suffice for the whole country. As for your Indians, they would be unnecessary except to search for those who were in hiding."

The Inca smiled in his turn. Hernando Pizarro's own comment was that he did so "like a man who did not much esteem us." It is easily believed.

Refreshments were now brought. Two girls came carrying golden goblets of *chicha,* a fermented drink made from maize; but the Inca signalled to them with his eyes, and they went back quietly and brought larger vessels.

The captains were a little shy of drinking, fearing poison, and explained that they were keeping a fast;

but, upon being importuned by the girls, and fearing still more of seeming afraid, they drained their golden goblets.

All this while De Soto's white horse, a magnificent animal, had been champing his bit and pawing the ground, much to the interest of Atahualpa and his attendants. The captain, noticing this, thought he had a good opportunity for exhibiting his charger; so, digging in his spurs, he went wildly over the plain at full gallop. Then, wheeling him in, he showed off all the grace and spirit of his mount and his own skill. Returning, again at full tilt, he reined in the horse, pulling him back almost to his haunches, right in front of the Inca — so near that a fleck of foam from the animal's straining flanks was thrown upon the royal robes. The chiefs who stood around fell back in alarm, and the women screamed. But Atahualpa never moved an eyelash. Those who had flinched were put to death that night for showing such timidity. Their bodies were found by the Spaniards, and the Inca, when questioned about their death, calmly said that it had been by his own orders.

The sun that, during the clearing of the sky that afternoon, had come from behind heavy clouds, now began to sink behind the enormous snow-capped mountains. It was the god of the Peruvians, and the emblem of the Inca, who was the Child of the Sun.

Its setting reminded the two officers that their mission was still uncompleted. Good-humor now having been restored by the exhibition of De Soto's horsemanship, they ventured to bring their business to an issue. What answer were they to take back to the Governor?

The Inca told them that they were to occupy the houses in the square — those and no others. In the morning he would come to visit them.

De Soto and his companion, delighted at their success, made their courtliest bows and rode back to Caxamarca.

But when the situation of the army was discussed that night in the council of officers, the words of Atahualpa took on a sinister significance. They were to occupy the houses in the square — those and no others ? Which meant that they were obligingly to pack themselves into a trap.

The barracks that had been assigned was a large low building of three wings, enclosing three sides of a square, though two sides sloped somewhat together. Like all the Incan buildings of the better class, it was built of enormous blocks of stone, had no windows, or very few, and all its heavy doorways opened on to the large central court. It is evident that the Inca's plan was to occupy the only means of egress, and so take the whole of the Spanish force prisoners.

Atahualpa intended their barracks to be their prison. He had overlooked the fact that it was perfectly adapted also for a very different kind of *coup de main*. The Spaniards determined to spring the trap first.

That night the guards in Caxamarca were redoubled and the rounds were gone with extraordinary care. Upon the slope where the Indian army was encamped, the watch-fires glittered through the night "as thick as the stars of heaven." But no discernible movement of attack was made. With the break of day, however, the Spaniards noticed that half of the Peruvian army had been marched under cover of the darkness to a new position and was now guarding the pass by which the Christians had entered and by which they now could not escape. This decided Pizarro.

Mass was sung, and at its close all joined in the martial psalm *Exsurge Domine*. The troops were assembled in the square and the Governor addressed them. His speech is reported, or summarized by Xerez. "You must all be of good courage to-day, and make fortresses of your hearts. You have no help but God, but remember that He never fails those who work in His service, even in their most sore need. For every Christian here, there are five hundred Indians. But we shall triumph, because God will fight upon our side." Every man, after listening to the General's words, felt equal to fighting a hundred.[2]

The Governor now posted his men. Into the two side wings he concealed his cavalry under De Soto and Hernando Pizarro. At the base of the square, Sebastian de Benalcazar (who was later destined to be famous as the conqueror of Popayan) was stationed in charge of the main body of the infantry. The Governor with twenty halberdiers occupied a stratgeic point, from which he could act as the occasion demanded. In a tower, overlooking the whole position, Pedro de Candia waited with the three arquebusiers and the "artillery." This consisted of two tiny cannon called falconets.

This admirable disposition of the forces was made

[2] So says Hernando Pizarro. But his cousin Pedro records that the terror of many of the Spaniards while waiting for Atahualpa to come was such that they were unable to contain their water. If they were afraid they did not show it in any other way.

only as a precautionary measure. Atahualpa was to be given his chance peaceably to accept the overlordship of the Emperor. But if he resisted, the Spaniards were determined to carry him off in the face of his whole army. They would thus disorganize it by depriving it of a head, and at the same time give themselves the most valuable of hostages.

Atahualpa seems to have been suspicious and hesitant. At noon he set out from his camp but, instead of entering the city as he had promised, pitched his tent a quarter of a league away, and brought up his men in three divisions. He then sent a messenger to say that as it was now the afternoon, he would stay the night where he was and visit the Spaniards the following morning. The lame excuse was obviously intended to cloak his intention of besieging the city.

Pizarro acted with decision. It would never do to keep his men on edge indefinitely. They had been in an exalted mood and the continued tension would be too much for their nerves, and might bring a reaction of panic. He therefore dispatched a messenger to Atahualpa announcing that he had prepared a supper for him, and would be very disappointed at his absence. Thus urged, Atahualpa advanced with five thousand attendants and entered the city.[3]

[3] Pizarro has often been condemned for attacking unarmed men. But as a matter of fact the Indians were armed, though with concealed weapons. Hernando Pizarro, it is true, speaks of them as having no arms; but a page or two later he says they were armed. The contradiction is explainable. They carried no spears or bows, thinking that, in view of their numbers, swords and daggers, darts, slings, and clubs would be amply sufficient. Xerez distinctly tells us that this bodyguard had weapons hidden under their cloaks. We cannot believe that Atahualpa would have entered Caxamarca unprotected. And the fact that he brought so large a number of men with him confirms this.

It was a resplendent procession. Going before the Inca, clearing away the straw and other refuse from the road, went a body of three or four hundred Indians dressed in a livery of vari-colored chequers. Then came Atahualpa, borne in a litter in the midst of his chiefs, all of them crowned with gold and silver, and with large pendants from their ears. The palanquin of the Inca was lined with the feathers of the macaw and adorned with plates of gold. Round his neck was a string of huge emeralds; and he wore the crimson *borla*. Also in a litter, which was a signal honor, was carried "the Lord of Chincha," the feudatory prince of the southern part of the Peruvian plains. He probably would not have been treated with such distinction — which had never been accorded to him before — except for the need of overawing the Spaniards with a sense of the might and majesty of the barbarian chief.

Upon reaching the centre of the square, the Inca ordered a halt, and while the litters were held high upon the shoulders of the bearers, the troops fell in files to the sides of the square, making room for those who were still marching in. This was no rabble horde, but an army. It was easy to understand how their discipline had given them domination over the stupider and more cowardly tribes of Peru. But the casques made from the heads of wild animals, with the grinning fangs above the stolid faces of the warriors, indicated that they were savages after all.

No sooner had the formation been completed than an Indian chief ascended the tower where the artillery

ATHABALIPA
ullimus Rex Peruanorum

ATAHUALPA
[From Ogilby's *America*, London 1671]

was posted and lifted his lance.[4]   Candia and his artillery-
men were waiting there with steel, flint and tinder
ready beside their loaded falconets.   When the Indians
mounted the stairs the Spaniards assumed a careless loung-
ing air.

Now Father Vincent Valverde came forward in the
black and white garb of the Dominican order — the no-
blest of all religious habits.   From his girdle dangled his
large rosary.   In one hand he held a crucifix, in the other
a Bible.   With him was the Indian interpreter Martinello.

He threw back his cowl, blessed the Inca with his crucifix, bowed, and began to speak.   "I am a priest of God,"
he said, "and I teach Christians the things of God.   I
have now come to teach you.   What I teach is what God
says to us in this book." [5]

Father Vincent, who was afterwards the first Bishop
of Cuzco, then explained briefly the main points of Christian belief: the mystery of the Trinity, the creation of
man, the calamity of the loss of his primordial innocence,
the promise of a Redeemer, the incarnation and birth of
Jesus Christ, His crucifixion under Pontius Pilate, His
resurrection, and His ascension into heaven.

He went on to tell of the founding of the Church by
Christ, and of the vicegerency of St. Peter and his suc-
cessors upon earth.   Then he came to the point that most
immediately affected the Inca.   One of the Popes had

---

[4] Xerez took this to be a signal; but Hernando Pizarro regarded it as being
merely some sort of ceremonial gesture in honor of the Inca.

[5] The egregious Abbott observes with some surprise that the friar's preach-
ing upon this occasion was, despite its admixture of popish errors, "what
might be called evangelical."

commissioned the kings of Spain to conquer and convert the natives in this part of the newly discovered hemisphere; and it was for that purpose these Christians had come to Peru.[6]

Atahualpa did not answer, as did another Indian chief, that the Pope must have been drunk at the time he divided the New World between Spain and Portugal; and that the kings of those countries must be insane to think that they could take what did not belong to them. Instead he listened politely to the sermon, and with exemplary patience, though he could not have comprehended much of so general an exposition of Christian doctrine, which came to him through an interpreter who was not very expert in either theology or Castilian. Garcilasso says that what the Inca got out of the dogma of the Trinity was that "the Christians believed in three Gods and one God, and that made four."

The Friar concluded, "Therefore, on the part of God and of the Christians I beseech you to be their friend, for such is God's will. And it will be for your good."

Atahualpa then said, "You told me that your authority for all these things is that book you are carrying. Let me have a look at it."

The volume was fastened with a strong clasp, which the Inca did not know how to open. When Father Vin-

---

[6] The good friar was a missionary, not a theologian. Like many of the missionaries he had in him a good deal of the *Conquistador* just as most of the *Conquistadores* had in them a good deal of the missionary. Valverde more likely than not knew Francisco de Vitoria. He could hardly have known that his fellow-Dominican had just delivered a course of lectures in Salamanca, in which he flatly denied the right of the Pope to divide the New World between Spain and Portugal, and that on the ground that the Pope's temporal power was held "only as far as is necessary for the administration of spiritual affairs." In any case it did not extend to unbelievers.

cent courteously reached forward to help him, Atahualpa struck him for his presumption and wrenched open the Bible for himself. He stared at the pages, not understanding the purpose of writing or print; and in a fury threw the sacred volume five or six yards away.

The anger he had cloaked with suavity was shaking him now. He ignored the exposition of doctrine, and said in a loud scornful voice, "I know very well how you have behaved on the road, that you have maltreated my chiefs and stolen cloth from my warehouses. You even took the mats away from a room in which my father once slept."

Valverde tried to pacify him. "The Christians didn't steal anything. Some Indians took the cloth without the knowledge of the Governor, and he ordered it to be returned."

But Atahualpa replied angrily, "I will not leave this place until they bring it all to me." [7]

Vincent Valverde returned sadly to Pizarro with his report. It was perfectly clear to their minds that the complaint about a few bales of cloth, raised at that moment, was for the purpose of provoking a quarrel. The whole tone of the Inca had been belligerent. And he had offered a deliberate insult to the Christian religion. [8]

[7] Pedro Pizarro reports the Inca as saying at this point, "You are all scurvy rogues, and I am going to have you all put to death." Even if he did not use those precise words, it was undoubtedly what he meant.

[8] According to some reports (but not including those of Pedro Pizarro and Xerez, and specifically contradicted by Garcilasso) Valverde incited the Spaniards to attack. It is probable enough that he did so. But in his justification it must be remembered that he had done his best to persuade Atahualpa to peace, and it had been decided upon before hand that if he failed Pizarro's plan was to be executed. The "incitation" in all likelihood amounted to his saying, "I can do nothing with him. You'll have to strike at once."

The Governor, from where he was concealed, saw Atahualpa standing up in his litter to address his men; and
he could hear their answering murmurs, low at that distance, but harsh and ominous.

The hour had struck. Pizarro at once strapped on a
doublet of quilted cotton, belted his sword round him,
and waved a white scarf to Pedro Candia on his tower.
Immediately the falconets and the arquebuses were dis-
charged and the trumpets rang out, the echoes clanging
against the stone sides of the square.

The thunder of the firearms was intended to have only
a moral effect. After the first volley, the falconets were
fired in the air, lest a ball should hit a Spaniard. During
the momentary interval between the waving of the scarf
and the discharge of the artillery, the cavaliers had fastened round their horses necks large bells which had been
held in readiness. Leaping into their saddles they
charged towards the litter of the Inca.

From three sides of the square they came, the bells
clanging and the trumpets blowing to increase the uproar.
Close behind the dragoons pressed the foot-soldiers all
shouting the Spanish battle cry, "Santiago ! Santiago !"

The suddenness of the impact and the noise gave the
impression of numbers much greater than were really
there. But the Indians were less confused by the surprise
assault than at the sight of a horseman in the sky, seated
upon a milk-white steed, and bearing a drawn sword in
his hand.[9] It was nearly seven hundred years since the
first time that St. James had appeared, upon the field of

[9] So says the Dominican Naharro. Without questioning the possibility of
the miracle, one wonders if the horseman upon the milk-white steed might

Clavijo, to turn the tide of battle against the infidel.

As soon as they saw the dragoons charging upon them, the greater part of the Indians fled as best they could through the open end of the square. Such was the pressure of that tumultuous crowd of terrified men, that part of a wall was broken down, and any who stumbled were trodden to death by their panic-stricken comrades.

Those who chose, or were compelled, to remain in the square were hacked to pieces by the sabres of the cavalry or fell before the pikes of the halberdiers. The ranks that had deployed so showily earlier that afternoon were formed of men who lacked, after all, the inner core of discipline. But, indeed, civilized troops might have been pardoned for not knowing what to do at so terrible a moment.

Those who could not escape and a few braver warriors clustered round the reeling litter of Atahualpa. The Lord of Chincha was killed; the guards who had rallied about the Inca were cut down; and the bearers of the gold-plated palanquin let it drop. The Inca was saved from injury by Pizarro who caught him in his arms. In doing so the Governor received an accidental wound in the hand from a Spanish sword. This was the only casualty among the Christians on that day.

Far out into the country the dragoons pursued the fleeing Peruvians; for even the thousands of fully armed men beyond the walls of the city took to their heels when the Indians inside came out pell-mell, wailing that the Inca had been taken. De Soto and Hernando Pizarro again rode as far as the baths where they had been the

not have been De Soto, not of course in the sky, but striking the terrified imagination of the Peruvians as the apparition of some superhuman being.

[85]

previous afternoon. It was necessary to improve upon the good work of the day and to follow up the capture of the Inca by striking his subjects with salutary terror. Yet the fight did not last long. Sunset, and the doom of the Child of the Sun, had been near when it began; and the fugitives could not be pursued after the fall of darkness. Garcilasso puts the number of Indians slain at ten thousand; Xerez at two thousand. It was more likely nearer two hundred.

Atahualpa had been invited to supper. He fulfilled his engagement, though the meal was unavoidably delayed. It was also probably spoiled, but he had the compensation of drinking wine for the first time in his life, and pronounced it superior to *chicha*.

Sitting at the Governor's right hand in a hall facing the square, he could see through the doorway how choked the place was with the corpses of his warriors. But the Spaniards were innocent of irony: there was no other banqueting-hall available. They treated their guest with elaborate deference, and served a rough soldierly fare to him upon plates of gold.

During the meal Pizarro demanded of his guest why he had thrown away the Bible Father Valverde had shown him. Had he not known that that would be regarded as an unforgivable insult? Atahualpa admitted his arrogance; but he had been misled by his spies and advisers. They had told him that the Christians were no great fighters; [10] that the terrible horses were unsad-

[10] This is the significance of the remark: The Spanish prowess was underrated because, up to that time, they had avoided fight whenever it had been possible to do so. Their humane and conciliatory policy had been judged as a sign of pusillanimity.

dled at night; and that with two hundred Indians he would be able to defeat them all. In this expectation he had allowed the army to advance as far as Caxamarca because he was curious to see what kind of men they were. It had been his intention to select a few of them as his personal slaves and to take possession of their arms and horses. The rest had been destined for death.

As a prisoner he could afford to be candid; and he dispassionately applauded the skill with which the Spaniards had turned the tables upon him. It was clever of them to have caught him in his own trap.

Looking back upon it all, the Inca felt little shame at being so easily defeated. It is true that his troops had hitherto proved invariably invincible; but then they had never encountered Christians before. The invaders constituted, he acknowledged, a most remarkable race of men, probably semi-divine, certainly the people who, according to the ancient secret tradition of the Incas, were to conquer the country and to change its religion. It was not merely that they were bearded and fair, or that they shot thunderbolts from afar, or that they bestrode without fear those amazing monsters, their horses. Upon their faces the mild Peruvians saw a terrifying look. It was the energy of Europe — that quality which has always overawed the savage and the oriental. The Chinese express the common feeling when they speak of "Foreign Devils." The Inca thought of it in somewhat different terms: in these Spaniards had been fulfilled the long prophesied return of the gods.

CHAPTER VI

THE DOOM OF THE INCAS

FROM sunset of the 16th of November 1532, the
Spaniards were the lords of Peru. The Inca was in
their hands, and though his army was intact, it was
now without effective leaders and stunned by calamity.
The Indian warriors had withdrawn as rapidly as they
could to distant parts of the country.

The conquerors had taken a large number of prisoners. Someone now made the suggestion that their right
hands should be cut off to disable them, and to strike
terror into the country. The inhuman proposal was rejected. There was not likely to be any further resistance,
at least not for some time. And, as Pizarro said, they
should not desire to emulate the Indians in cruelty.
The prisoners were accordingly released.

In Caxamarca the food supply was abundant. The
military granaries were well stocked; and the herds of
llamas provided meat in plenty, despite reckless waste.
The army determined to remain where it was until the
arrival of reinforcements — which could be safely counted
upon now, in view of what had been accomplished —
made possible the march to Cuzco.

Meanwhile the Inca cheerfuly accommodated himself to a captivity which was not disagreeable. He was given a magnificent suite of apartments for his private use; he was allowed to have there such of his servants and concubines as it pleased him to summon; all the deference due to his rank was punctiliously accorded him; and he was able to receive visitors freely. His imprisonment meant little more than that a guard was set over him night and day. He probably found it a pleasant relief from the boredom of his office; and he could afford to wait for his ultimate release. In the interval he cultivated the society of the amusing visitors to his land.

For their part, they came sincerely to like him; and their good-nature pitied his downfall. Except when he was among his own subjects, at which times he assumed his old demeanor of impassive gravity, treating the greatest chieftains with sublime haughtiness, Atahualpa turned out to be an amiable fellow. It was a relief to him to be able to unbend and to crack jokes with his captors. They taught him chess, at which intricate game he displayed a rapidly acquired proficiency; they also taught him to speak a little Spanish, and even to read a few words. The men with whom he was upon the most friendly terms were Hernando Pizarro and De Soto. The elaborate courtliness of the one cavalier, the brilliance and the knightly bearing of the other, pleased him immensely.

These men and the Dominican fathers all tried their hands at his conversion. It was difficult to get metaphysical ideas into the head of a barbarian, though Atahualpa was a very intelligent one; but they managed at least to convince him that his own idols were worthless. It was not hard to establish that point. The gods had given him no help; and the oracle, when consulted, had advised him to attack the Spaniards. But despite Valverde's zealous brandishing of the threat of hell-fire, the pagan chief shrugged his shoulders and said that he would live as his fathers had done.

Sitting one day with his captors after dinner, he offered for his ransom to fill the room in which they were with gold up to a point which he reached standing upon his toes.

As the room was thirty-two feet long by seventeen wide, the officers laughed, thinking this one of the Inca's many pleasant jests. To convince them that he was serious he improved upon his offer: he would fill a similar room twice over with silver. Then, seeing by the amazement upon their faces that he had named too high a price, he stipulated that the gold and silver were not to be melted into ingots — it must be accepted in whatever form it arrived, whether in bars or as beaten vessels. Pizarro closed with his offer and gave him two months in which to make it good.

Messengers were at once sent out to the various districts where there were royal residences, and the treasures of Peru soon began to pour in. Barbaric gold dazzled the eyes of the Spaniards. Day after day they saw some new splendors displayed. The designs of the goblets, platters, and images were not, as a rule, very elaborate; but in view of the Peruvian lack of iron — or rather of their failure to make use of the ore in which their soil abounded — their metal work was remarkable.

THE RANSOM OF ATAHUALPA
[From De Bry]

They had considerable skill in the process of smelting. Yet their alloys were all a matter of luck. They managed to make cutting tools of bronze, but no two were ever of the same temper, and the vast majority of their chisels were useless. But with others the Indian artist contrived to achieve, by his patience, works of sculpture and graving which were ingenious, if rarely lovely.

The Inca was playing for time. The appraisal of the ransom would keep his captors busy. And it would be a most difficult matter for them afterwards to transport all that treasure down the mountain paths for shipment to Spain. The men who brought in the gold and silver were sent out again with messages to the chiefs, and by this means Atahualpa could sit, though a captive, at the centre of the web into which the Christians were to be snared. So he went on jesting and playing chess with that charming young man De Soto.

After a time, the treasure began to come in very slowly, and the Spaniards began to be suspicious. The Governor decided to send out scouting parties to see if there was any valid cause for the delay.

One of these, under the command of Hernando Pizarro, was sent to Pachacamac on the sea coast to the south. It was there that the famous oracle had its seat in the temple.[1] The other was under De Soto and went to Cuzco.

In the great temple of Pachacamac Hernando Pizarro found very little treasure — only eighty-five thousand

[1] Pachacamac is not far from the present city of Lima, founded by Pizarro, which has the honor of being the birthplace of the only canonized saint of the Americas. She is St. Rose of Lima, an Indian girl, who was a member of the Dominican order.

castellaños and three thousand marks of silver, a disappointing haul. But he had another purpose, always present to the conquerors, besides that of gathering gold. He was anxious to convert the heathen. Much to the consternation of the Indians he penetrated into the inner shrine, where the oracles were delivered, and found in a dark chamber which had a close fetid stench, a "very dirty idol made of wood." The worshippers were waiting paralysed with terror for Pachacamac to destroy the sacrilegious violator of his sanctuary; but nothing happened, even when the officer ordered the shrine to be broken up and a crucifix erected instead. Then, as he himself tells us, "for want of a preacher, I made my sermon, explaining to them the errors in which they lived." The text, in effect, was that of *Dei gentium dæmonia*. He gave them some instruction in the Catholic Faith, and taught them how to make the sign of the cross in order to defend themselves against the Evil One. Good soldierly theology!

His piety was soon rewarded. He heard that Chalcuchima, the Inca second in importance to Atahualpa, was near Xauxa a four days' march away, and that with him was a large convoy of gold.[2]

On the way across the mountains the horses needed new shoes. As iron was lacking, the Spaniards shod them with some of the silver taken from Pachacamac. It was typical of the mingling of romance and realism in the conquest of Peru.

Chalcuchima, though outnumbering Hernando Pi-

[2] Xerez, Estete, Hernando Pizarro and others give a full account of this most interesting expedition.

zarro's band by several hundreds to one, was found in a state of abject fright. He had been deliberately dawdling the time away at Xauxa. He could do so no longer. The captain drove the pusillanimous warrior before him; and in his train were two hundred and sixty llama-loads of gold.

Hernando de Soto was not less successful. Three common soldiers, along with one of the numerous half-brothers of Atahualpa,[3] had preceded him to Cuzco. Pizarro had given the men strict instructions that they were to do nothing displeasing to the chief, and that they were not to injure the natives or lay their hands upon private property. But, with the consent of the Inca, they were to hasten the sending of the gold in the temple.

Unfortunately these men were of a type of which there were only too many among the *Conquistadores,* and behaved in Cuzco like drunken sailors on shore-leave. Accordingly De Soto and another officer were sent after them to see that they exercised some restraint.

The two officers made their journey of six hundred miles in unfamiliar luxury, and were carried in litters along the mountain trails. At Xauxa, which they reached some time after Hernando Pizarro had left it, they encountered no less a personage than Huascar, the deposed Inca. He piteously addressed De Soto, begging that he would turn back and accompany him to Caxamarca. In the hands of his Indian captors he feared for his life. If only they would take his part against Ata-

[3] The father of Atahualpa, who was the possessor of a huge seraglio, might easily have been the father of fifty sons. Garcilasso says that some of the Incas had three hundred children.

hualpa he would give the Spaniards twice as much gold as it was in his brother's power to offer.[4]

A good deal of, this was lost upon the two Spanish officers, though not upon the Indian custodians of Huascar. The speech got to the ears of Atahualpa, with what result we shall see presently. In any event De Soto did not feel justified in going back. His instructions were to proceed to Cuzco. So, ordering the Indians to take Huascar to Caxamarca, he went upon his way.

As soon as he arrived in Cuzco he put a sharp stop to what the three soldiers already there were doing. Their business, he reminded them, had no connection with the Virgins of the Sun, but only with the temple of the Sun. The safety of their own skins was of no great moment to him, but they were exasperating the Indians and so endangering the Governor's policy. They had better confine themselves to stripping the temple of its gold, for which they had the warrant, however reluctantly given, of the Inca himself.

From the walls of the great building, therefore, were taken some of its plates of gold. Seven hundred of them were taken down, the smallest of which, says Sancho, weighed four or five pounds, the larger ten to twelve pounds. They found also a seat of pure gold which was valued at eighteen thousand *pesos,* upon which the Sun was supposed to rest himself when weary. They did not molest the image of the Sun which, upon an enormous plate of gold, blazed upon the inner shrine, or that of the

---

[4] The promise, extravagant as it may sound, could possibly have been fulfilled. Huascar was the rightful Inca and inherited the bulk of his father's treasure. He is said to have hidden these during the civil war, and to have killed the Indians who buried it.

Moon, his sister-wife, confronting it. And they left undisturbed the mummies of the predecessors of Atahualpa, each sitting in its golden chair.

De Soto and his companion now had an opportunity to view the marvels of the Inca's capital. It was the largest of the Peruvian cities, though it probably had nothing like the two hundred thousand inhabitants credited to it by the perfervid imagination of one of the chroniclers. Father Valverde estimated the number of its houses at twenty-three thousand, which would cut the other figure in half.

It had many fine stone palaces, but the vast majority of its buildings were adobe. The streets were laid regularly at right-angles, but were so narrow as hardly to give two horsemen room to pass.

The object for which De Soto naturally felt the most admiration was the fortress on the hill overlooking Cuzco. Pedro Sancho was afterwards to pronounce that "neither the bridge of Segovia nor any other of the edifices which Hercules or the Romans made is so worthy of being seen as this." He calls it "beautiful," and so no doubt it was from a soldierly point of view. Being higher than any other building in the country it possessed at any rate a symmetry which the other sprawling and squat Inca structures lacked.

When De Soto got back with his convoy he found that Hernando Pizarro had just arrived with spoils as opulent as his own, those which the tardy Chalcuchima had been bringing in; and the Governor decided to wait no longer. Almagro had arrived with over two hundred men, so the Spaniards now felt themselves in a position to extend their power over the whole country. But they had first to distribute the ransom of Atahualpa.

Some time was necessarily taken in melting down and weighing so huge a treasure, but by the 18th of June 1533 the whole business was completed. Atahualpa was released from further obligations; though it was thought necessary, for the safety of the army, to keep him in custody a little longer. A fifth share was reserved for the Emperor, with which Hernando Pizarro, of the hot temper but courtly grace, was dispatched to Spain. The rest was divided among the army, Almagro and his men getting (because of their absence in November) only a bounty of twenty thousand *pesos*. To each officer and man the Governor assigned the amount which, in his judgment, his individual services had been worth. Francisco Pizarro's own share amounted to fifty-seven thousand two hundred and twenty *pesos* and two thousand three hundred and fifty marks of silver. Hernando Pizarro was given a recompense rather more than half his brother's, and De Soto seventeen thousand seven hundred and forty *pesos,* and seven hundred and twenty-four marks of silver. His share may be taken as a standard; a first-class cavalryman got about half of what he received, and a foot-soldier about a fourth, some a little more, and some a little less. The poorest paid was made rich.

With such an influx of wealth coming into the hands of men who were not used to it, absurd prices prevailed. A horse sold for from two to three thousand gold pieces, a sword for fifty, and a pair of boots for forty. Men settled their debts by going from house to house followed by an Indian laden with gold, and handed out lumps with complete indifference to their weight.

This saturnalia of spending by men without a care in the world suddenly received a check. The news came that Huascar had been murdered, and it was taken to be a sign, of which there were soon to be others, of a stiffening of purpose on the part of Atahualpa and his partisans.

Pizarro had always intended to go into the claims of the rivals for the Incaship, but he had been busy with other concerns and had put off doing so. In fact, while Atahualpa remained in his hands, it suited his purpose to have him regarded as the Inca. It was enough for him that Huascar should be in the safe custody of his Indian enemies. When a conclusion had been reached over a difficult case — and that depended upon the devious intricacies of Peruvian politics — it would be time enough to send for him. He contented himself, therefore, with warning Atahualpa that he would be answerable with his own head for his brother's death.

The wily Inca hit upon an expedient for finding out if Pizarro really meant what he said. One day when he went to dine with the Governor, he pretended to be in deep affliction and wept. When Pizarro asked him what was the matter, he would not answer, but wept more copiously. Finally he sobbed out, "I am crying because you are going to kill me."

"Kill you!" cried the governor. "What do you mean? I am not going to kill you. Let me know what your trouble is."

Then in great agitation, Atahualpa said, "My Lord, you

gave me orders that Huascar was not to be killed, and you said you would kill me if any harm came to him. Now he has been killed; but it was done without my consent. And you will take my life."

Pizarro tried to comfort him. He need have no fear. If this had been done without his consent, he could not be held responsible. This was exactly what the Inca had wanted to know. He had tested the ice and found that it would bear. The same day he sent a secret message to Huascar's keepers, and the unfortunate man was at once drowned in the river Andamarca. Atahualpa had heard a few days before of his brother's meeting with De Soto.

The truth about this murder came out before long. And other disquieting reports reached the Spaniards in Caxamarca. It was said that the Inca had been in communication with Rumi-ñacu, "the stone-eyed," one of the Peruvian war-lords, and that the tribes were mustering for the attack.

Counting Almagro's reinforcements, the Spaniards were still only a handful against a host. It was small wonder that even these men of iron found the situation getting upon their nerves. There began to be a demand that Atahualpa be brought to trial; and in this the newcomers under Almagro were notably insistent.

The proposal was vigorously opposed by a group of officers, who were led by De Soto. They argued that whatever Atahualpa's guilt might be, he came under the jurisdiction of no lesser court than that of the Emperor. De Soto offered to be the Inca's escort to the coast, from where he could be sent to Spain; he denied that Pizarro possessed any competency in the matter.

This was regarded by many others as pedantry, and with some justification. It was not a time when men could afford to be hampered by the technicalities of normal legal procedure. Feeling ran high between the Almagroists and the group led by De Soto.

Indian runners at this moment came in with news that Rumi-ñacu was on the march, or so Felipillo interpreted them. De Soto was therefore sent out to reconnoitre. He was always the man chosen for such dangerous duties. But it was work in which he delighted. Meanwhile orders were given that the guard should be redoubled in Caxamarca, and that every man was to sleep with his sword within reach, and his horse saddled.

It has been suggested that De Soto was sent on this scouting expedition to get him out of the way. That may have been the motive; for De Soto was now, since the departure of Hernando Pizarro for Spain, Atahualpa's main support. On the other hand, we must remember that reconnoitring was in the line of his special aptitude. He was the obvious man for this operation. What is more likely is that the Almagroists took advantage of his absence to press for the trial of the Inca.

The whole garrison was in a state of "the jumps." At any moment they expected to see the passes full of Rumi-ñacu's warriors. The punishment of the Inca was the Spanish trump card. Pizarro was obliged, however reluctantly, to play it.

Probably no one, not even De Soto, had much doubt

of Atahualpa's guilt. The only question was one concerning the jurisdiction of a court-martial. The consensus of opinion — which De Soto's absence facilitated — was that as the offence of the prisoner was a military one, the officers had competency over it. This view was prompted by panic, and prevailed. The Inca was brought to trial for his life.

The indictment was drawn up by soldiers, not jurists, and was therefore clumsily worded. One of the charges — that Atahualpa had many concubines — was ludicrous. He was a pagan, and so not bound by Christian law. And in any event he had received his women at Caxamarca with the full consent of the Spaniards. Moreover, many of the Spaniards had themselves taken Indian girls as concubines. Pizarro later had one of Atahualpa's daughters as his mistress. The gravamen of the Inca's criminality was that he had murdered Huascar, after usurping his office, and that he had treacherously used the privileges he enjoyed of receiving his chiefs in order to organize a revolt against Spanish rule.

The Inca had learned a little Castilian during his captivity, but it was too little to be of much service to him in the trial. For lack of any other available instrument, the services of Felipillo had to be used. It so happened, however, that this young Indian, who came from the island of Puna, belonged to one of the oppressed tribes that hated the Incas. And he is said to have been engaged in an intrigue with one of Atahualpa's concubines. He was well aware that, if Atahualpa ever regained power, a death full of unimaginable tortures would be his own portion. He therefore twisted both questions and answers to suit his own purpose.[5] Even apart from any intention to deceive, he was not a satisfactory interpreter. Quechua was not his native tongue, though cognate to it; and his Castilian was vile. He may have blundered through ignorance. But whether through ignorance or malice, the Indian youth had both the Inca and the Spanish judges at his mercy.

Twenty days earlier, before any warning had come about the rising of the natives, Atahualpa had sat one evening, talking cheerfully and joking, as was his custom, with the Christian officers. He pointed out a comet which had appeared in the sky over the direction of Cuzco. This, he told them, indicated that a very great lord would soon have to die in the land. No sinister meaning had been attached at the time to the remark by any one present. But Atahualpa's words were now remembered against him.

He was found guilty on what the court-martial believed to be amply sufficient evidence, and was condemned to death by burning.[6] It is certain that the Governor deplored the hard military necessity which obliged him to carry out the sentence. He, in common with all the conquerors, felt a sincere liking for the Inca; but he could not allow personal feelings to stand in the way of what he conceived to be the safety of the army.

---

[5] Just before he was hanged by Almagro, as happened to him later, he is said to have confessed to this.

[6] Burning was the mode of execution for the crime of heresy. But the *Conquistadores* used it sometimes for military offences which demanded exceptionally severe punishment. This, in their opinion, was such a case.

Many men saw him weep at not being able to spare Atahualpa's life.[7]

Two hours after sunset the trumpet rang out in the square, and the army was assembled by torchlight to witness the execution of the sentence. In the centre of the wide court, upon the very spot where he had been carried in his golden palanquin, eight months previously, Inca in fact for the last time, a strong pile was stuck upright in the ground, with faggots piled up. To this Atahualpa, attended by the Dominican chaplain, Valverde, was led in chains.

Father Vincent, who had spent the time between the sentence and the execution in pious exhortations, at last had the fruit of his labors. Atahualpa asked for baptism, and received the name of John. It was the 29th of August, the day upon which the Church commemorates the beheading of St. John the Baptist.

His tardy conversion saved him from the rigor of the sentence of burning. He might be strangled instead. As he was being fastened to the great stake, he committed his sons to the care of Pizarro — a signal act of respect for his executioner. He felt no resentment. He recognized the military necessity for his death. If guilty he must have accepted his execution as his deserts. But in any event the mind of a barbarian tyrant was not likely to have been much affected by abstract considerations of

[7] The sugggestion has been made that Pizarro had a personal grudge. The Inca is said to have expressed contempt for the Governor, when he found that he lacked the accomplishments of some of his subordinates and could neither read nor write. A soldier of that time would have been little troubled at not being able to do what many stupid men of his day (and ours) find easy. The idea can be accepted only by a mind remote from reality.

justice. He certainly died with Indian indifference.

As he gasped his last under the hands of the garrotter, the soldiers, among whom he was universally popular, led by Pizarro, solemnly intoned for his solace at that awful moment, the Apostles' Creed. The Dominican friar, holding his book close to his eyes in the flickering torchlight, read the Prayers for the Dying: *Proficiscere, anima Christiana, de hoc mundo.*[8]

Had De Soto returned that afternoon the sentence upon Atahualpa might not have been carried out; but he went further than he intended, and did not reach Caxamarca until a couple of days later. He was aghast at the news waiting for him. Blazing with anger he strode over at once to the Governor's quarters. He found Pizarro sitting gloomily in his room "with a great felt hat, by way of mourning, slouched over his eyes." Drawing his sword De Soto knocked the hat off, and bitterly reproved his commander. "Sir, you have done a serious injustice. You should in any case have waited for our return. As a matter of fact the accusation against Atahualpa is false. There is no gathering of armed men." [9]

The body of Atahualpa was buried with every mark of respect, and with the ceremonial due to his rank, in the church of St. Francis, where a requiem mass, due to him as a Christian, was sung by Father Valverde, one of the signers of his death warrant.

---

[8] "May God take him to His holy glory," prays pious Pedro Sancho, "for he died repentant of his sins with the true faith of a Christian."

[9] This was perhaps too much to say. De Soto had found no armies assembled for attack; but it was soon to be made apparent that the military organization of the Incas remained undestroyed.

From the friar's lips came the heart-shattering verses of the *Dies Irae:*

> *Tuba mirum spargens sonum*
> *Per sepulchra regionum*
> *Coget omnes ante thronum.*
>
> *Liber scriptus proferetur*
> *In quo totum continetur*
> *Unde mundus judicetur.*
>
> *Judex ergo cum sedebit*
> *Quidquid latet apparebit;*
> *Nil inultum remanebit.*
>
> *Rex tremendæ majestatis,*
> *Qui salvandos salvas gratis,*
> *Salva me, fons pietatis.*

The sublime dirge of Christendom was interrupted by the women members of Atahualpa's household, who wailed at the church door that this was no way to bury an Inca. As they were not allowed to throw themselves into his grave, some of them hanged themselves with their own hair in order to follow him into the land of shades.

CHAPTER VII

THE NAVEL OF THE WORLD

IT WAS now necessary to have a new Inca. Pizarro, thinking in terms of European dynasties, picked To-parca, a brother of the executed war-lord. He invited the *caciques* to name another if they wished to do so, but they hurriedly assented to the Governor's choice.

The time had come for pressing on to Cuzco, and with a force augmented to just under five hundred men, the Governor marched early in September 1533.

It was De Soto's second visit to the capital. On the previous occasion, when he had gone to stop the escapades of the three soldiers with the Virgins of the Sun, he had been carried in a palanquin; now he had to go slowly, painfully, burdened with armor, ready for attack at any moment. Along trails cut in the mountain sides the army advanced, up rocky ledges where the horses found a foothold with difficulty and had often to be led by the bridle, across the swaying bridges of osier, and through narrow defiles where there was always danger of an ambush.

The military foresight of the Incas in building granaries was now of material aid to the Spaniards. Being made of stone these structures could not be burnt. But the villages along the line of march were for the most part destroyed, and as often as not the bridges were found with holes torn in them.

These signs confirmed the Spaniards in their suspicions of the hostile intentions of the Peruvians. Chalcuchima was still in their safe keeping; but they heard that Quizquiz, another great chieftain, was waiting with his forces near Xauxa. Though the absence of tents in the cold rains that were now steadily falling made campaigning difficult, they determined to oust him from his position without delay.

Once again it was De Soto who was selected to clear the way. He was sent on ahead with sixty men and found the bridge broken. The stream was swift, and it was one considered impassable. But the impetuous officer was not to be kept back. He boldly rode his horse into the torrent, to the amazement and consternation of the Indians upon the opposite bank, who had been jeering at him, but who now took to their heels. He had won an important action without striking a blow.

He did not always find victory so easy. As he drew near to the sierra of Villaconga he received intelligence that the main body of the enemy was waiting for him in a mountain pass a few leagues north of Cuzco. He should have waited for reinforcements; but as Herrera says of him, "he was not a whit more prudent than high-spirited," and he determined to go on, despite inadequate support and the fact that some of the passes were already full of snow.

In a steep and winding defile in the mountains the savages rushed down upon him yelling, and carrying aloft derisively, as a banner, the head of a horse killed by their darts. From every rock and tree and bush they came, brandishing their spears and battle-axes. There was no room free for the full weight of a charge: it was as much as the dragoons could do to retain their seats. The Indians tried to drag them from their saddles, and clung round the legs of the mounts. Upon their naked bodies the Spanish sabres did deadly execution, many men falling, cut through from neck to groin. But the horses were tired after the ride and bewildered; and the soldiers were becoming disorganized.

Rising in his stirrups, and lifting his sword to heaven, De Soto gave the battle cry that had been heard upon more than three thousand battlefields from León to Peru. "Santiago! Santiago!" It never failed to fire a Spanish heart. Not once had the warrior-saint deserted them; he would not desert them now. New strength came to the dispirited Christians. With blows more than human they cut through the files of their antagonists, shaking them off, and sending sundered limbs and bodies toppling down the precipices. They gained a little space, charged again at short range against the mass; hacked their way on; were checked; but rallied and pressed forward. At last, having lost five men killed and eleven wounded, as well as several horses, they succeeded in reaching the plateau, where they had room to make the impact of their horses felt.

Night was falling. Watching in their armor through the night, they waited for the disastrous dawn.

The savages had withdrawn only two bowshots away. In the darkness the Spaniards could hear their guttural voices. Sometimes the taunt came, "Wait, Christians, till day, when you are all to die. Then we shall take away from you just as many horses as you have."

De Soto, having looked to the wants of the wounded, addressed his men. His words have been preserved. He said, "Tomorrow we must attack at daybreak, without delaying an instant. Quiz-quiz is coming with reinforcements, and we are lost if we allow him to arrive before we have crushed the men who are encamped over there. I believe the day through which we have come safely was one full of worse perils than the one which awaits us tomorrow. And God, our Lord, who has delivered us from danger in the past, will grant us victory." To which came the mocking answer from the Indian encampment, "Tomorrow, Christians, you die."

That might well have happened, in spite of all De Soto's brave words, except for the arrival of Almagro. The Governor, alarmed by the prolonged silence of his Captain, had sent the Marshall forward with thirty men. Almagro, coming upon evidences of a bitter battle, dead men, Spanish and Indian, forced his march through the night; and before the first break of light glimmered in the east, he ordered the trumpeter to announce his approach to the heights where De Soto waited for the dawn. No sweeter music was ever heard than that of the shrill bugles pealing from crag to crag in the pass below. They answered it with an exultant fanfare.[1]

Pizarro afterwards sent De Soto a message congratu-

---

[1] The blowing of the trumpet in the mountain passes reminds us of Roland, though in this case it was the rash Roland who heard the horn. To him might be applied Oliver's reproof, "Vassallage comes from sense, not folly."

lating him upon his victory, but administering a mild re-
buke for his having been so reckless. He instructed his
subordinate to be guided by prudence in the future; and
ordered him to wait with Almagro at the last bridge, so
that the whole army might enter Cuzco together.
Pedro Pizarro, writing no doubt as spokesman for the
family, suggests that De Soto was trying to steal a march
upon his commander, and had pressed on with the intention of snatching to himself the glory of taking the
capital unaided. It is possible; but equally likely De
Soto was animated merely by innocent impetuosity.

On November 15th, "at the hour of high mass," two
months after setting out from Caxamarca, and a year to
a day since the taking of that city, the Spanish army
entered Cuzco, "the navel of the world."

While they were upon the march the young puppet-
Inca Toparca had been killed, in circumstances so suspicious that everything pointed to murder. It was believed that Chalcuchima had ordered the assassination,
and that he was at the bottom of the Indian insurrection.
Pizarro had appealed to him to urge the natives to lay
down their arms, and had threatened to burn him alive
if hostilities continued. To this Chalcuchima listened at
first, to quote Sancho, "without saying a word." Afterwards he protested that he had advised peace, but had
been disregarded.

The Spaniards refused to believe him. They knew
how great was his influence in the country, and traced to
him the ambush that had been laid for De Soto. That
officer was among the most insistent of those who urged
Chalcuchima's court-martial. He had befriended Ata-

hualpa to the end, but he was now quite cured of trusting Indians.

Father Valverde, while the Indian servants of the chief were bringing the faggots for his pyre, pressed upon him, as he had upon the Inca, the necessity in his extremity for baptism. But Chalcuchima refused, and perished calling upon his gods. He had certainly been playing a deviously treacherous game.

The conquerors would have been embarrassed without an Inca. Toparca had never possessed any authority, because the *caciques* had not really wanted him, and had merely tamely acquiesced in his appointment. A much stronger candidate now come forward in Manco, another of Huayna Capac's sons. He had what Toparca lacked, the spontaneous support of the council of chiefs, and he was friendly to the Spaniards.[2]

It was possible on this occasion to carry out the customary Indian ceremonies — to which were added the Christian rites — much more completely than with the unfortunate Toparca. Mass was sung by Father Valverde, now nominated Bishop of Cuzco; and Pizarro himself bestowed the *borla*. Manco and the chiefs present lifted up the Spanish banner in token of their submission to the Emperor.

After this was over the mummies of the previous Incas were brought out of the temple, paraded through the central square, and put in their golden chairs for the drunken feast with which the Indians crowned the day. Strictly speaking, only one mummy was brought out —

[2] Quintana says of him that "suddenly despairing of the destiny of his country, he went over to the Spaniards."

that of Huayna Capac — for, despite what Garcilasso says, the process of embalming was imperfectly understood among the Peruvians. Even this mummy had lost the tip of its nose, and so the attendants, standing behind with brushes of brightly colored plumes, had to drive away the flies that were eager to settle upon the slowly decomposing flesh. The ancestors of Huayna Capac had reached a stage where they had become unendurable even to the devotion of the Indians and their indifference to stenches. These, therefore, were represented by plaster or clay effigies, to which the original hair and nails, being incorruptible, were fastened.

At the great banquet table food and drink were placed before the departed; and, to quote Pedro Pizarro, "the dead pledged one another as well as the living, and the living pledged the dead."

Though Manco was now Inca, Quiz-quiz was still recalcitrant; and Almagro and De Soto were sent against him, while the Governor remained in the capital to consolidate Spanish power. With them marched the new Inca, who at this time seems to have been sincerely loyal, and a large force of Indian levies. These were probably of not much use except in scouting, and as guides through the mountains. But there were occasions when, in that capacity, they were invaluable. Pedro Sancho tells of a time when the little Christian army found itself surrounded, and was saved only because Manco knew of a road out of the trap.

Soon the responsibility for the military operations fell entirely upon the shoulders of De Soto, Almagro having been obliged to ride north to turn Pedro de Alvarado, who landed in March, away from his designs upon the province of Quito. But it is exceedingly difficult to give any coherent account of a campaign which consisted of hide-and-seek skirmishing in a broken, unfamiliar country. All the reports are confused. Only one thing is clear, that De Soto did efficiently what needed to be done. He checked Quiz-quiz and forced him back; whereupon his followers, disgusted at being driven to a war which they despaired of winning, assassinated him.

But even De Soto was not always engaged in fighting. He found time for other adventures. A large part of Miguel Cabello Balboa's *History of Peru* is devoted to a romantic story in which he figures. The Inca Huascar had a favorite concubine to whom he gave the name of Curicuillor, Star of Gold, because of her beauty. But he loved her so much that the other members of his seraglio, resenting his neglect of them, poisoned her. The Inca's sister, fearing that the dead woman's daughter would meet with a similar fate, brought her up secretly, at some distance from the court. Later a young chief named Quilaco-Yupangi fell in love with her; but before he could marry her civil war broke out in Peru, and Quilaco, who sided with Atahualpa, was called to the command of his tribe. The war raged four years, and Curicuillor, after the death of her aunt, cut her hair short and, wearing male attire, joined the camp-followers of Quilaco's brigade. In a battle her lover was defeated and wounded. He would have died had not Curicuillor (now going under the name of Titu) carried him from the field and nursed him back to life.

De Soto, at the time he was on his first journey to Cuzco, met these two lovers, who told him their story and threw themselves upon his protection. He interested himself in them; converted them; and had them baptized, Yupangi taking the name of his patron, Hernando, and Curicuillor that of Leonora. Then he had them married according to the laws of the church.

Two years later, Yupangi having died, De Soto put the beautiful young widow still more securely under his protection by making her his mistress. By her he had a daughter named Leonora, who about 1580 (according to Balboa) was still living in Cuzco as the wife of the royal notary Carillo. By him she had had several children. The names of two of them are given — Pedro and Juana.[3]

No doubt De Soto's life with the lovely Princess was pleasant. He had other reasons to congratulate himself. His share of the ransom of Atahualpa had been enormous, and he had added to it— out of the spoils of Cuzco and during his other campaigns — until it reached the gigantic figure of a hundred thousand *pesos*. Allowing for the increase in the value of money, Peru had made him a millionaire.

But a new stage had been reached in the conquest which was not much to his taste. The quarrels between the Pizarros and Almagro were becoming more and more

---

[3] The story may be taken for what it is worth. It appears to be well authenticated, and is certainly very precise. De Soto, however, makes no mention of this daughter in his will, in which he remembers other illegitimate children. But the child may have been born after he had left Peru, so he may not have known of her existence.

serious, and it was hardly possible for an officer of high rank to be in the country without being drawn into them.

Pedro Pizarro gives — of course as a family partisan — his version of an incident that happened in Cuzco. De Soto was at that time *Corregidor;* and Almagro was claiming that the city fell within the limits of his province. He also believed that dispatches were about to come from Spain confirming him, and that Juan Pizarro, who also was in the city, was preparing to seize and suppress the expected documents. De Soto decided to support Almagro against unwarrantable interference. This provoked Juan Pizarro's anger and, according to his cousin Pedro's story, he attacked De Soto with a lance, and would have killed him had not the *Corregidor* galloped away upon his horse. If De Soto really did run away that day, it could not have been from fear; for he always showed himself the most valiant of men. It is much more likely that he felt about young Pizarro as Abner felt about Asahel.[4] Juan was the Governor's brother.

There is reason, rather, to believe that De Soto was the agent of reconciliation, when the frequent quarrels between Francisco Pizarro and the Marshall were patched up. For this he was well qualified by his gifts of personal graciousness, and in a position to be of use because his bosom friend, Hernán Ponce de León, was Almagro's second in command.

---

[4] "Then Abner said again to Asahel, Turn thee aside from following me: wherefore should I smite thee to the ground? how then should I hold up my face to Joab thy brother?" II Samuel, ii, 22.

On the 12th of June 1535, a solemn contract was entered into by the jangling officers. They signed a document protesting undying friendship; they undertook not to disparage one another's work in their letters to the Court; and agreed that all the profits of future discovery should be equally shared between them. The wrath of God was invoked against the breaker of this compact, which was sealed by the taking of an oath upon the Blessed Sacrament, administered to them at mass.

Fifteen days later in Cuzco De Soto also signed a document. It was a renewal of the former partnership with Hernán Ponce de León, and obviously an adjustment of business matters with his friend before parting from him.

It would seem to have some connection with the Pizarro-Almagro agreement. De Soto may have felt that hope of lasting peace in Peru had finally been reached, and that his friendly services were now no longer needed. Or he may have seen the beginning of new strife, and given the men up in disgust as hopeless — which is what Herrera suggested. What is reasonably certain is that soon after this he said good-bye to his old comrades and the beautiful Indian princess, and sailed, via Panama, for home.

CHAPTER VIII

THE SOUL OF A CONQUEROR

IT was sixteen years since De Soto had last seen Spain,
and during them he had lived the hardest sort of military life. Even to him, with his body toughened to
all privations and his soul to the endurance of all dangers,
the prospect of rest was alluring. No one could say that
he was not entitled to take his ease — though he was still
young — after the manful services he had done his King.
He intended to enjoy the huge fortune he had won with
his sword.

There went back with him to Spain several other young
men who also had seen service in Peru. They had not
gone out with Pizarro, but accompanied Alvarado three
years later. No great wealth, therefore, had been acquired by them, so they were glad to attach themselves to
De Soto.

He soon added to these officers Juan de Añasco, a
hidalgo of Seville, as a fourth gentleman-in-waiting, set
up a splendid establishment, and cut a great figure at
court. He and his entourage went everywhere in costly
apparel,[1] though he was not by nature profuse, or a

[1] In the Congressional Library at Washington there is a tailor's bill for a
large number of black velvet and taffeta suits — apparently formal court dress
— ordered and paid for by De Soto for his retainers.

waster of money. But he understood that a lavish scale of living was expected of one who had been enriched by the gold of the Incas.

The personal bearing of the *Conquistador* was magnificent. His portrait in Herrera's *History* is crudely executed, but at least it catches perfectly his impetuous eagle look, and shows a man whose sword seems to grow from his hand. He was at the height of all his physical and intellectual powers, conscious of his fame and his achievements.

A curly head of hair and a beard set off the martial carriage of the long narrow head; his drooping mustachios and his brooding deep-set dark eyes suggested the poet more than the soldier. Even his somewhat swarthy complexion, though it could not have made him more handsome, added mystery to his countenance. There was here a curious combination of the man of action and the dreamer.

Like all very rich men he was flattered; and the Emperor signified his favor by borrowing a large sum of money from him. But he was too much of a realist to be greatly affected by adulation. His character had been tempered by stern experience.

Yet his own sternness, which was inflexible, was concealed. He struck everyone as being very affable. Herrera describes him as being kindly, generous, and forgiving, and always willing to please — so long as no harm was done to his position or his plans. Even Oviedo, who did not like him and who underrated his abilities, admits that he was a man of good impulses, a gentleman, and a fine soldier who would have left an unblemished name had he not been brought up "in the bad school of Pedrarias Davila, in the destruction and dissipation of the Indians of Castilla del Oro, graduated in the deaths of the inhabitants of Nicaragua, and canonized in Peru as a member of the order of the Pizarros."

Whatever justice there may have been in Oviedo's words, to the nobles and ladies around the Court De Soto appeared always brilliant and charming. Something romantic hung about him. His were the first Christian eyes ever to have looked upon the already half-fabulous Atahualpa. He had seen the temple of the Sun, gorgeous in gold, and the convents of the heathen and their mosques and bishops. He had been the first Christian to climb the stupendous mountains of Peru, and the first to cross, with nausea in his stomach, the frail trembling bridges of osier stretched across the infernal chasms. It is true that Hernando Pizarro had already told the Emperor and the grandees, with the smouldering eloquence he had at his command, of the same things. But if the elder Pizarro had had the advantage of being the first to relate these astonishing stories, no one got tired of hearing them. And to the ladies of the court a handsome captain of thirty-five was a far more fascinating *raconteur* than an ungainly middle-aged man with drooping lips and a bulbous nose and a most ridiculous affectation of courtly manners.

De Soto enjoyed telling his adventures; he would have been less than human if he had failed to enjoy being admired. Though his wanderings and conquests were all over now, he could still recall them vividly. He could hear, almost with his physical ears, the clangor of the bells and the shouts of "Santiago !" as the horsemen thundered against the mass of the Inca's warriors in the square of Caxamarca, or the ominous cries in the darkness upon the plateau of the sierra, "Tomorrow, Christians, you die !" He had only to shut his eyes to picture sharply upon the retina of his memory the skyline of the Andes; and in the turquoise heavens a condor winging towards the sun.

He sighed a little, as men always do when they think of familiar scenes, but only a little. He was content. He could afford to live the rest of his life upon his incredible glory. If he had come to it early, that was because he had packed so much into a few years. The world had no right to ask him for more than he had already done.

It was time for him to marry. The light loves of Nicaragua, like the princess of Peru, belonged to the past. He was now in a civilized land again, and it was necessary for him to be the founder of an illustrious line. His sons should bear his honored name and do deeds worthy of him and of Spain.

Among the ladies of the court [2] was one whose parents had at one time destined her for a royal marriage. But that had somehow fallen through, possibly because her father before his death had lost a good deal of his former prestige. He was Pedrarias. She was Isabella de Bobadilla, keeping, in accordance with frequent Spanish usage, her mother's maiden name, made famous by Beatrice de Bobadilla, the Marchioness of Moya, the intimate friend of Isabella the Catholic. Ranjel, De Soto's secretary, says

[2] What romancing Wilmer and Abbott do here !

finely of her, "She was a woman both good and great and truly noble in mind and bearing." All that we hear of her clearly indicates that she was compounded of intelligence and passion, large-hearted, and valiant.

Doña Isabella, the mother, the widow of Pedrarias, no doubt knew all about the escapades of De Soto in Panama and Nicaragua. A Governor's wife generally does know a surprising amount about the young men in her settlement. At any rate we know of the Princess Curicuillor and of two illegitimate children in Central America, whose mothers were, doubtless, Indian women. Our captain of dragoons had behaved like the majority of other soldiers lost in the loneliness of savage lands.

But whatever the mother knew, she was not going to take youthful pecadillos too seriously. De Soto, rich and renowned, was a catch; Isabella, though beautiful, was no longer in her first youth. The widow was glad to agree to the marriage.

We have the Conveyance of Dower, under which all the cattle that had belonged to Pedrarias in Panama, the estate and the slaves and the horses were given in "pure and perfect gift irrevocable in favour of the said Doña Isabella de Bobadilla, that she might thereby the better and more honourably marry." The document was signed at Valladolid on the 14th of November 1536. The wedding probably took place the following day.

But though fêted by the Court and adored by his wife, De Soto soon found Spain, with its stiff splendors, dull compared with Peru. He noted himself getting soft and flabby and in danger of sinking down into a comfortable life. Hard riding and bouts with the foils were no ade-

quate substitute for the ardors and endurances of real war.
When he took down his sword from its hook he found
it slightly tarnished with rust; yet the same sword had
once flashed in the tropic sun and smitten hundreds with
terror. He was still only thirty-seven, good for another
thirty years. Why, his father-in-law at eighty-five was
the Wrath of God! What would he think, were he
alive, of his daughter's husband growing fat and old as
he sat by the hearth ?

He had kept Tobar and Moscoso and the others with
him; and more and more their talk turned wistfully to
the old days of strenuous action. Cavaliers whom he
had known in Castilla del Oro, Peru and Quito sought
him out when they visited Spain. And as they spoke his
hand itched for the sabre.

He had reached the point of being unable to endure
idleness any longer, so wrote to a councillor, close to the
Emperor, asking for permission to lead an expedition
into the interior of Quito. He knew that Almagro and
Pizarro had definitely parted company, and did not want
to be involved in their quarrels. But there was plenty of
room in South America for his own conquests.

It was, however, all very vague; and De Soto, in the
same letter, went on to say that, in the event of this
being denied him, he would like to try for the Governorship of Guatemala with permission to make explorations
in the South Sea. He concludes by begging the mantle
of Santiago for himself and also (loyal friend !) for Hernán Ponce de León.

This was being too indefinite. His request was not
granted; or it is possible that De Soto himself withdrew

it. There is also the possibility that, upon its being presented, the Court brought forward the counter-proposal of Florida. At any rate by April 1537 he had been duly appointed *Adelantado* of that province.

Florida, by which was then meant not only the state bearing the name, but all the country lying to the north of Cuba, whose extent was only dimly guessed at, was supposed to be an island. It was also regarded as an extremely hard nut to crack. But if anyone could conquer it — and after all, nothing was ultimately able to resist Spanish valor — De Soto was the man. Though all his predecessors had failed, he was quite willing to try, and was quite confident of his success.

Ponce de León has the honor of having discovered the country. He arrived there on the 27th of March 1513; and because the day was Easter Sunday, *Pascua Florida,* and because the magnolia trees were in bloom, he called it *Tierra Florida.*

He did little more upon this visit than to take formal possession of the province for Spain; and when he returned in 1521 with the title of *Adelantado,* to settle it, to acquire some of its wealth, to convert the heathen, and to locate the fabulous Fountain of Youth, he was wounded in a fight with the Indians and died a little later. Over the grave of this brave man in Porto Rico was inscribed the following epitaph:

> *Here lies the* LION. *Mighty was his fame.*
> *His deeds were even greater than his name.*[3]

[3] *Mole sub hac fortis Requiescunt ossa LEONIS,*
Qui Vicit factis Nomina magna suis.

Meanwhile Alonzo Álvarez de Pineda, the pilot of Francisco de Garay, while upon the search for the strait leading to the South Sea, had explored the Gulf of Mexico and, in 1519, had crossed the estuary of the river Espíritu Santo — now, after having borne at various times various names, known as the Mississippi. And in the year of De León's death, Vásquez de Ayllón led an unauthorized expedition in the Cape Fear district. He returned seven years later with the King's commission, and attempted to found a colony. He has the distinction of having built the first ships constructed upon the coast of North America, but his settlement did not prosper, and he died before the year was out.

Eighteen months later Panfilo de Narváez, a tall, red-bearded, powerful soldier — but one-eyed as a consequence of his conflict with Cortés — tried again. He was gallant, able, gracious in his manner, but unfortunate; and has since been grossly maligned. His adventures at several points parallel those of De Soto in Florida. His fate should have been taken as a warning. His career is therefore instructive.

After a stormy voyage he landed at Tampa Bay, where he found a little gold — a very little — and read the Requisition. Then, with three hundred men, he pressed inland. But encountering only "great lakes, dense mountains, immense deserts, and solitudes," he turned southwestwards once more in the hope of regaining his ships. When at last, after having severely suffered in its scuffles with fierce Indian tribes, the army reached an inlet of Appalache Bay, the ships had sailed for Cuba.

There was only one thing to be done: new boats had to

be built. Just one carpenter was among them, and they possessed no iron, no forge, and no tools — to say nothing of sails or rigging. And while they were at work there was no food for them to eat.

Yet the energy of despair triumphed over all obstacles. Bellows were made of wooden pipes and deer-skins. From their stirrups, spurs, and cross-bows the Spaniards painfully constructed nails, axes, even rude saws. Their shirts were made into sails; their horses' tails and manes were twisted into ropes. The horses themselves were killed, their skins being taken off entire to serve as bottles for water. Their carcasses were used for food. Upon leaving, Narváez named the harbor the Bay of Horses.

On the 22d of September 1528, they put to sea in five small boats, all so overloaded that the gunwales remained only a span above water. In this way the two hundred and forty survivors crawled slowly along the coast of the gulf, in their miserable state being often molested by the savages.

They crossed the mouth of the Espíritu Santo, whose powerful current carried them far out to sea; and it took them three days to come again within sight of the shore. Eventually every one of the boats was wrecked, and though eighty men found refuge on an island, nearly all of them died. The others who had set out from the Bahía de Caballos perished from wounds or exhaustion or "found sepulchre in the open sea."

This example of courage would have been altogether sterile, this disaster complete, except for Cabeza de Vaca. He, along with four other men, was captured and enslaved by the Indians, but eventually rose to high esteem among them because of his gifts of healing. Once, to the grateful astonishment of his barbarian masters, he performed a successful operation with an oyster shell. But at other times, in his capacity of medicine-man, he was expected to effect his cures by the customary method of magic. Accordingly he satisfied the natives and at the same time eased his own conscience by saying an Our Father and a Hail Mary and by making the sign of the cross over the sick — who were so often cured by the Christians' prayers that Cabeza de Vaca and his companions gained enormous prestige among their captors.

Cabeza de Vaca also developed skill as a trader, and being allowed to go considerable journeys without guard, contrived to escape, after six years spent as a slave. Enduring terrible sufferings, he made his way westward, ever trusting in God and cheering on the companions who had joined him on the prickly-pear plains of Texas. Their clothing was the skins of dogs, and their food the scrapings of uncured hides. When they were exceptionally lucky they got a scrap of raw meat thrown to them by the Indians through whose territory they passed. They never dared to go to the trouble of roasting this, for if they did so the first man who came along would take it away and eat it himself. It was upon this journey that the American buffalo, "the hunchbacked cow," was seen for the first time by a European.

The fugitives crossed the Colorado, the Rio Grande, and the Conchos rivers; and, after having reached a point probably as far north as El Paso, struck southwards until they came to the Gulf of California, reaching Culiacan in Mexico in the spring of 1536. Soon afterwards Cabeza de Vaca set out for Spain, with the intention of asking to be appointed *Adelantado* of an expedition to Florida, but arrived too late. De Soto had already received his commission to explore and conquer the country.

But the successful candidate felt some compunction about having stolen, however unwittingly, another man's project; and, with the candid generosity so characteristic of him, offered his rival a partnership. This was accepted, but upon a disagreement later arising over the claim that De Soto had promised his new associate a ship, Cabeza de Vaca withdrew. He gave it out that he did not feel inclined to serve as a subordinate; so would seek an independent command in another province. With his knowledge of the geography, languages, and customs of Florida he would have been invaluable to the expedition, especially during the westward march of the army.

He did, nevertheless help it in other ways. His written *Relación* does not paint a very enticing picture. There is not much mention in it of gold; there is a great deal about desolation. Even in his conversations in Spain, he generally described the poverty of the country and the hardships he had undergone. At the same time he managed somehow to give the impression that Florida was the richest place in the whole world.

It does not appear that he actually said it in so many words. It was rather that his evasiveness put that idea in his hearers' heads. The man had a way of breaking off in the middle of a sentence, or when he was pressed too closely by questions, and saying with an air of solemn mystery, "That's something that has to be reserved for the ear of the Emperor. I have sworn not to divulge certain facts."

There was a good deal of the charlatan about him, but, nevertheless (or in consequence), he impressed his contemporaries. Yet it would seem that he really had brought himself to believe his own romances about northern gold, because when his kinsmen, Baltasar de Gallegos and Cristóbal de Espíndola, went to him asking his candid opinion about their accompanying De Soto, he once more wrapped himself in the mystery of his oath of secrecy, but strongly advised them to go. And when his reserved information — whatever it was — had been disclosed to Charles V, the Marquis de Astorga, who was informed, thought so highly of the prospects in Florida that he sent Don Antonio, his brother, and two kinsmen to join the expedition.[4]

De Soto soon came to be absolutely convinced that Florida was all that it was popularly supposed to be. For he not only had Cabeza de Vaca's word, but the sensational success of Cortés upon the same continent to set his imagination on fire. Hundreds of other young men were similarly inspired. If this was the richest country upon earth, why, it was just the right country for them. There was a rush to mortgage or sell estates to provide equipment. They were all going to come back to Spain De Sotos. It was one of those curious recurring instances of speculative fever. At the end of the rainbow was the pot of gold.

[4] The fact that the Cardinal of Ciguenza sought (and obtained) the post of Treasurer for his nephew, Juan Gayton, indicates the confidence of those "in the know."

The concession to the new *Adelantado* stipulated that he was to raise five hundred men with the necessary arms, horses, munitions, and military stores. His salary was to be fifteen hundred ducats a year, but was to come out of the profits of the enterprise, and was not payable unless the conquest paid. All of this was in line with the policy of the Spanish Crown, which, while authorizing exploration, risked as little money upon it as possible.

The inhabitants of the province were to live tax-free for ten years; and the general regulations governing the treatment of the Indians in the colonies were to be carefully observed. The importation of negro slaves was permitted, but strictly limited.

A hospital for the poor was to be built, to be supported by the fines imposed by the courts of justice; but no lawyers were to be permitted to go out, as their presence always resulted in the fomenting of litigation. Priests, on the other hand, were to accompany the expedition "for the instruction of the natives of that province in our Holy Catholic Faith." This was a matter to which the Governor was ordered to bestow grave attention: "anything otherwise we shall deem contrary to our service."

De Soto was given the coveted knighthood of Santiago. A marquisate was to be his reward, and for his territorial possessions he was empowered to select any piece of land twelve leagues square, so long as no part of it rested upon the sea. In other words the temptation of his attempting to grasp independence was removed.

The stipulation about the number of men De Soto was to raise was unnecessary. We have seen what difficulty Pizarro had to find men to join him. There was no such difficulty now. Enthusiasm was spontaneous. Cabeza de Vaca was the oracle. But De Soto's prestige drew by reason of its own strength. Everyone had heard of his brilliant exploits in Peru. Though young in years he was old in experience of Indian warfare. His athletic presence, the decision of his voice, his abounding energy, all inspired confidence, and his affability charmed all those who came into contact with him. The conqueror's star was leading him on. He was obviously destined to achievements which would eclipse even the epic story of Cortés and Pizarro.

De Soto thought so too. His two years in Spain, during which, so far as external magnificence was concerned, he had seemed to be on the very crest of the wave of glory, now appeared to him as having been merely the trough into which a wave must fall. He had really swept upward with the conquest of Peru; he was now gathering strength and volume to climb to a still higher summit. Nothing would be able to stand before the impact, the sweep of the tumultuous flood. Alexander, Cæsar, Charlemagne — what other names would the world compare with his?

Not only Spain but neighboring Portugal sought him out. André de Vasconcelos rode across the border with a picked company of cavaliers, and came to De Soto in Seville begging to be allowed to enlist under his command. And when the time came for the review nearly twice the number De Soto's commission had called for offered themselves.

He had provided ships for only five hundred, "a noble fleet of nine vessels, five navios, two caravels, and two brigantines;" it was impossible to accommodate all who clamored to go with him. The best men only should be chosen.

The Castilians — according to the Portuguese hidalgo's story — rode out to the muster "very showily, in silk over silk, pinked and slashed," whereas his own countrymen came in polished armor. As the General was not wanting a fashion parade, he ordered another review for the following day, when every man was to appear in arms. Then it was seen that under many a flashy silken corslet there had been rusty mail; and many a pretty fellow held a poor lance. These, and all the men who appeared to lack the necessary military qualifications, were at once rejected. But after a thorough sifting, six hundred and twenty excellent soldiers, two hundred and twenty-three of whom were mounted, were left. To take them all meant overcrowding the ships; but De Soto could not bear to leave behind any first-class material. Fortunately — as the sequel will show — not all these were of the hidalgo class. The fact that a certain number of lowly-born adventurers were in their company, men who had skill as artisans, later saved the expedition from total loss. They were accompanied by twelve priests, eight of them seculars, two Dominicans, a Franciscan, and a Trinitarian. The conversion of the heathen was to be properly attended to.

Nuño Tobar was appointed second-in-command, with the title of Master of the Camp; and, all the arrangements having been completed, the ships bearing that brilliant army passed over the bar at San Lucar. It was the 6th of November, the feast of St. Lazarus. On that same day, far off in Peru, Almagro was defeated at Las Salinas by Hernando Pizarro.

With "great festivity" they sailed, banners in the breeze, trumpets sounding, and the artillery firing salvos. Every heart was high; every face flushed with joy. They were off to the conquest of Florida.

CHAPTER IX

FURTHER PREPARATIONS

THE SHIPS had orders to keep close together, because, since Spain was at war with France, there was danger from French privateers. And the pirates of Barbary were a perpetual menace. But a gay spirit prevailed. Not all the corsairs in the world could frighten men who were going to conquer Florida.

Fourteen days later, on Holy Saturday, they reached Gomara in the Canaries, where they landed to celebrate the greatest festival of the Christian year. There the Governor of the place, a Bobadilla and a cousin of Doña Isabella's, came to the docks to greet them. He was clad in white from head to foot, and everyone was amused by his singular appearance. They thought he looked like a gipsy.

But he entertained them handsomely and, when they left Gomara, he gave De Soto's wife his natural daughter, Leonora, to be her waiting-maid. Several of the officers had brought their wives, including Carlos Enríquez who was married to De Soto's niece. And the presence of ladies upon the flag-ship added sparkle to the brilliant weather.

On Whit Sunday the ships came to anchor in the harbor of Santiago, and the new Governor of Cuba — for he was that as well as *Adelantado* of the Florida expedition — was welcomed by the firing of whatever ordnance the city of eighty houses boasted.

The settlers had not forgotten their courtly manners in the wilderness. They came in a body to welcome De Soto, to whom they presented a splendid roan horse, well caparisoned; and they had a mule for Doña Isabella to ride. For everyone free quarters were provided, either in the town or in the ranches around.

The Cubans, who were anticipating a great increase in their own wealth as a result of the opening up of Florida, gave themselves over to a long period of festivity. Cuba was an island where horses flourished amazingly. With the advent of so large a body of cavaliers, tilting, racing, and bull-fighting absorbed for a time all the thought and energy of a new-comers.

The young men of De Soto's army, who had arrived in holiday mood, thoroughly enjoyed the long picnic. They were left undisturbed in their pleasures all that winter, because the Governor had a good deal of business to attend to on the island. He had to take over the reins of office; and he wished to organize in Cuba a base of supplies. With his ships he would be able to establish rapid communication with Havana. In this respect he was in a far more fortunate position than Pizarro had ever been.

In Cuba one event that was destined to have a considerable effect upon the fortunes of the expedition occurred. Nuño Tobar, the Master of the Camp, having little of importance to do, whiled away the time by engaging in an amour with Leonora de Bobadilla. She was now with child by him.

When the Governor heard of it he was deeply incensed. The girl had been put under his protection and was the ward of his wife, whom he considered gravely insulted by this affair. He instantly dismissed Tobar from his office, and not even when he had made reparation by marrying Leonora, would De Soto restore him to favor. And Tobar remained degraded, not until the end holding so much as a captaincy.

The punishment, though no doubt just, did harm to the morale of the army. And that for two reasons. Tobar's services were lost; and he was an excellent soldier, who on several conspicuous occasions showed himself prompt and resourceful in a crisis. His position was occupied by men who were not nearly so good, first by Vasco Porcallo de Figueroa and, later, by Luis de Moscoso.

Porcallo joined De Soto in the island. He was a man who had had considerable military experience in his youth, but for some time he had been a planter and miner, in which occupations he had grown rich. He was too old for hard campaigning, as he soon discovered, and was "of a galliard disposition."

Moreover, his main object in accompanying the expedition was to procure slaves for his plantations and mines. And while De Soto had no conscientious objection to a little slave trading — for, as we have seen, he had once been engaged in that line of business himself — he had no intention of allowing it to interfere with his purpose in Florida.

[134]

The Gentleman of Elvas tells a story of how the over-
seer of Porcallo, having learned that the slaves of his
employer intended to hang themselves in a body in order
to escape their miseries, went cudgel in hand to their
rendezvous. There he told the surprised and trembling
wretches that it was impossible for them to do anything,
or even to think of anything, that he did not know
beforehand. As for their hanging themselves, well, he
would hang himself too, so that he could give them in
the next life a much worse time than he had given them
in this. He seems to have caught something of the
humor of the jovial but cruel Porcallo.

Unsatisfactory as the appointment of Porcallo as Master of the Camp proved to be, it had one immediate advantage: De Soto's new lieutenant contributed stores
upon a lavish scale, and gave the army fifty horses. He
took with him to Florida also a number of Spanish servants and negro and Indian slaves; and he was instru-
mental in securing a few recruits in the island.

If no expedition to the New World had ever consisted
of better human material, so also no expedition was ever
better equipped. Above all else in importance, there
were a great many mounts available. By the time De
Soto sailed from Cuba half his men had horses. Packs of
bloodhounds and Irish greyhounds for the pursuing of
Indians were taken, their usefulness for such purposes
having been fully demonstrated in Central America and
La Española.[1]

[1] The print of Spaniards throwing Indians to the dogs represents Balboa
executing men guilty of unnatural vice. He possessed a famous hound, red
in color with a black snout, that was named, with some justice, "Little
Lion." This dog, which was the son of an animal hardly less redoubtable,

The example of Cortés during his march to Honduras was followed. A herd of thirteen pigs was transported to Florida; and there came times when carefully husbanded rations of pork saved the army from perishing of starvation. In readiness for the melting into ingots of the prospective gold, furnaces were prepared and anvils and forges for the repairing of damaged armor and for the making of such chains as might be needed. Nothing that the previous experience of those who had been in the Indies showed to be serviceable escaped De Soto's foresight.

Preparations so elaborate had taken time. Another cause for delay was due to the fact that Havana, at the other extreme of the island, was burned by a marauding band of the French. Before the expedition could leave, the town had to be rebuilt, and a bastion begun.

The Governor also saw that it was necessary to visit all the settlements under his jurisdiction; so while his nephew Carlos Enríquez sailed with the ships for Havana, taking with him the ladies and the infantry, De Soto rode with his horsemen the entire length of Cuba. The Gentleman of Elvas tells us about some of the things he saw upon this journey, of the "monstrous alligators" and of "snakes, the size of a man's thigh and even bigger," as well as of the curious fruits and vegetables of the country, the "batata," the "plantano," and the "ynhame." It was not, upon the whole, a pleasant excursion. The mosquitos were exceedingly troublesome,

the Beçerrico of Ponce de Leon, took a soldier's share of the plunder, and was worth it. He could tell a good from a bad Indian, and had so much intelligence that he used to take captive those who offered no resistance, but tore the others to pieces.

and marshes had to be traversed. Through one stretch of water that needed to be forded they trod on clams whose shells cut the Spanish riding-boots to shreds.

The ships also had been in trouble, and were carried out of their way by storms to within sight of the shores of Florida. But the whole force was safely gathered in Havana in March.

During the period of waiting Juan de Añasco, the Royal Treasurer, had been twice sent out with a caravel and two pinnaces and fifty men to explore the coast, and to find a suitable harbor. He picked a spot further south than that at which Narváez had landed, at what is now known as Charlotte Harbor.[2] Upon his return he brought with him two captured Indians, knowing that the expedition would need guides and interpreters. As these men said, by means of signs, and with Indian mendacity, that the country abounded with gold, the Governor and his men became greatly excited and longed for the hour of their departure. The pleasures of Cuba had suddenly become insipid to them in view of the conquest of a land which all firmly believed would prove to be the richest that had ever been discovered.

While De Soto was still in Cuba his old friend and partner Hernán Ponce de León paid him a visit. Garcilasso de la Vega is the only one who records the fact, and that might make us skeptical, did not certain clauses in the will drawn up by the Governor while he was in Havana seem strongly to support it. But we may reasonably doubt the rest of Garcilasso's story. Accord-

[2] See Hodge and Lewis' *Spanish Explorers* — p. 146. Tampa Bay is often given incorrectly as the landing place.

ing to him, Ponce, when he arrived, was unaware of his friend's presence in Cuba and was very much embarrassed by it, because he was bearing with him the treasure he had acquired in Chile. He therefore most unhandsomely attempted to cheat his partner by burying his gold.

The will seems to be decisive evidence against this. For it indicates the greatest possible trust in Hernán Ponce de León, who was appointed one of the Governor's executors. Not even the magnanimous De Soto could have referred to Ponce in the terms he uses, had his friend been guilty of the baseness Garcilasso describes.

Isabella, a brave-hearted woman, wished to accompany her husband to Florida. It was, she urged, only what her mother had done when she went to Darien with Pedrarias. But her husband would not permit this. He had seen too much suffering in Castilla del Oro and Peru. He had heard, too, of what the army of Alvarado had had to endure during the march through the province of Quito: of men frozen in their saddles and of women and children lost in wastes of snow in the mountains. For all he knew Florida would be full of the same dangers: he was certain that the dangers, whatever they were, would be too great for him to allow women to encumber the expedition. Nuño Tobar and Carlos Enríquez and Baltasar Gallegos all were obliged to leave their brides behind. Only one exception was made. Or it may be that the woman went as a stowaway. Her tragic history amply proved the wisdom of De Soto.

After all — so he assured Isabella, believing it himself — they would not be gone long. The distance between the shores of Cuba and Florida was short. He would be able to go backwards and forwards frequently. And he had occupation for his wife in his own absence. She should act as his deputy, with Juan de Rojas, a hidalgo of Havana, to exercise the function of *Alcalde Mayor*.

On the 18th of May 1539, a Sunday, the army for the conquest of Florida sailed. Isabella was never to see De Soto again.

CHAPTER X

FIRST ADVENTURES

OWING TO the dropping of the wind the voyage took a whole week. On Whit Sunday, the 25th of May, the ships came to anchor in blue brilliant weather in Charlotte Harbor. The name given to it by De Soto, however, was that of Espíritu Santo, in honor of the day.

The Spaniards had to keep their ships a league from shore in four fathoms of water because of the shoals. But they were happy to have reached their destination, and were content, for the time being, to bask in the languid air. This army of young men — Porcallo's were the only grey hairs among them [1] — though so eager for adventure and conquest, were bound by the enchanting beauty of the sea, sky, and shore, and remained wrapped in a dream. The magnolia, the tulip, the rhododendron, and the azalea shone against a background of cypress, live-oak, and ash. The scent of lily and jasmin filled the air. The palm swayed in the breeze. The palmetto was in bloom. Well was this country named *Tierra Florida.*

[1] Garcilasso mentions one other grizzled cavalier killed by accident while fishing. Being so much older than his young comrades he was affectionately known as "father."

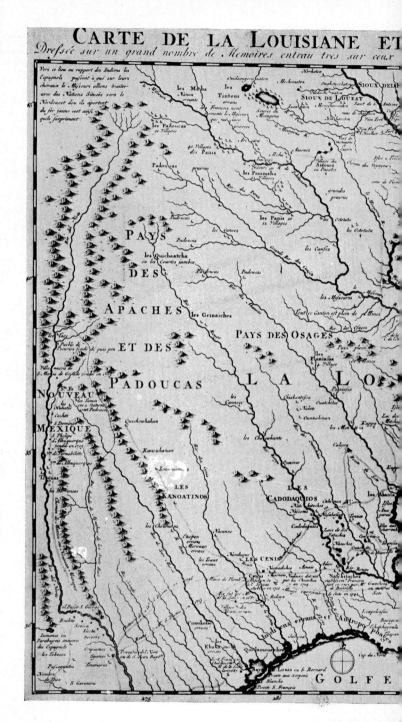

THE DELIS

[Made in 1718 and included in the 172

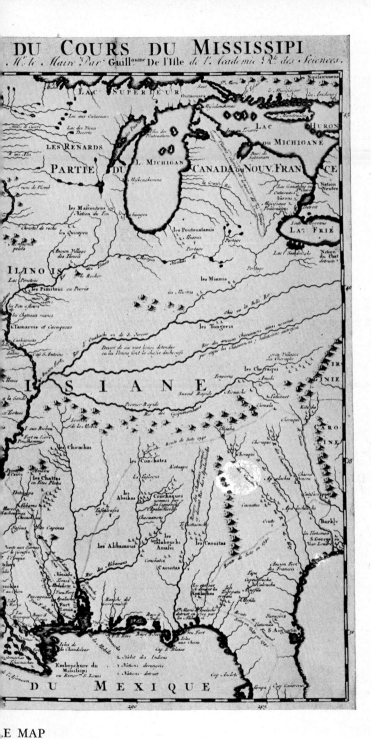

E MAP

[edition of Garcilasso de la Vega]

But from their ships riding at anchor in the bay the invaders could see another sight — one plume of smoke after another going up along the shore, signals of warning. It is easy enough to imagine the consternation of the savages. The sight of those floating castles and men in armor filled them with very different feelings from those of the entranced Spaniards on board.

De Soto should have taken to himself the significance of the warning and have proceeded cautiously. But he was a man impetuous by nature, most fully himself when leading a charge of cavalry, and he was impatient to land. As the larger ships could not follow, because of the shoals, he took one of the brigantines of shallow draught and steered for the shore. Quite insufficiently attended, he put his foot upon the country he had come to conquer, indifferent to his danger, forgetting that it had proved disastrous to his predecessors, ignorant that it was to be his own grave.

Ranjel, his secretary, reproved this lack of prudence in his *Relación*. The Governor, he says truly, should not have conducted his own reconnaissance, but have sent a subordinate. And Biedma only expresses the general view when he says that the whole army grew uneasy before the recklessness of its commander. He had gone where it was impossible for them to bring any help, had he needed it.

We have in this initial moment what was to be so typical of the unlucky campaign. De Soto, than whom no one could be more reliable as a lieutenant or more dashing in a charge, was not fully fitted for a position of supreme command. His courage and his devotion were never questioned; he often displayed resource; but his judgment was almost as often at fault. And his intrepidity, though invaluable in extremity, was a frequent cause for alarm.

As soon as De Soto had landed he came upon traces of the Indians. Indeed his little party found one of the large communal huts used by the local tribe, but it was deserted, the natives — fortunately for the Governor — having vanished into the woods at his approach. Not even when he pushed imprudence to the very verge of folly, and went riding after deer into an unknown country, did he encounter any of the natives. That he should have hunted at such a time shows that he began by taking the conquest as a holiday.

At last the army landed, five days after the arrival. The men and horses were taken off in pinnaces so as to unburden the ships, and, with the lessening of the draught of water, to enable them to go closer to the shore. Only the sailors remained on board, and these had to rely upon the tide to carry them each day a little nearer in.

This took another eight days. Even so the manœuvre does not seem to have been performed with sufficient deftness. Two ships scraped bottom, and though, because of the sand, they received no damage, there were high words between the Governor and Juan de Añasco, the pilot.

That day and the next they encamped upon the seashore. De Soto's reckless mood imparted itself to others. So Porcallo de Figueroa went off in company with Añasco and five other cavaliers to see the country. Immediately came their first brush with the Indians. Ten warriors armed with bows and arrows attacked them, and succeeded in killing two horses, but fled after two of their own number were run through.

Juan Lobillo and about forty foot-soldiers went out reconnoitring in another direction. They also tasted the prowess of the savages. Coming to some huts, they managed to capture a couple of women, whom they took back with them to serve as guides. But all the way into the camp they were followed by Indians, who despite being only nine against forty, slew one Christian and wounded three or four others. Well might Ranjel say of them, "These Indians are as agile and as good fighters as can be found among all the nations of the world." Elvas bears the same testimony: "The Indians are exceedingly ready with their weapons, and so warlike and nimble, that they have no fear of footmen; for if these charge them they flee, and when they turn their backs are presently upon them. They never remain quiet, but are continually running, traversing from place to place, so that neither cross-bow nor arquebus can be aimed at them. Before a Christian can make a single shot, an Indian will discharge three or four arrows; and he seldom misses his object."

This was the beginning of four years of almost incessant skirmishing.

The scouting parties discovered also that the country was a difficult one, full of ponds, bogs, and bushes. The Spanish horses became caught in the morasses, covering themselves and their riders with mire. This too was to be the constant portion. Beautiful the country might be, but it was not a beautiful one for mounted men.

Upon the next day the army began its march round the bay. The cavalry was divided into three squadrons; and in this order the Spaniards advanced that Saturday and Sunday, fording the long creeks that ran up from the harbor, and floundering in the swamps, until they reached the village of Ucita, about which their guides had told them.

Weary with their laborious march through the muddy country — how much mud these unlucky men were to see in Florida and upon the banks of the Mississippi ! — they slept that night scattered about, without discipline, "not at all in the order of war." Again gross imprudence on the part of the general.

The neglect was afterwards atoned for. The cavalry was arranged in four companies, with André de Vasconcelos, Pedro Calderón, Arias Tinoco, and Alfonso Romo as captains; while Francisco Maldonado and Juan Rodríguez Lobillo were put over the infantry.

The village of Ucita consisted of eight large huts of timber and palm-leaves, with the chief's house upon a mound[2] thrown up artificially for defensive purposes, and of a "temple" at the top of which perched a wooden fowl with gilded eyes. This was really the burial house. The fowl which was taken to be an idol was nothing of the kind, for these savages had no god and no religion in the true sense of the term. They attached magical properties to certain things, and had a sort of confused veneration for the Sun and the Moon.[3]

[2] An old burial mound in all probability. These mounds are often mentioned by the chroniclers.

[3] *Nullam Dei habent notitiam, neque ullam religionem; quod illis conspicuum est, veluti Sol & Luna, illis Deus est."* De Bry.

To prevent a surprise attack, De Soto ordered the woods around, which were of high trees and dense thickets interspersed with fenny places, to be cleared by the axe to the radius of the range of a cross-bowshot from the encampment. Along the paths, at every strategic point, a couple of foot-soldiers were stationed as sentinels and horsemen were kept in readiness to support them at the first shout of alarm.

De Soto's situation was a very perplexing one. It is possible that he had a rough map of the coast. But he knew absolutely nothing about the interior of the country — except what he had derived from Cabeza de Vaca's vague report — and apparently he could expect no reliable information. Pizarro, when he actually began the conquest of Peru, had possessed the invaluable services of interpreters. The long delay had been of use to him, by giving several natives time to learn Castilian. Cortés also had had the intelligent help of his mistress Marina, with her command of both the Nahua and Maya languages. De Soto had nobody.

The two Indians whom Juan de Añasco had taken back to Cuba after his voyage of exploration, had mastered only a few elementary words, and communication with them was still mainly a matter of signs. They did not seem to know where any of the trails through the thick woods led, or could not or would not tell; and in such a district of swamps and tall timber it would have been fatal to have proceeded by guesswork.

In complete ignorance, therefore, of what it was he had to take possession of, De Soto went through the requisite formalities, and on June 3d annexed Florida to the Spanish Crown. This done, he sent one of his interpreters (such as they were) with pacific messages to the local chief, who so far had kept carefully out of the way.

The man never came back. And that same night, owing to the carelessness of those who had charge of them, the two women captured by Lobillo managed to give their guards the slip under cover of the darkness. And it was only by great good luck that the fourth and last Indian in their custody did not also escape.

The army was greatly concerned over so serious a loss. Not less than Columbus were they going into the unknown. Their plight was in many ways much worse than that of the first Atlantic voyager, for at least he had a clear horizon before him, and the elements that his trade had made familiar to him to master. The soldiers of De Soto had before them quagmires and thickets and dark woods and trails that led — no man knew where.

Something had to be done, and at once. They could not stay indefinitely in their little clearing of the forest and wait for guides obligingly to come in. So De Soto ordered Gallegos to take a strong detachment — forty cavalry and eighty infantry — and the one Indian left to show them the way if he could. Let him go out and find whatever there was to find. Lobillo, with fifty foot-soldiers, some with cross-bows and guns, proceeded in another direction.

The Indian who was with Gallegos promptly behaved after the almost unvarying fashion of Indian guides: he deliberately led the party astray. Sunset was flaming in the sky, and the Christians were confused and perturbed before the threat of night approaching in that swampy wilderness. Just at that moment, at some distance away, appeared twenty braves, having upon their faces "a kind of red paint which the Indians put on when they go to war or wish to make a fine appearance." They wore plumes of feathers, and carried bows and arrows. Like all the Indians of this part of Florida, they were naked.

Immediately the Spaniards charged, not so much with the intention of slaughtering their foes, as in the hope of taking a few of them prisoners, and so getting new guides. The savages made no attempt to stand against the onslaught, but fled nimbly into the woods. All except one. He, naked and feathered and painted and tattooed like the rest, ran forward with outstretched arms, and cried out to the lancer who was about to run him through, "For the love of God and of holy Mary, do not kill me !"

Astounded at these words coming from an Indian, unable to believe his own ears the soldier held his lance still aimed at the speaker's heart, but stayed the shaft.

The savage, struggling with Castilian, which he had not used for eleven years and had almost forgotten, told the Spaniards, now gathering around, a story so strange as to seem impossible. Yet it was all absolutely true.

His name he said was Juan Ortiz, and he had been born in Seville, of good family. He was last survivor of the expedition of Narváez. But would they mind stopping the pursuit of the fleeing Indians ? They were his friends and intended the Christian no harm. Upon his calling to them in their own language they came peaceably towards him.

They were even reassured sufficiently to go with him

to the Spanish camp, since Ortiz was going too. And mounted behind the cavaliers, and wondering at the strange beasts, bestrode by them for the first time in their lives, they came to where De Soto was waiting for news.

His delight knew no bounds, and he embraced Ortiz as though he were a long-lost son. Here was a man who had been with Cabeza de Vaca, who knew him well, and who could corroborate his story. That fact alone gave them encouragement. But they had also rescued a Christian. And "God had given them a tongue and a guide."

It took Ortiz some time to get accustomed to the use of his mother tongue. He told them that it had been as much as he could do to speak the name of God and Mary. If he had hesitated over the unfamiliar words a moment longer, he would have been dead. He would get it all back eventually. But for several days he could not connect one idea with another except by putting in for every word of Spanish four or five of Indian.

This meant that he had for so long spoken and thought in the language of the savages as to have become the perfect interpreter. But his knowledge of the topography of Florida was limited, extending no farther than a radius of twenty leagues. His definite assurance as to the absence of gold in the country was, therefore, lightly dismissed as based upon manifestly insufficient information. From him, however, De Soto learned that the village was the headquarters of a chief named Ucita.[4]

[4] The Spaniards here, as elsewhere in the Indies, called the chief after his his village, or the village after its chief, with perfect indifference. The names are, of course, only approximations to the guttural Indian words. Ranjel calls "Ucita" "Ocita," and Garcilasso renders it "Hirrihigua." Ucita

Juan Ortiz had good reasons for knowing all about Ucita, as was evident when he told his story. This chief, upon capturing him, had him bound hand and foot to four stakes, beneath which a fire was lighted, that he might be slowly roasted to death. A daughter of the chief — a prototype of Pocahontas with Captain John Smith — took pity upon his sufferings, and begged for his life, giving the somewhat naïve reason for mercy that while one Christian might do no good, he certainly could not do much harm. Moreover, she confessed to a fancy for having one as a slave. His life was therefore spared.

But in captivity Ortiz was made so miserable by the cruelties of Ucita, that he often longed for the death he had barely escaped. It was only his Christian faith that prevented him from commiting suicide.

He lived on among the savages, partly a drudge and partly a clown. The chief on great festivals, or whenever he felt in the mood for amusement, used to have arrows shot at him, but by men skilled enough to avoid a vital spot. The entertainment consisted in seeing the captive run from the archers, dodging the arrows when he could, and writhing in anguish when hit. The wounds upon his limbs attested to the truth of his story; and the scars upon his back showed where he had been burned.

Ucita, ever fertile in torture, invented a new torment for his captive. Ortiz was put to watching the burial-ground. This was at some distance from the village and there, alone through the desolate nights, the Christian slave was set to guard the corpses from the wolves

would be the head of the tribe of that name. We have similar cases still in Ireland and Scotland, with *the* O'Donnell and *the* MacDonald, the titular heads of the ancient clans.

and lynxes. They reposed upon platforms, and were in rough boxes, covered only with loose planks.

He was given four darts to keep the marauders away. Commending himself to God — for he understood perfectly well that Ucita planned his ruin, and that one stolen corpse would mean death — the wretched lad stationed himself at the appointed place.

The very first night he heard the pad of feet, the clattering of scattered timbers, the crunching of bones. He ran swiftly in the direction of the sounds, and an animal, barely visible in the darkness, leaped to the ground and scuttled away with its spoils. With all his might, but mainly at random, Ortiz threw one of the darts, without being able to know anything about the result of his shot.

In the morning he found to his terror that the body of a small child, the son of one of the most important men in the village, was missing. He therefore gave himself up for lost.

Ucita heard what had happened, and told his slave that he had to die for failing in his trust. But the Indians, upon going a little farther along the trail, found first the corpse of the little boy, and then that of the wolf, with a dart in its side. After that even Ucita had to treat him with a decent show of forebearance.

Again the life of Ortiz came into imminent jeopardy. Ucita was driven from his village by an enemy, a chief of the name of Mococo, and fled to his fastness by the sea, the place where the Spaniards were encamped. Here there was no outlying burial-ground to guard, so Ortiz, in losing his occupation, lost also his master's reluctant favor.

The girl who had rescued him from the pyre now again befriended him. She told him that her father "designed to appease the thirst of his god" by offering his slave up as a sacrifice. For, as the Gentleman of Elvas remarks, the Indians were worshippers of the Devil.[5] The kindly daughter of a ferocious father begged Ortiz to flee at once, that very night. He could go to Mococo, who would be sure to protect him. She even went with him part of the way, to put him upon the right road, and gave him directions as to the path he should follow for the rest of his journey.

By Mococo he was well received, and was even admitted to membership in the tribe. He was given at the same time a promise that, in the event of Christians ever again coming to those shores, he might go to them. And for nine years Mococo had faithfully protected him, despite frequent demands made by Ucita that his slave be returned. As soon as he heard of De Soto's landing, Mococo redeemed his promise.·

But Ortiz laughed, when he was told that he could go to rejoin the Christians. He thought the chief was jesting with him. It was several years since he had abandoned all hope of seeing civilized men; and, as he assured his Indian friends, he never thought any more about his own people, but was quite content to remain as one of the warriors of Mococo.

The chief gravely assured him that Christians really had come to their district. If Ortiz wanted to go he

[5] Elvas could not be expected to know very much about the cloudy religious ideas of the Indians. But he was probably not far from the truth. These savages, like all others, found it necessary to appease malignant spirits.

had better do so at once, as they might not stay long. In that case he would not be to blame, for he had carried out his undertaking. The "Spanish-Indian" had been on his way to the Christian camp when he ran into the scouting party of Gallegos.

If Castilian came back to him only gradually, he took still longer to accustom himself to the wearing of clothes. In consideration of running sores, and wounds which were still painful after having been treated by the medicine-men, the Governor presented him with one of his own suits of soft velvet. But the heat of it was too much for a body inured to cold; and he went for twenty days wearing nothing but a long loose linen garment. Then by the aid of the Spanish infirmarian, and with the slow return of old habits, he was able once more to endure the garb of civilization. In the end he became the complete cavalier, encased in armor and mounted on horseback. As an interpreter he was worth a hundred men to the expedition.

It was now necessary to repay Mococo for his generosity. The Governor sent some of the Indians to the chief to announce his coming, and rode over to his village.[6] There the chief with all his warriors and his sons and his wives received De Soto with profound honor, kissing his hands, and asking for an alliance against his enemies. The Gentleman of Elvas reports his speech — or rather summarizes it. Like all Indian orators Mococo loved high-flown language and elaborate courtesies. He dep-

---

[6] Garcilasso is followed here, because Ranjel confirms him. But the embellishments of the Inca are omitted. Elvas has Mococo visit De Soto. Biedma says nothing about it.

recated his own trifling services, and informed De Soto that "as much as in your bodily perfections you excel all, and in your command over fine men you are superior to others, so in your nature you are equal to the full enjoyment of earthly things." And more to the same effect.

De Soto thanked him for his care of Ortiz, and assured him that it would never be forgotten. The chief could count upon his friendship and the protection of all Christian men. Even though, the Governor went on, he had done no more than keep his plighted word, there was nothing more that he could have done.

The remark was a trifle clumsy, and no doubt disappointing to men who so keenly relished the courteous phrase. And when De Soto went on to inquire if Mocoço knew of any part of the country where there was gold or silver, he may have further dampened the chief's fraternal love.

It would seem that the question was disquieting; at any rate Mocoço answered that, while he did not know of any gold, there was a chief named Paracoxi [7] who lived thirty leagues away who could tell him all about it. He couldn't feel quite comfortable while these new brothers of his were in the neighborhood. Paracoxi was the man to ask.

With reciprocal presents, and more of the speeches beloved by Indians, the two men parted.

[7] "Paracoxi" was really a word meaning chief. Laudonnière, who understood this, always speaks of *the* "Paracoussy," as we should say Pharoah or the Shah.

CHAPTER XI

BOGS AND PITFALLS

IT is very difficult, if not impossible, to trace with any degree of certainty the exact route followed by De Soto. While there is substantial agreement among the contemporary chroniclers as to the general direction and distances and the order in which the various localities were visited, it must be remembered that these men were in a totally unfamiliar country, without maps, and with very simple astronomical instruments, if any at all. The distance between two given points could be computed only roughly by the time it took to follow a winding trail.

Moreover the names of Indian villages and chiefs were rendered into a vague approximation to Indian sounds. Thus the name of Paracoxi, which is that used by Elvas, becomes in Biedma Hurripacuxi, and in Garcilasso Urribarracaxi. Castilian togues evidently found it difficult to get round these harsh gutterals.

Indian tradition identifies several of the places visited by the army. But this, though not valueless, is highly unreliable.

Nevertheless, we can plot the line of the route, if not with precision, at least with a fairly good idea of where it went. That must suffice us. Much more important now is the magnificent spectacle of the explorer's inflexible will, and the courage shown by him in the face of danger that was from day to day absolutely incalculable.

To say that no man ever grumbled during those three years with De Soto at the bitter deprivation and suffering endured by the army would be false; soldiers always grumble. But it is a fact that the records of the expedition all show the same spirit of great-hearted cheerfulness. Stained though this page of history may be with occasional deeds of cruelty, it is also resplendent with heroism. Great dreams and great deeds — the contemplation of them never fails to make men noble.

De Soto was now preparing to march north. With this in mind, and to prevent any desertions, he sent the six larger ships away, keeping only a caravel and a couple of brigantines in the harbor. In doing so, he followed the example of Pizarro and Cortés.

Before setting out with the whole army, the Governor ordered Gallegos with fifty cavalrymen and thirty or forty foot-soldiers to go to the province of the Paracoxi.[1] Upon the arrival of the Spaniards there, the Indians came to the officers on behalf of the absent chief to ask their intentions. Gallegos answered that he wished only to establish friendly relations between himself and the Paracoxi. But when he enquired where gold and silver might be found, the savages, who, like Mocoço, were uneasy at the presence of Christians in their midst, told them that towards the west there was a province called Cale, with which the Paracoxi was always at war. In those territories the

[1] Eighty horse, and a hundred foot, says Ranjel.

greater part of the year was summer; and there was so much gold that the warriors wore golden hats like casques. The Spanish helmets had given the Indians an idea. It was with tales like these that these crafty savages always tried to get rid of their unwelcome visitors.

Meanwhile Añasco, cruising in the remaining boats, dispersed a demonstration of hostile Indians with his light cannon, but lost a number of men from the deadly aim of the native bows. And Porcallo de Figueroa was sent out to find, and to bring in, the coy Ucita.

That chief, whose village De Soto had been occupying for a month, steadily resisted all friendly overtures and kept hidden in the recesses of the forests and swamps. But now that De Soto had Mocoço's men as guides, and Ortiz as an interpreter, he sent his second in command, the middle-aged Porcallo, to bring Ucita with him, by force if necessary.

This was an adventure which the rich Cuban thought would prove very much to his taste. His secret motive in joining De Soto had been the securing of slaves for his plantations and mines; and he felt disappointed that the local chief Mocoço and his people had made an alliance with the Spaniards. There had, therefore, been no Indians available for capture. If Ucita could be surprised in his hiding-place, it might be that a large number of prisoners could be taken at the same time.

He set off, in the gay expensive clothes he loved to display, at the head of a company of horsemen hardly less brilliant than himself. Ucita should be brought back. He pledged his word on that.

It was easier said than done. Ucita had a very shrewd

notion of what would happen to him if he fell into the
hands of the Spaniards, especially after the way he had
treated Juan Ortiz. He took care to conceal himself in
impassable country. Messengers from him came out to
ask Porcallo to turn back. They warned him that Ucita
was too strongly entrenched to be taken, even if they
could find him; but the Master of the Camp took the advice as being due to panic, and persisted in going on. He
even increased his speed, for fear that, after all, the chief
might escape.

The galloping of dragoons was in vain. They soon
arrived at the edge of an immense bog. Looking upon
the wide stretch of dismal mire, they were for giving up
the hope of capturing Ucita in face of such an obstacle.
But Porcallo's blood was up. He had not come all that
way for nothing; so he set the example by charging forward straight into the mud. His men, swearing heartily
at their leader's obstinacy, could do nothing else but
follow.

Before long, however, Porcallo found himself in a deep
hole, where he floundered in a morass from which he
could not extricate himself. His horse slipped, throwing
the rider headlong; and when, after frantic exertions, he
succeeded in dragging himself and his mount out, man
and beast were covered from head to foot in grey slime.

The order for the return to camp now had to be given.
In such a district of bogs Ucita was secure. So Porcallo
rode along crestfallen in bedraggled finery, secretly fum-
ing at the sniggers of his men. Yet he was a genial old
fellow, well liked for his generous spirit by all the army;
and his wrath gradually became transformed into a comic

ruefulness. After all, he reflected, he was too advanced
in years for such adventures, and a man of too substantial a dignity to subject himself to the inglorious dangers
of these infernal swamps. It served him right. He
should have stayed upon his estates in Cuba and left the
conquest of Florida to younger men. His soldiers heard
him muttering whimsically "Hurri-harri! Hurri-higa!
Burra-coxa! Hurri-harri! The Devil take a country
with such names!" It was as near as he could get to the
one that Garcilasso renders "Hirrihigua."

A man floundered with such words almost as badly as
in the bogs. Porcallo had had enough of it. He determined to go home. And De Soto was quite willing that
he should do so. For he and his Master of the Camp had
opposed objects in view.

When the time for parting came, however, good-humor
was restored all round. Porcallo distributed presents to
his many friends, and — what was more important —
agreed to act as agent in Cuba for the army. He would
superintend the gathering of stores and the enrollment
(if possible) of fresh volunteers. As a recruiting ser-
geant he might not be, after his unlucky experiences,
convincingly enthusiastic; but being a Cuban and a man
of business he could be counted upon to serve the army
well as a manager of supplies.

The ship that took Porcallo back to the island was
probably the same that carried a letter, dated July 9, 1539,
to the justice and board of magistrates in Santiago. In
it De Soto gives an account of his doings since arriving
in Florida, but assures his officials that he has not forgotten them or the love he owes "to objects at a dis-

tance." In general he instructs them, as their Governor, to maintain the repose and well-being of the public, and, in particular, to hasten with the building of the bastion begun before his departure. He also announces that he is on the point of leaving for Cale, where "they say" there is an abundance of gold and silver, and many pearls. "May it please God that this be so; for of what these Indians say I believe nothing but what I see . . . although they have it for a saying that if they lie to me, it will cost them their lives."

Six days later, on Tuesday the 15th, the Governor, leaving a hundred men behind with Calderón, marched northward to join Baltasar de Gallegos in the search for the province where the natives wore hats of gold. He was already, as we see, strongly inclined to disbelieve anything told him by the natives; but on one point his faith never faltered until the end. "As Florida was so wide, there could not fail to be a rich country."

It was a curious procession that he led — brilliant, high-spirited, nobly bred young cavaliers, and a large drove of pigs. The sows he had brought had farrowed. Their presence necessitated a ragged and disorganized advance, for the horsemen and dogs were continually obliged to go off to round up a refractory porker.

This was not good for discipline. But the pigs later saved the expedition. And the newly appointed Master of the Camp, Luis de Moscoso, a good-natured, indolent officer, was often very careless. Ranjel notes this disapprovingly, and tells how, upon the second day of the march, while the riders had dismounted to rest, a rabbit starting up in the long grass frightened the horses, so that they scattered in all directions, and were with difficulty recovered. Had any Indians been around at the time, he grimly notes, they would have had the army at their mercy and the war would have ended shamefully then and there. Yet the gay-hearted young men treated the incident as humorous, and called the tract of water near which they were the Lake of the Rabbit.

They were soon sobered. Under a blazing sky the next day several of the foot-soldiers collapsed, and one man died of thirst. But a little farther on they came to a plain and saw, for the first time in Florida, fields of maize. They were cheered by the sight, for they were hungry as well as thirsty. As Indian corn was still somewhat new to them, however, they did not yet know that the pleasantest way of eating it was to boil it on the cob. Instead they laboriously made bread of it, pounding it in wooden mortars with a pestle, and sifting the flour through their shirts of mail.

As they neared Cale, De Soto again behaved with a recklessness which his secretary blames. In his impatience to reach his destination and to find out if there really was treasure there, he rode on ahead accompanied by only ten men.

Cale when reached yielded nothing but food, of which the army was badly in need. There was no sign of gold; and the Indians when questioned about their "casques" looked blankly amazed.

In this district the Spaniards ate for the first time "little dogs that did not bark." The chroniclers set down the fact for the purpose of indicating the privations of the army in being reduced to such meat. They were not usually given to self-pity, and in this instance it was comically misplaced. The "little dogs" were opossums. That the Spaniards found them good to eat, they set down to their own starving voracity.

From this time on De Soto steadily followed the policy of getting by hook or by crook the local chief into his clutches and of keeping him as a hostage until the invaders were well out of his territory. It was a policy which had proved successful in Mexico and Peru; in Florida, among warlike savages, it aroused fierce resentment. Yet, even so, that seemed better than leaving the chiefs at liberty to organize attack.

The hounds were used to bring in fugitives. Ranjel and Elvas both give the story of a chief who ran off with other Indians into a wood. In pursuit of him was released an Irish greyhound, which was so well trained that he passed by all the other warriors and hung on to the arm of the one man he was after until the Spaniards could come up.

These bloodhounds were also used as executioners. The flinging of men to the dogs is horrible to think of, but it apparently was regarded as a necessary military measure. The guides would often deliberately lead the army out of its way into impassable country or into ambushes. Hanging seemed to do no good, for that the Indians endured with stoical indifference. The one form of punishment that they feared was that of being torn to pieces, and this the Spaniards employed.

Another harsh practice of the Governor's was to compel the chiefs to furnish him with carriers for the baggage, and with cooks. The Indians, however, were quite accustomed to being burden bearers for their own lords. They were not treated badly, unless they attempted to escape, but many of the women taken from among the natives as servants were maltreated by the more brutal elements among the soldiery.

Abandoning Cale, since there was no gold there, the army marched on to Caliquin,[2] which the Christians reached on August 17th. There they heard of Narváez having been in the vicinity in 1528. The memory of his dismal fate, of which they had learned the details from Cabeza de Vaca, depressed every soul, and "all counselled the governor to go back to the port that they might not be lost." But De Soto was constitutionally incapable of turning back. To every argument he turned a deaf ear. All pleading was useless. He answered "I will never return until I have seen with my own eyes the rich country which I have been told is somewhere here." Having so spoken, he curtly ordered his officers to get their men in readiness for the saddle.

The *Cacique* of Caliquin[3] was trapped by a deplorable stratagem. Riding out one day trying to capture Indians for guides, Gallegos captured seventeen of them, among whom was a young girl who turned out to be the daughter of the chief. They held her in close custody. She should be the decoy. The father, a handsome, magnificently built warrior of thirty-five, arrayed in all his savage panoply of head feathers, came in as they had hoped to ask for his daughter to be restored. He was

---

[2] Aguacaleyquen in Ranjel.

[3] Garcilasso calls this chief "Vitachuco." The name appears in Elvas as "Uitachuco," an Appalachian village where De Soto encamped in October, as we learn from Ranjel who calls the place "Ivitachuco."

DOGS AS EXECUTIONERS

[From De Bry]

told that he would have to accompany the army until
it had reached the next province. The man proved to
be a most dangerous hostage. The Spaniards would have
done better to have left him alone.

At Napetaca, De Soto was met by Indians playing upon
reed flutes. The hideous noise they made,[4] according
to Ortiz who understood these matters, was intended to
be taken as a sign that they came in peace. All they
wanted was to get the chief back.

De Soto put them off by saying that they would get
their chief back all in good time, and that he was not
a prisoner but a guest. The answer naturally did not
satisfy the Indians. As the Spaniards had employed a
ruse, they would use another. Secretly they laid their
plans for rescuing their leader and for wiping out the invading army. Ortiz luckily discovered the plot; and De
Soto, informed as to what was in the wind, determined
to strike first in the *Conquistador* manner.

The minor chiefs begged for a parley to discuss the
matter further. Both parties were to meet unarmed, and
in the middle of an open plain at a little distance from
the two armies. Their intention, as Ortiz had discovered, was to have their bows and arrows hidden in
the long grass, in which many picked warriors were also
concealed, and then, at a signal from the hostage, to kill
De Soto and the men with him.

The Governor took the captive by the hand and led
him out to meet the other chiefs. A saddle was provided for De Soto to sit on during the palaver. He was
accompanied by six soldiers, one of whom was a trump-

---

[4] Bartram calls the music of Indian flutes, "a howling melancholy discord."

eter. Two horses were held in readiness in the rear with the necessary arms.

Moscoso, who was waiting impatiently for his general's signal, began to discern movements in the grass. Indians were closing round. Without waiting for the blast of the trumpet, he dug spurs into the flanks of his horse, and shouting to the cavaliers, "Come on, gentlemen! Santiago! Santiago!" charged full tilt at the braves. They at once sprang for their concealed bows, and the plain became alive with naked warriors. But Moscoso's cavalry was upon them almost before the first shaft could be fitted to the string.

Leaving the chief to the custody of his guard, De Soto ran back to his charger, and put himself at the head of the thundering horsemen. The Indians fought valiantly, but at a disadvantage. The General's horse fell riddled with arrows, as did several others; and a few of the Spaniards were wounded. But it was impossible for the Indians to stand for long against mounted men.

Forty or fifty of them having been thrust through by the lancers, the rest fled for safety to two large ponds, where they could swim in the centre, out of the range of quarrel from cross-bow or bullet from arquebus.[5] Garcilasso, embellishing the story as usual, says that every now and then an Indian would get up on the backs of other swimmers, to shoot an arrow at the Christians on land. Even if it were possible to perform such a feat, the bowstrings, being wet, would have made the shots

[5] Garcilasso says, with characteristic exaggeration, that there were ten thousand Indians. It is his favorite estimate, but is manifestly absurd. Ranjel and Elvas put the number at four hundred.

ineffective. It is probable enough, however, that the fierce warriors waved their bows in defiance.

What happened was sufficiently remarkable without all that. Throughout that day the swimmers in the ponds refused to surrender; and guards had to be established at night to prevent any escape in the darkness. The footmen were supplemented by cavalrymen and bloodhounds. Neither side took any rest.

During the night the Indians attempted to outwit the Spaniards by swimming noiselessly to the shore with lily-pads over their heads. It was a clever ruse, but proved useless. At the sight of any ripple upon the surface of the water, a lancer would charge into the pond up to his horse's chest; and the swimmer would go back hurriedly to his companions.

At last, urged by Juan Ortiz to give themselves up, since escape was impossible, many of them, one by one, overcome by weariness and the chill of the water, came to the bank and surrendered. By the first light of dawn all except twelve, who still obstinately refused to leave the ponds, were captured. This dozen, however, would apparently have gone on until they collapsed and were drowned, had not the Spaniards sent in their Indian carriers and guides after them. The swimmers were now too weak to resist and so were pulled by the hair to land.

The last of all to be taken out was a young chief. Though half dead with cold and fatigue, his courage remained unquenched. He said proudly to the Indians around, "Go to my people and tell them to take no thought of me. I have done what a brave man should do, and if I took refuge in the pond it was not to escape death but to encourage the others there. Tell them that they may be assured that if I have to die it will be as a valiant man."

The assurance was hardly needed. And he did not have to die, for the Spaniards, connoisseurs in these matters, applauded his courage. It was not safe, however, to let the captives go; but De Soto promised them fair treatment for good behavior. He needed their services as carriers.

Nevertheless, it would have been safer, as events showed, to have released them all, and even to have given back their chief. Because these men had a determination quite as great as that of the Spaniards, and immediately hatched a new plot.

The chief was exempt from all menial service and continued to dine at the Governor's table. He took advantage of his favored position to organize attack. The youths whom he had been allowed to keep with him as his personal attendants were sent round the camp to the captives, who were almost as numerous as their masters, telling them that at the dinner hour each should spring upon the Spaniard he served, who would be off his guard, and kill him by any means available. The chief himself undertook to deal with De Soto, whom he felt quite capable of handling. And at the instant of assault he would give the tribal war-whoop as a signal.

On the appointed day, the chief attacked De Soto during the meal. Without warning the tall athletic warrior struck the Governor with full force in the face. It was a terrific blow, that knocked out several of De Soto's

THE INDIANS BEING TAKEN FROM THE PONDS

[From *Voyagie van Don Ferdinand de Soto na Florida, Leyden 1706*]

·teeth and bathed his face in blood. He reeled before it, half stunned, and the chief sprang upon him to strangle him. But De Soto was also a very strong man and he rallied, landing in his turn a hard punch upon the chief's nose. Hearing the noise of the scuffle, several men outside rushed into the hut, and ran the assailant through with their swords.

Throughout the camp it was the same story. As one man the Indians rose, howling for blood. Those who could seize a Spanish spear or sabre did so; those who had no better weapon took up anything that came to hand, a hammer or a cudgel, a cooking-pot or a brand from the fire, or one of the heavy pestles used for pounding grain.

The Christians were taken completely by surprise. Four of them had their brains dashed out, and nearly all received some hurt, a broken head, a scalded back, or a burnt face. But as soon as they had recovered from the shock of the first impact, they settled down coolly to scotching the insurrection.

Luckily few weapons were seized by the Indians, though those who succeeded in getting hold of any used them manfully. One man, for instance, climbed up into the loft of the granary with a lance where he defended the entrance, says Elvas, "with the uproar of ten men" until a battle-axe brought to a close his glorious but brief career.

There was only one thing that could be done with the Indians after they had been subdued. The sullen scowling faces made that much clear. De Soto angrily burst out, "I wish to God that those lords of the council in Spain who are always instructing us how we should treat these people could see what kind of men they really are!" He could not let them go; and there were too many of them to be kept in confinement. The Governor therefore determined to make a frightful example of them.

Some of the younger and, presumably, more tractable of the Indians were spared. These were handed over to such soldiers as possessed good chains and could be trusted to be vigilant guards. All the others were ordered out to execution. They were brought into the open space in the middle of the camp and there shot to death by the Indians from Cale — the Spaniards themselves disdaining the butchery of unarmed men.

One gigantic warrior was being taken out to execution by a Spaniard of the name of Saldagna, according to Garcilasso. When he saw what was happening in the square, fury seized him, and he turned upon his captor. Taking his neck in one hand and his thigh in the other, he lifted him above his head and dashed him to the ground. Then he proceeded to jump upon the man's stomach, and would soon have killed him had other Christians not run up to the rescue. But the savage had not yet finished. Drawing Saldagna's sword he "fought like a bull in the arena," says Elvas, until the halberdiers dispatched him. At any rate, it was a better way of dying than his fellows found.

CHAPTER XII

THE WILDERNESS

HAVING quelled this uprising, the bruised and scalded army — hardly a man among them had got off scot free — proceeded northwest, limping upon its march. The winter was near, and there was need to find better quarters than those they possessed, as protection against the cold.

It was the third of September when the march began in that superb autumn weather which marks the western hemisphere. The country was still difficult, being swampy and full of woods of pine and of live-oaks festooned with Spanish-moss — the same district in which the Seminoles were later to hold the United States Army at bay for seven years. The savages, because they had heard of the fate of the chief of Caliquin and his men, were careful to keep out of the way.

A wide river had to be crossed, the Suwanee. This the Spaniards named the River of the Deer, because it was there that they were met by messengers from Uzachil, whose territories they were approaching, who bore some excellent venison as a present. The chief himself, mindful of what had happened a few days before, did not venture to come in person to greet the Spaniards. And the villages all the way along the route were deserted.

The crossing of the Suwanee, as of other rivers, called for the exercise of a good deal of ingenuity. Sometimes, of course, they proved fordable; but often they were too swift for safety. In that case the horsemen held their mounts with their breasts against the current to break it, while the infantrymen went over supporting themselves by holding on to the manes and tails of the animals. At other times the mounts had to be swung across on hawsers. But in some places bridges could be made. And Nuño Tobar distinguished himself by recommending a method of laying the timbers criss-cross, for which he was laughed at, but which, upon trial, proved eminently satisfactory.

A bridge was practicable only in the case of small streams. Many were too wide for that; and too deep for fording. Over such the army was transported on rafts.

Rivers presented only an occasional problem. The permanent need was for carriers for the baggage and domestic service. Under their excessively hard work many of the Indian porters died; and many more managed to escape. The few surviving followers of Caliquin were led in chains with iron collars round their necks; for, after their recent experience, the Spaniards meant to take no chances. Even so, the Indians often got away. If one of the soldiers got behind or if he went out to bring in wood or corn, the manacled captives with him — did they get the opportunity — would overpower their master, knock his brains out, and run off into the woods, chains and all.

Others managed to file their fetters through with a

flint at night. But if they were caught, they were punished with death, as a deterrent to those who were meditating flight. As Hakluyt's translation of Elvas grimly puts it, "They paid for themselves, and for the rest."

It was observed, however, that as soon as the younger men and the women had been taken far enough from their own country, they became tractable; for, despairing of seeing their homes again, they seemed no longer to care and resigned themselves to their fate.

As the army moved farther north it became more frequently attacked, for it was entering the Appalachian lands, where the tribes were renowned for their valor. There was rarely or never a massed assault; but stragglers were cut off, and a perpetual annoyance was kept up. In that wooded country no man knew at what moment an arrow would come flying at his face or at his horse's side, shot by a warrior concealed in a clump of trees. And on the first of October a stiff skirmish took place in which three men were killed before the Indians were dispersed by the cross-bowmen.

These savages also, as the Spaniards found, were first-rate fighters, especially in a broken country. Carrying bows which no Spaniard could so much as bend they shot with terrific force their crude but carefully constructed arrows. Some of these were tipped with fish bone, as sharp as a needle. Others had flint heads, many of which were serrated and caused ugly festering wounds. Generally, however, these would break, when they struck upon armor.[1] The most dangerous kind to the Span-

[1] Garcilasso tells us a number of stories about these arrows. Such as that of an Indian who shot right through a breastplate hung up as a target. And a second breastplate being hung up, he penetrated both at a single shot.

iards, were the cane arrows that had been pointed and hardened in the fire. These would split against iron, and the splinters find their way between the gaps in chain-mail. But any arrow was a formidable weapon. The Christians learned the truth of what Peter Martyr wrote to Pope Julius II, "The inhabitants of Terra Florida have sharp nayles."

A few days' further marching—still through boggy lands, but now with a sandy bottom — brought them to a much pleasanter district, one more open and with many cornfields. There were plantations of beans and pumpkins, too, and orchards of plums and walnuts. So finding a town that suited their purpose, they determined to stay in it for the winter. Like all the others it was deserted. Its name was Anhaica.

Finding that the sea was not far distant — it was only eight leagues away — De Soto dispatched Juan de Añasco on a scouting party to find a harbor for the caravel and the two brigantines which were still with Calderón at Charlotte Harbor. The cavaliers came back with a story that terrified everybody. Everybody, that is, except De Soto. He was not to be moved by such things.

They had found a huge tree that had been cut down and hollowed into a manger. The skulls of horses were lying scattered about; and the place where a forge had been set up was discernable. Upon the standing trees crosses had been cut. This was the Bay of Horses where the ill-fated Narváez and his men had lived upon horseflesh while they were making their frail disastrous ships.

The discovery shattered the morale of the army. This would be their fate too. Why should they fare better

than Narváez ? He had been a stout captain, but he
had perished and all his men with him. De Soto was
implored to turn back. His officers urged that they had
been five months in Florida, floundering all that time in
mud, with never a glint of gold to gladden their eyes.
Could he not see that the enterprise was hopeless ? No
man could make headway in such a land, or conquer
Indians of such a breed.

His answer was characteristic. If his men thought that
they were in the position of Narváez, let them do what
Narváez had done and build boats — and suffer his fate.
He sent Añasco to bring up Calderón with the hundred
men left at Ucita's settlement. When the greater number of these had been landed, he sent the remainder in
the brigantines back to Cuba with twenty women slaves
as a present to Doña Isabella, and the caravel under Maldonado to explore the coast farther west. The army was
therefore left without a means of leaving.

By the time Maldonado had returned De Soto's men
had got over their panic. His exploring party reported
the discovery of an excellent harbor, well sheltered and
with deep water — what is now Pensacola Bay. De Soto
proposed making it the centre of his operations in the
summer. Maldonado was accordingly ordered to go back
to Havana (for which he sailed on February 26, 1540),
where he was to gather badly needed provisions and military supplies. He was instructed to bring the brigantines
and the caravel to effect a juncture with the army in the
western harbor discovered by him.

The plan was obviously sound, though it entailed a
certain amount of risk. It depended, of course, upon De

Soto's being able to reach Pensacola by the summer, travelling through he could not know what dangers, and facing unforeseen delays in an unfamiliar country. If the plan could have been carried out, the history of the expedition would have been very different. But it was November before the soldiers came within reach of Maldonado's ships; and by that time the situation had entirely changed. De Soto by then had found reasons for not informing his subordinate that he was near at hand.

In Anhaica, the Spaniards, though spared the fatigues of the march, were incessantly beset by the savages. Twice their encampment was set on fire, and it was always unsafe for any small body of men to to go far from the settlement. The Indians made light account of the drastic penalties they received when caught. And as death had no terrors for them their noses and hands were cut off. But it was no use. Their ferocity actually seemed to increase as a consequence of such measures.

Their pride equalled their courage. Not one of them was ever known, for fear of death, to deny that he belonged to the tribe that was giving so much trouble. When asked where they came from, they used to draw themselves up and answer haughtily, "From where? I am an Indian of Appalache." And they gave their captors to understand that no more deadly insult could be offered them than to suppose that they were anything else but Appalachians.

The Conquerors could not but admire such arrogant stubbornness. But they found it inconvenient and unexpected. It was worse than the fierceness shown by the men of Caliquin. Was it possible, they could not help wondering, to bring their projects to success in the face of such opposition ?

Even De Soto must have been troubled in mind; but he never would admit having any doubts about subjecting Florida to the Spanish Crown. And by his single unmovable will he held the army steady. All through the dreary winter it was his strength alone that sustained them.

And now confirmation of his hopes seemed to come. One of the Indians captured during the autumn told the Spaniards that he did not belong to that part of the land, but to a province a long way off in the east which was governed by a woman. He added that she was a person of astonishing size, and — what was more to the point — that she exacted a tribute of furs and gold from all the neighboring chiefs. The Spaniards, accustomed by now to the tall stories and downright lying of the savages, might have been skeptical except for one circumstance. The youth completely convinced them that he was speaking the truth by giving a demonstration as to how gold was taken from the ground, melted and refined, "exactly as though he had seen it all done." It was impossible that he could be so accurate in his details unless he had had personal experience of the smelting of the metal. Everyone who witnessed the signs he made took that as certain. And Ortiz, who could talk with him in his own language, testified his belief. Ranjel, compiling his diary, and knowing later that the whole thing was pure fabrication, could account for it on no other ground than that the Devil had taught the young Indian how to be so convincingly explicit.[2]

The story excited the army to the highest possible pitch. De Soto went about radiantly triumphant. He could now afford to chaff Moscoso and the other officers who had been in favor of abandoning Florida. He had always told them that gold in vast abundance was here. If it hadn't been for him, they would all have gone back to Spain upon the very verge of success.

Much earlier than they had intended they broke camp. They were eager to find this princess and her treasures, and they had to leave at once if they were to get back in time to join hands with Maldonado at Pensacola in the summer. On the 3rd of March the army set out in search of Cutifachiqui.

They marched through what is to-day the state of Georgia, making in north-easterly direction. A difficult and hazardous journey was expected, and they were not disappointed. It was made all the more laborious because during the winter the greater part of the captive Indians, who had been naked and in chains, had died. And the Appalachian Indians were so fiercely intractable that they could not be used as porters. Therefore each man had to carry his own supply of maize in addition to his personal *impedimenta*. But they did so the more cheerfully in view of the gold with which they were so soon to fill their hands.

---

[2] The Conquerors often encountered such instances of ingenious imagination among the Indians. The savage named by Coronado, El Turco, on account of his appearance, told him of a land where the fishes were as big as horses, and where the chief took his siesta under a tree upon which were hanging a number of golden bells which put him to sleep as they swung in the breeze.

The country was, for part of the way, pleasant enough; though at the beginning swampy districts had still to be gone through. And a great many rivers had to be crossed, among them the Ockmulgee, the Oconee, and the Ogeechee. And these called for all the ingenuity of Nuño Tobar and the other amateur engineers.

While they were still among the Appalachians there were frequent skirmishes, but as they approached the territories of the Creeks they came across a gentler, more refined race, and one with more of the amenities and appurtenances of decent living. Elvas gives us this description of the new group of tribes.

"The houses of this town were different from those behind, which were covered with dry grass; henceforth they were roofed with cane, after the fashion of tile. They are kept very clean: some have their sides so made of clay as to look like tapia. Throughout the cold country every Indian has a winter house, plastered inside and out, with a very small door, which is closed at dark, and a fire being made within, it remains heated like an oven, so that clothing is not needed at night-time. He has likewise a house for summer, and near it is a kitchen, where fire is made and bread baked. Maize is kept in a *barbacoa,* which is a house with wooden sides, like a room, raised aloft on four posts, and has a floor of cane. The difference between the houses of the masters, or principal men, and those of the common people is, that besides being larger than the others, they have deep balconies on the front side, with cane seats, like benches; and about are many *barbacoas,* in which they bring together the tribute their people give them of maize, skins of deer, and blankets of the country. These are like shawls, some of them made from the inner bark of trees, and others of a grass resembling nettle, which, by threading out, becomes like flax.[3] The women use them for covering, wearing one about the body from the waist downward, and another over the shoulder, with the right arm free, after the manner of the Gypsies: the men wear but one, which they carry over the shoulder in the same way, the loins being covered with a *bragueiro* of deerskin, after the fashion of the woollen breechcloth that was once the custom of Spain. The skins are well dressed, the colour being given to them that is wished, and in such perfection, that, when of vermilion, they look like very fine red broadcloth; and, when black, the sort in use for shoes, they are of the purest. The same hue is given to blankets."

In this country, too, they came across something of a systematic attempt at agriculture, performed under difficulties by instruments of bone or stone or wood or shell. And the baskets, which they found useful to their porters, were admirable for their beauty.[4] It is curious that no mention is made of what one might have supposed would have specially excited the Spaniard's curiosity — the use of tobacco.[5]

[3] Ranjel also admiringly notes this cloth woven from mulberry bark. He says it looked like home-spun linen.

[4] Adair in his *History of the American Indians* (1775) writes: "They make the handsomest clothes-baskets I ever saw, considering their materials. They divide large swamp-canes into long thin narrow splinters, which they dye of several colours, and manage the workmanship so well, that both the inside and outside are covered with a beautiful variety of pleasing figures." See also Mason's *Indian Basketry*.

[5] Cabeza de Vaca, however, speaks of the way the Florida Indians "produce stupefaction with a smoke, and for that they will give whatever they

They now encountered in the person of Patofa a chief who professed friendliness, but whose amiability towards the Spaniards was based upon the fact that he hoped for their aid against his enemies, especially against the chieftainess of Cutifachiqui. He was so delighted when he heard that De Soto was marching in search of her, that he supplied the Spaniards with a large number of porters and all the baskets needed.

With Patofa, De Soto took a new line, and, borrowing a page out of his Peruvian memories, gave him to understand that he was "the Child of the Sun."

Although he was not above playing upon the savage's heathen superstition, he saw in his friendliness an opportunity of the sort that, so far, had rarely occurred. He made an attempt, therefore, to instruct the people in the elements of the Christian religion.

The day happened to be, by a coincidence of dates, both Holy Thursday and the "Day of the Incarnation," that is of the Annunciation, the 25th of March. And, though no man in the army, as Ranjel tells us, was so strict a Christian as to abstain from flesh meat on that day — and after their long privations the roast venison and turkey provided by Patofa were an irresistible temptation — Spanish piety set up a cross in the centre of the settlement. The Indians were told that the Governor had come to make known to them the faith of Christ; and De Soto and his priests urged them to yield obedience to the Apostolic Church and the Supreme Pontiff. They were also to acknowledge themselves to be vassals

possess." Possibly he had been stupefied, like other people, trying to smoke a pipe for the first time, or perhaps narihuana was smoked.

of the Emperor, and were assured that they would be treated well and with the justice accorded to all of His Majesty's Christian subjects.

One of the friars explained to the natives the significance of the cross. "It is put there," he said, "to commemorate the sufferings of Christ, who was God and man, and the creator of heaven and earth. This is the sign of your salvation. Therefore you should revere it." However much the Indians understood of this exposition, they did at least join, to the best of their ability, in the devotions of their visitors.

As they proceeded on their journey through a country of tall timber, which was succeeded by a wilderness and then by another forest, the soldiers again suffered from the scarcity of food. They lacked altogether the savages' skill in stalking or trapping game; moreover, they had no time to linger upon it. And the lack of flesh meat seems — very strangely — to have been no more serious a deprivation than the lack of salt. Without these, many wasted away and sank under sheer debility. Such sufferers would moan pathetically, "Oh, if I had only a slice of meat or a few lumps of salt, I should not die like this!" When one of the "little dogs" was killed, its flesh was so highly valued that if the lucky hunter failed to send a share of it to his officer, he would be sure to feel the sting of his superior's spite, and be assigned to some disagreeable duty. They had got over pitying themselves for being reduced to such food. The man who brought one of the dogs down with his cross-bow thought himself a very fine fellow.

They saw of course no buffaloes. In fact only once,

and then when in the farthest point west reached by them, did they ever see the "hunchbacked cows." These would have been of enormous benefit to them, for upon their horses they could have killed as many as they pleased. But turkeys and wild rabbits and deer wandered all about them with general impunity.

On April 15th the young Indian who had told them of the country of the chieftainess and had offered to guide them there — he who had given through the power of the Devil so vivid a demonstration of the mining and smelting of gold [6] — began to make believe that he was possessed of evil spirits. One of the friars exorcised him, and the fit passed; but others regarded the whole thing as a hoax. The fact seems to have been that the poor lad had lost his way, and was terrified, knowing as he did what happened to false guides. Fits or no fits he would have been flung to the dogs except for the circumstance that he was the only Indian with them whose language Juan Ortiz understood. A few days later the youth took the additional precaution of asking for baptism, after which the iron collar was struck from his neck.

The Spaniards were now in the middle of an immense pine forest, in which no path could be found, or any sign of a habitation. The guide had no idea where they were, and the carriers lent them by Patofa could give them no help. It was a desperate pass, for their food was ex-

---

[6] Perhaps the Devil had nothing to do with it, after all. The German traveller, Johannes Lederer, who visited North Carolina and Virginia in 1669, says that the Spaniards were at that time working gold and silver mines in the Appalachian Mountains, and that he saw specimens of the ore. There are certainly traces of mining operations to be seen in Upper Georgia.

hausted and soldiers and horses alike were all lean with hunger.

Had they been attacked by any considerable body of savages just then, they must inevitably have been wiped out in that labyrinth. But it was a wilderness that even the Indians avoided.

Most of the officers were now in favor of going back by the path by which they had come; but De Soto insisted, as he always did, that they must go forward. Yet, like everybody else, he had no knowledge of where they were, or of what they were aiming at — except that they had to find the golden land of Cutifachiqui. Not altogether justly, but with some degree of reason, does Oviedo (it is clearly his note) interpolate in Ranjel's diary: "I have wondered many times at the venturesomeness, stubbornness, and persistency or firmness, to use a better word for the way these baffled conquerors kept on from one toil to another, and then to another still greater; from one danger to many others, here losing one companion, there three and again still more, going from bad to worse without learning by experience. Oh, wonderful God! that they should have been so blinded and dazed by a greed so uncertain and by such vain discourses as Hernando de Soto was able to utter to these deluded soldiers." Yet it was this "firmness, to use a better word," this ability to keep on in the face of danger and disappointment, that made De Soto and the *Conquistadores* so great.

In these straits he sent out four of his captains, each with eight horsemen, in different directions. But they all came back at night, having found no road or any sign of a settlement. The horses were so jaded that the riders had to lead them in by the bridle.

The following day four other officers were appointed to the same duty, each again with eight men, but this time men who could swim. Gallegos was ordered to go up the river bank; Añasco down it; and Romo and Lobillo into the country on either side.

Some of the pigs brought from Cuba — which had at one time increased to three hundred, but whose numbers were now greatly diminished — were slaughtered for food. They had been kept for just such an emergency. With rations of a pound of pork, and a few herbs and wild spinach, the soldiers kept themselves from perishing of starvation. "Dying of hunger, with no trail, drenched with continual rain, the rivers always rising and narrowing the land, and without hope of villages or knowledge of where to find them, lamenting and calling on God for mercy;" — such was their state, as Ranjel describes it. Garcilasso tells how four soldiers once resolved to divide a handful of corn between them. This they parched, in order to swell it, and each man got exactly eighteen grains.

In this crisis De Soto suffered as much as the lowliest there. And all looked to their young commander as to a father. "He concealed his distress," says Garcilasso, "he caressed the soldiers, and encouraged them with a gaiety that charmed them and made them forget a part of their troubles; so that, in their turn, they showed a countenance as contented as if they had everything in abundance."

The extremity may be gauged by the fact that they

[183]

dismissed their native porters in order to husband their supplies of food, which were rapidly nearing the point of absolute exhaustion. Porters for military stores were always a necessity; but they were less of a necessity than something to eat.

At last three of the officers returned, two of them with locally captured Indians, and one of them, Juan Añasco, with the good news that he had found a village some twelve or thirteen leagues down the river. "At which," says Elvas, "the governor and his people were as much delighted as though they had been raised from death to life." Because of this De Soto gave orders that the rations of pork be stopped at once — the extremity having passed. The remaining pigs were to be kept in reserve: the men were to subsist as best they could on such herbs and roots and berries as they could gather in the woods.

Lobillo now came back with four Indian prisoners, but having lost two of his men. Even the welcome intelligence that he brought of trails did not save him from his general's anger. Without allowing his captain to rest or eat, De Soto ordered him to go out again and find the missing men under pain of death.

Worse befell one of the captives, who like all the others said that he knew of no village except the one already located. The unfortunate wretch was burned alive, whereupon the surviving Indians, whose memory had been marvellously stimulated by what they had just witnessed, said that the province of Cutifachiqui was only a two days' journey away. That was what the Spaniards wanted to know. They rejoiced to hear that they were so near their goal.

On the 26th of April, a Monday, the army set out for Aymay, the settlement discovered by Añasco. Before leaving, De Soto buried at the foot of a tree in the camp a paper of instructions, which he put into a pumpkin gourd. With a hatchet he cut into the bark of a tree these words, "Dig here, and at the root you will find a letter." It was the means for letting Lobillo, and the others still absent on reconnoitring duty, know where the main body had gone. There was still no other road than the one Añasco had made — a trampling through the undergrowth, and here and there trees freshly notched with hatchets to indicate the way taken.

Towards evening of that day the Governor, with a few of the better mounted of his men, reached the village; but the great bulk of his army was too exhausted, man and beast alike, to reach the place that night. Yet every heart was cheered, and they gave the cluster of huts the name of *Succor*.

They found there a *barbacoa* loaded with corn; also more than thirty bushels of *pinol,* or maize already parched. There were besides a large number of mulberry trees full of fruit; and in the clearing around were strawberries, "very savoury, palatable and fragrant." Ranjel notes that in that savage paradise countless wild roses were growing, "like those in Spain." It is a poetic touch, similar to others in his narrative. The secretary of De Soto, like Ruth, was sick for home.

CHAPTER XIII

THE PRINCESS AND THE PEARLS

AFTER these hardships, there followed what was the most charming and romantic incident of the whole expedition. On the last day of April the Governor took such of his soldiers as had recovered most completely from the privations they had been obliged to suffer, and, with an Indian woman as a guide, set out along the trail that lead to Cutifachiqui. He had already been told by some of the natives that the chieftainess, or *cacica* as the Spaniards called her, was waiting for him in her town. In view of the stories he had heard about her wealth, he was consumed with eagerness to meet her. We are not told what her feelings were. She must have felt some trepidation; she may have felt some curiosity to see the pale-faced, bearded men in iron, and their monstrous steeds.

On May Day the Spaniards reached a clearing on the bank opposite to her settlement. This is generally supposed to have been several miles below the place now named Silver Bluff, South Carolina, on the east bank of the Savannah River, about twenty-five miles below Augusta.

As soon as De Soto was perceived, four canoes crossed

over to meet him. These were not the light and graceful vessels of birch-bark, such as the northern Indians made, and with which we are familiar, but cumbersome dug-outs, hollowed by fire.[1] But what they lacked in beauty they made up for in size. In one of them was a young girl, whose easy dignity of bearing excited the admiring wonder of the Spaniards. They took her to be the *Cacica* they had come so far to see.

She was, however, only a niece of the chieftainess.[2] The reason, she explained, the *Cacica* had not come in person to greet her visitors was that she had stayed behind to prepare for their reception. But her canoes would soon arrive to carry the Governor to the other side.

De Soto made a courteous reply and she was paddled back to her aunt. Then, after a short interval, the chieftainess herself came out of the village, carried in a chair, which was covered with the "delicate white cloth" woven from mulberry bark. Some of her principal men bore her with the greatest respect upon their shoulders to the landing place, where she entered the state canoe. At the stern was spread an awning under which she sat upon cushions. The dug-out came straight across to the Christians. It was a pretty spectacle, but De Soto's keen eye was disappointed at not seeing any sign of gold ornaments, such as the Inca had worn when he was carried in his litter into Caxamarca. He noted, however, that

---

[1] De Soto certainly never saw a birch-bark canoe, for the dug-outs were also used, as Hennepin tells us, on the lower Mississippi.

[2] Garcilasso of course has a pop-eyed embellishment of this. The young girl, according to him, was the daughter of the chieftainess, but the mother refused to visit De Soto. Indeed when a young Indian was ordered to go to the obstinate lady to beg for an interview, he killed himself rather than bear what he knew would be an unwelcome message.

both the girl and the woman who was now crossing the river wore ropes of pearls round their necks.

The story of this *Cacica* is very astonishing, and there is no other instance known of a woman in such a position among the Creeks. But the details are given, though with some minor discrepancies, by all three of the chroniclers upon whose records this portion of De Soto's history has been based. And Garcilasso adds his testimony.

Pedro, the Indian lad who had first told them about Cutifachiqui, had described the lady as being of enormous size. This was now seen to be an ungallant exaggeration. The *Cacica* was stately, truly, but neither of gigantic height nor obese. She struck the Spaniards as being a very handsome woman of about thirty-five.

There was much more to admire in her than her good looks. Her intelligence, her tact, and her gracious kindness so enchanted De Soto that, as Garcilasso says, he did not think of inquiring her name.

While she was speaking to the Governor, she unstrung, one after another, some large pearls she had upon a chain, which went three times round her neck and descended to her waist. Then she made a sign to Ortiz, who was doing the interpreting, to take them and give them to De Soto.

Ortiz made the suggestion that she should give them with her own hands, for then the pearls would receive an added lustre; but to this she replied that the modesty of her sex forbade such a liberty.

Her words were translated to De Soto, and still further charmed him. He bowed and assured her that since it was a ceremonial gift made as a sign of good-will,

A FLORIDIAN PRINCESS

[From De Bry]

there could be no stain upon modesty. It would please him very much if she gave them to him herself.

At this she rose up from her seat, and went forward with her present to the Governor, who politely approached to receive it. He bent down his head, and she ventured, after this encouragement, to put the rope of pearls round his neck. Then he drew off a fine ruby ring, and gave it to her as a sign of peace. This she, with equal politeness, accepted, and put on "with remarkable grace."

The *Cacica* did much more for her visitors. She gave them comfortable quarters in her village — half of the houses being put at their disposal — and sent them abundant food of wild turkeys, dried venison, maize, walnuts, and mulberries. Salt, too, of which they stood in great need, and blankets and furs were provided. Everybody was delighted with such a welcome.

The people in the village appeared to the visitors to be clean and polite and naturally well-conditioned — in strong contrast to the savages of the Floridian peninsula. All were modestly dressed in clothing made from tree fibres and in feather shawls and deer-skins with colored designs. But the Spaniards noted, less approvingly, that the skins of "wild cats" which gave out a strong smell, were also used. The Creeks had evidently not perfectly mastered the curing of skunk hides.

When De Soto inquired about gold, the princess answered that it was quite true, she had a lot of it. In proof of which she sent messengers to bring some in. But this turned out to be copper, though of so light a color that many of the Spaniards believed gold was mingled with it. Having no *aqua-fortis* or quicksilver, however, they could not assay it. As for the "silver" which was brought to them in long slabs, it crumbled at the touch. It was only mica.

Yet there was some consolation in the large number of pearls in the place.[3] Garcilasso tells of a soldier who while eating an oyster (more probably a mussel) found a pearl caught between his teeth. As it was a very fine specimen, he offered it to De Soto as a present for Doña Isabella. The General civilly declined accepting it, and told the man to keep the pearl and use it to buy horses when they got back to Havana. As for himself he was as much obliged as though he had accepted what had been so kindly offered, and would one day make a suitable return.

In a country and among a people where the only things of real value were game and corn and the skins of wild animals, a necklace was regarded as of little consequence. But the good-natured *Cacica* noticed how the Spanish eyes sparkled at the sight of pearls. So she told De Soto, that if he really was interested in these trinkets, he might help himself. There were plenty, she said, in the sepulchres. And by sending to the graveyards of the uninhabited villages, he could find more than it would be possible for his horses to carry away.

[3] A. J. Pickett says in his *History of Alabama*, "There can be no doubt about the quantity of pearls found in this state and Georgia in 1540; but they were of a coarser and less valuable kind than the Spaniards supposed." They came as often (or more often) from the mussel as from the oyster. Their abundance is revealed by the many shell-dumps along the Tennessee and other rivers. The Tennessee mussel, says Brinton, was margaratiferous. In recent years freshwater pearls from this region have commanded good prices.

De Soto took her at her word, and on May 7th he and his secretary Ranjel visited "the mosque and oratory of this heathen people." It was, of course, the house where the dead reposed. All around the wall went a platform raised about two feet from the ground, and on it what appeared to be mummies were lying. As a matter of fact there was no true embalming practised among the American Indians. The method here was no doubt that used elsewhere: that of taking the flesh from the skin, which was then stuffed with sand, the other remains being cremated or dried and put with the bones at the "mummy's" feet.

The "mosque" was full of pearls, many of them woven together in the figures of babies or birds. But most of the pearls were discolored by the process used for opening the oyster shells, that of fire, and damaged by having been bored with red-hot copper spindles.

Their value must have been problematical; yet undoubtedly there were some good specimens among them. It was the only treasure ever found by De Soto. He took away a load three hundred and fifty pounds in weight.

While Ranjel was looking over the pearls, so he himself tell us, he came across a green stone which he took to be an emerald of good quality. He immediately called De Soto's attention to it, and the General ordered him to summon Juan de Añasco, the royal treasurer, who was outside, to hand it over into his custody. The secretary admits saying, "My Lord, don't let us tell anybody about this. Let us keep it ourselves. It may prove valuable."

De Soto turned on him angrily saying, "And if it *is*

an emerald — are we to be thieves ?" But after the expert Añasco had examined it carefully, he pronounced it to be only colored glass.

In the same cemetery De Soto found something of a very different sort. It gave him a shock to come there — where he would never have expected them — upon relics of Ayllon's expedition, Biscayan axes of iron and rosaries of jet beads. But the Spaniards now had the pearls to cheer them. The signs of their ill-fated predecessors did not prove nearly as disquieting as had the skulls of the horses of Narváez.

Again the princess suggested a further expedition in search of pearls. Another village of hers, Talimeco, had many that he was welcome to take. But De Soto smiled and answered with a proverb which could not have been very intelligible to her, "Let them stay there. To whom God gives a gift, may St. Peter bless it !"

This was interpreted by Ranjel to mean that De Soto proposed, after further explorations, to go back to Cutifachiqui, since that district was by far the best they had so far seen, and to carve out there the personal estate bestowed upon him by the terms of his agreement with the Spanish Court. The pearls could wait until he got back. He did not wish to burden his horses with more than the three hundred and fifty pounds of pearls he already possessed.

Thinking the matter over, De Soto decided that it might after all be as well to go to Talimeco, to look it over. He found it situated by a beautiful stream on a hill covered with trees of walnut, pine, live-oak, liquid-amber, and cedar. The house of the local chief was large, broad, and high, decorated above and below with very fine handsome mats, arranged so skilfully that all of them appeared to make a single one.

The "temple" was also of mats, and was of considerable size, a hundred paces in length and forty in breadth. At the entrance stood wooden statues, the largest of which was twelve feet high. These were armed with copper axes. They were represented with an aspect so ferocious and menacing, says Garcilasso, that the visitors stood looking a long time at these figures, "worthy the admiration of ancient Rome."

Inside, plumes of various colors were fastened to the roof, from which also drooped festoons of pearls. And the walls were decorated with a cornice of shells above life-sized carvings of men and women, the men holding weapons. "As for the statues of women, they held nothing in their hands."

The Spaniards examined with professional curiosity the weapons they saw there. In addition to the axes and hammers and maces — most of which were of stone, but some of which were of copper [4] — pikes were found, decorated with tassels near the blade and at the handle, and shields of bison-hide, which must have been brought from some distance away, and of interwoven canes. They closely observed the arrows, tipped with stag's horn, or with "a flint stone as keen as a dagger." With such weapons they were already well acquainted, and of their

[4] Copper was rare among the Indians. The melting of the metal was not understood, and it was regarded merely as a kind of malleable stone that could be hammered into shape for their hatchets. The people of this territory seem to have been comparatively well supplied with it. Most of the implements of agriculture or war were made of stone or wood, though bone and shell were also used.

effectiveness they were destined to learn still more later. The pearls of Talimeco were left untouched. There were more there than nine hundred men and three hundred horses could have carried away.

In so pleasant a place everybody, except De Soto, says the practical-minded Biedma, the factor or quartermaster of the army, wished to stay and establish a colony. It was well-stocked with food, had excellent water and was near the sea — further away than they imagined, but still near. They could not do better.

And Biedma was right. The whole history of America might well have been completely different if De Soto had established himself in South Carolina. The Spaniards could have entrenched themselves there and in Virginia, and so have prevented the English from driving their wedge between Spain in the South and France in the North. The opportunity was lost, though De Soto must be pardoned for it, just as Biedma cannot be credited with an imagination capable of foreseeing future developments on the continent.

The Governor would not hear of making the suggested settlement there. He had only just begun his conquest. Good as this territory was, there were undoubtedly better ones still to be found. And it still was not the land of gold. "It was his object," grumbles Elvas, "to find another treasure like that of Atabalipa, lord of Peru. He would not be content with good lands or pearls." He further describes his commander as "an inflexible man, and dry of word." De Soto, he fully admitted, always liked to hear what other people had to say about a plan:

"but once he had made up his mind he was not to be moved, and all had to bend to his will."

In this case De Soto had made up his mind. Cutifachiqui was obviously not the place of which Cabeza de Vaca had so mysteriously spoken. He would find that place; and he would not rest until he had found it. There were two arguments with which he met any brought against him — and both were unanswerable. The first was that he had to join hands with Maldonado, according to agreement, on the shore of the gulf. The other was that they could always return to Cutifachiqui in the event of not finding a richer district.

Yet when he gave the order for the army to march it was not in the direction of the gulf but to the north, where he had heard of another great chief. Perhaps this would prove to be the wealthy potentate for whom he was looking. On the 13th of May he set out from Cutifachiqui.

Most ungallantly he obliged the chieftainess to go along with him. He did not have the excuse in this case of actually fearing any treachery. On the contrary he had been treated with unfailing kindness and courtesy. Really the *Cacica* could not have done more for him. But he needed to have carriers, and as portage was work intensely disliked by the natives, his hostess would have to use her authority to secure them, and to keep them after they had been secured.

She was treated with delicacy and consideration — which were no more than her due; but, however much the fact may have disguised by a show of deference, the good woman was held as a hostage. As the Gentleman of Elvas caustically remarks, this was an ill return for a hospitable welcome, and only showed the truth of the adage, "For well-doing, etc."

The army struck a northwesterly course, no doubt along the Indian trail, following the Savannah river; and reached Xuala, near the head of the Broad River in North Carolina in the territory of the Suwali tribe, about the 22d of the month. Despite the forcible detention of the indignant princess, the Indians along the route came to meet them with presents of turkeys and skins, and with friendly protestations. But the country was sparse in cornfields and the horses were growing lean again.

At Xuala a rich and amiable chief — though he occupied a town more like a fortress than any they had encountered, and so could have resisted them — gave the Christians whatever they asked for: carriers, *petacas*,[5] corn and the "little dogs" that did not bark and tasted so good. In that region, according to Ranjel, there were clearer indications of gold than in all the country through which they had come; but even there the Spanish hopes were falsified.

On the 25th of May the army crossed the Blue Ridge mountains, and, descending to a plain the following day, suffered from severe cold, despite the season. It was on this day that they forded the river which they took to be the Mississippi, "by which later they were to depart in the

---

[5] *Petacas*, says Ranjel, were baskets covered with leather and fitted with lids.

brigantines they had made." It was probably either the Chattahoochee or the Coosa.[6]

But before they got so far north the *Cacica* of Cutifachiqui managed to escape.[7] De Soto must have had some compunction about forcing her to accompany him, and on that account allowed her privileges he would hardly have accorded to another. Moreover, she had natural good manners. He could not do otherwise than treat her as a lady. One day "she made an excuse of going into a thicket" with her women attendants, and was never seen by her captors again. Elvas says that she was later heard of as living with an escaped negro slave of Vasconcelos as his wife. A somewhat dismal ending to the romance.

She took with her a *petaca* full of pearls. And these, being unbored and therefore unspoiled by inexpert handling, were the most valuable part of the loot. The lady could have had little use for them, but she probably thought that their loss to the Spaniards, who strangely regarded those beads as something precious, would teach them a little lesson. One likes to think that the search for her was perfunctory.

It was not the first time that De Soto let a captive slip out of his hands, if Garcilasso, who is the sole authority

[6] Elvas says, "We discovered the source of the great river whence we were to take our departure, believed to be the Espíritu Santo." His notion of its course is indicated in the map facing page 268 made by a member of the Expedition.

[7] Ranjel says that she got away at the source of the river they took to be the Mississippi; Elvas says that it was on the journey there. This is more likely; because so far north the chieftainess would have been out of her territory and could hardly have arranged for a band of her own subjects to be at hand to whisk her away.

for the following story, is to be believed. According to his account De Soto got hold of a chief of the name of Capasi as a hostage. The man was so monstrously fat that he could not walk, and had to be carried everywhere in a litter. One day he suggested to the Governor that, if he were allowed to go near a certain stronghold of his men, he would personally order them to submit to the Christians, for without word from his own mouth they would continue to be enemies.

The Governor consented, and the chief went off, under an escort of soldiers. But one night he slipped away. Whereupon the escort, frightened lest their carelessness should be severely punished, concocted a yarn that the obese Capasi had been spirited bodily through the air (that of all mediums of escape for him !) by devils. Hearing which De Soto was very much annoyed. But seeing that the damage was done, and that his own trust-fulness had really caused it, he affected to believe them, and gravely agreed that the heathen necromancers could do very wonderful things indeed.

CHAPTER XIV

DISASTER

ON THE fifth of June the army reached Chiaha at the point where the Little Tennessee and Tennessee rivers meet. A large part of the way from Xuala the road had been more or less mountainous, and the horses were worn and thin. Therefore the Spaniards determined to rest themselves in a land where corn abounded, and where the weather was so pleasant. They received from the friendly chief of the district supplies of lard stored in calabashes.[1] This they discovered was bear fat, and they found it agreeable to the taste. The chief also gave them some beautifully clear oil extracted from walnuts, and — what they had never seen before in Florida — honey in the comb.

For these supplies of food the Spaniards were grateful. Even more they appreciated the good-will of the Indians. It was evident to everyone that if the inhabitants attacked them there they could hardly have hoped to defend themselves with success.

The Indians would probably have not been so amiable had they known what was coming. When De Soto's

---

[1] Another method of storing this fat was in deer-skins. They were taken off whole, and all the orifices stopped up with cement.

men had rested enough and were prepared to resume the march, some of the officers made exorbitant demands upon the savages by whom they had been entertained, and with whom they had disported themselves by fishing and swimming in the river. De Soto asked for carriers for the baggage and — yielding to the advice of his lieutenants — for thirty women as domestic servants. The chief was naturally disturbed by the request, and answered that he would first have to confer with his principal men.

That night the whole population of the village decamped.

De Soto, taking thirty cavaliers and as many infantrymen, immediately went in pursuit of the people. He found them at last huddled upon an island in the middle of the river, where they were safe from the cavalry. A native messenger was sent to explain the situation: that carriers had always been supplied along the route and that they would be well treated. As for the women, De Soto told the chief, after he had been persuaded to cross over to the bank, that he would not ask for any, "seeing how very dear they were to them."

No less than five hundred carriers were supplied, and, as the Spaniards were satisfied as to their good conduct, they did not put them, as was sometimes done, in chains to prevent their escaping.

On the 28th of June, a Monday, the army resumed its march, and came that same day to a swift river which was crossed by a method already found effective. The horses were put in line, with their masters mounted, so as to break the force of the current, while, upon the lower side, the foot-soldiers forded holding on to the animals by their tails, manes, stirrups, breastplates — anything they could reach.

Three days later the advance guard reached a village of the chief of Coste. They immediately incensed the people, who had received them peaceably, by taking some of their corn away without permission. De Soto, who arrived the following day, found it hard to avert serious trouble. But although the warriors were threatening attack, he went into the village accompanied only by a handful of soldiers, all of them unarmed. To the men who had preceded him there he shouted that no weapon was to be drawn. And, further to impress the natives, he loudly berated the Spanish marauders, and hit several of them over the head and shoulders with his cudgel.

This had the desired effect. The chief and his leading men came forward, and the Governor told them, that as he wished to avoid the possibility of further trouble, he would go out into the open country to camp. Unsuspectingly a small body of Indians and their chief followed them; and were clapped into irons as soon as they were well out of the settlement. The conduct of De Soto here was cool and resourceful, but the trick he played upon the chief cannot be admired, even if it was employed out of necessity. Elvas, who criticizes De Soto freely enough at times, said that this strategem was quite contrary to the frank and straight-forward nature of the Governor, who was sincerely grieved that a difficult situation should have called for action of so discreditable a kind.

The chief, after having furnished the necessary guides

and carriers,[2] was released, and the army, continuing upon its way, entered the province of Coça, reaching the village of that name in what is now Talladega County, Alabama, on the 16th of July. They were already late for their meeting with Maldonado.

At Coça the chief came out to receive De Soto at a distance of a couple of bowshots from his collection of huts, borne in a litter, seated on a cushion, and covered with a mantle of marten skins. Upon his head he wore a "diadem of plumes," and he was surrounded by a company of attendants who were playing upon reed flutes and singing — a howling melancholy discord. De Soto, according to his custom, detained him and some of the Indian notables.

This time, however, the capture of the chief, instead of having the effect of making the Indians docile, caused the flight of the entire settlement. As new carriers and guides were urgently needed, bands of horsemen were sent out in every direction to round up the fugitives. Others, in fear of the Spanish anger, returned of their own accord. All were put in chains, and none of them, says Elvas, ever got back to their own country, except some few who were able to file their fetters through at night, or slipped away while on the march.

It was now August; and the delay in joining forces with Maldonado was becoming serious. If they did not hurry, they feared that they might find the ships gone. So on the 20th the army moved again, losing here, as

[2] One would think that with the five hundred carriers supplied a little while before by the chief of Chiaha, the Spaniards ought to have been well supplied. But perhaps this indicates that they had been allowed to return home.

elsewhere, deserters in ones and twos, despite the risk of hanging that these incurred.

Ten days later the army entered Ulibahali, a strongly palisaded village; and though no overt resistance was offered, the General discovered that the Indians were planning to rescue the chief of Coça. He therefore used the utmost caution in taking possession of the place, and obliged his hostage to order the inhabitants to lay down their arms, and to furnish carriers and women as servants. Yet the local Indians could not have been a badly disposed set of people, for several men deserted there. A negro slave belonging to Lobillo is mentioned as one; another was a Levantine named Feyada. The most serious defection was that of a gentleman of Mancano who had long been subject to melancholy and had contracted a habit of walking by himself.[3]

Had these deserters remained with De Soto a little longer, they would have heard, as he did upon reaching the Alabama river, of a negro and of Don Teodoro, members of the Narváez expedition, who had lived for some time among the Indians. The savages confirmed the story they told by displaying a dagger that had belonged to the dead cavalier.

The Spaniards now took their course along the banks of the Alabama, at the rate of five or six leagues a day, and at Tuscaloosa on October 15th met an Indian chief of gigantic size. He and his son, a youth of eighteen, were a foot and a half taller than the tallest of their sub-

---

[3] In 1560 the Friar Anunciación heard that these men, who were then dead, had lived eleven or twelve years among the Indians. They preferred exile among savages to the sufferings of the unending march.

jects, who were themselves all strapping, stalwart men. The only way that Ranjel could describe Tuscaloosa was by saying that he was as tall as "that Tony of the Emperor, our lord's guard."

He received the Master of the Camp, Moscoso, in great state sitting under a large umbrella made of deer-skins quartered red and white so skilfully that it looked from a distance like taffeta. The meeting was in a small way similar to that of De Soto and Atahualpa. The gigantic chief received the envoy with contemptuous gravity, and hardly condescended to look at him.

When De Soto arrived, however, he refused to be embarrassed by Tuscaloosa's display of disdain. Instead he took him by the hand and drew him to his feet; then, sitting beside him on a bench near by, he made him courteous speeches.

All this was lost upon the chief. Even when the Spaniards got up some jousting matches and horse-races for his entertainment, he affected to regard it all with calm indifference. He gave, however, or caused his braves to give, an exhibition of dancing in return. Ranjel says, somewhat quaintly, that it was in the fashion of rustics in Spain; by which he probably means that it had bucolic clumsiness.

When all these amusements were over, the Governor came to the point and asked for carriers. The chief's haughty answer was that he had never been accustomed to serve any man; but rather that it was for all men to serve him. So as Tuscaloosa felt like that about it, De Soto promptly took him into custody.

The chief was incensed. Though a hostage he proved

powerful enough to do considerable — indeed, almost ir-
reparable — harm to the Spaniards. He was by far the
most formidable enemy encountered during the whole of
the expedition.

Secretly he sent out messengers to summon his warriors. But with a show of conciliating his captors, he
furnished them with four hundred porters. Another
hundred and some women servants he promised would
be delivered as soon as they had arrived at Mabilla. It
was to that point that he was luring the invaders, since
it was there that the concentration of his own forces was
to be effected.

Suspecting nothing of this, and still hoping to win
him over by minor courtesies, De Soto gave him a scarlet
cloak and some buskins, and a horse to ride. The only
animal suited to his weight was a heavy-boned pack
horse. Astride this beast, which was held in the greatest
terror by most Indians, Tuscaloosa experienced a fierce
joy. It was to him, says Ranjel humorously, exactly as
though he were mounted upon a lion or tiger. The horse
must have been equally disturbed. The giant's feet almost touched the ground as he sat in the saddle.

On October 12th they set out for Mabilla, near the present city of Mobile, Alabama. The next day at Piache,
where they crossed the river on rafts, the local chief attempted to resist their passage and a Christian was killed.
Another, who had wandered off alone to look for an
escaped slave, failed to return. De Soto therefore threatened Tuscaloosa, saying that should the missing man not
be given back, and those responsible not at once handed
over to punishment, he would take his life in forfeit.

The tall chief's one object was to get the Spaniards into his stronghold. So he concealed his anger at being addressed in such terms, and gave an assurance that the man was quite safe and would be handed over at Mabilla. The simple-minded De Soto believed him.

At nine o'clock in the morning of the 18th, St. Luke's day, the army arrived at Mabilla, a small town, but very strongly stockaded, situated on a plain. De Soto himself rode forward in company with Tuscaloosa and his son, taking as his escort fifteen lancers and thirty foot-soldiers.

As he neared the stockade he was met by a soldier sent out three or four days before, ostensibly as a messenger but really to discover the temper of the Indians. This man warned De Soto to proceed cautiously. Hostile preparations were being made. Weapons had been brought in. There seemed to be a concentration of warriors from the country round about. The stockade had just been strengthened. De Soto could see for himself that such huts as were outside the fortifications had been demolished, so as to leave a clear field, and to give the Spaniards no cover did they try to storm the place.

Nevertheless, a chief came out to greet them with songs and flute-playing and a present of three cloaks of marten skins. But Moscoso's eyes could not be diverted from the ominous signs of warlike readiness, and he begged his commander not to enter the town. It would be the height of imprudence. He pointed out that there were only two narrow entrances through the stockade, and that the place was a trap.

De Soto, rash as usual, answered lightly that he was tired of camping in the open, and that he meant to go

HAVANA BEING BOMBARDED BY THE FRENCH
[From De Bry]

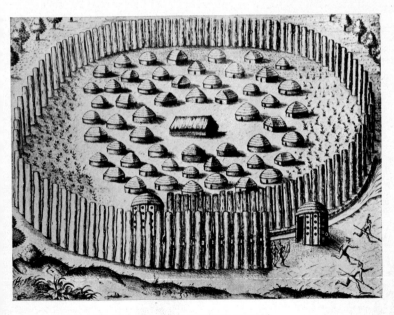

AN APPALACHIAN FORT
[From De Bry]

where he could sleep once more with a roof over his head. He came near to sleeping under a still more substantial shelter.

Further to show his disdain of danger, or as an act of conciliation, he left most of the members of the advance guard outside, and entered Mabilla accompanied only by seven or eight men, a couple of priests, and a few officers, among whom were Moscoso, Espíndola, and Gallegos. He took also a cook and some Christian Indian women to prepare a meal to which it was his intention to invite the chiefs. With the soldiers left outside were the four hundred porters, all of whom were in chains. The main body of the army was out of sight, but not far away.

No sooner had De Soto entered, than the two entrances through the stockades had bands of Indians posted by them to prevent any egress. He did not notice the fact, and he could not know that about three thousand warriors were concealed in the town. The belligerent disposition of the settlement was masked by an exhibition of dancing on the part of fifteen Indian women, which was cleverly designed to distract the attention of the Spaniards from what they were not supposed to see.

What very soon became noticeable, however, was the changed demeanor of Tuscaloosa. He resumed his original arrogance and demanded his immediate release. When De Soto told him that this could not be granted until he had completed the promised tally of porters and servants, he jumped to his feet, very angry. In that case, he said, he would have to consult with the other chiefs.

The Governor tried to placate the furious warrior with

soft words, but he was in no mood to listen. "With great contempt and haughtiness," he shook De Soto off and withdrew to the council house near at hand.

They waited for him a long time and as he showed no intention of coming out, first Juan Ortiz and then Espíndola, the captain of the guard, were sent to summon him. This officer found on reaching the entrance that the large cabin was full of excited Indians, all armed with bows and arrows, and he did not dare to enter. He beckoned to Tuscaloosa to go with him, and received a bellow of refusal. If the Governor wanted to go in peace he had better do so at once — that was the final warning.

As he went back to De Soto he noticed that other cabins were crowded with concealed braves, and, as the Alachua Indians built their huts with an open loft at one end, they had excellent posts for their bowmen. The situation was alarming, and growing worse every minute. He advised De Soto to retire while he had the chance.

But retreat was not in De Soto's nature. To go out — if they could get out without a scuffle — would be regarded as a sign of weakness. If only he could see Tuscaloosa again for a moment.

He called to a chief who was on his way to the council, and attempted blandishments. The man replied loftily that he would not listen to him, and strode off towards the cabin. Gallegos was insistent, and tried to detain him, holding on to his marten-skin cloak. The chief slipped it over his head and went on his way, leaving the cloak in the hand of the Spanish officer.

Gallegos, very annoyed at this, ran after the chief, sword in hand. As the man still refused to stop he slashed at him, lopping off an arm.

The blood of Gallegos was now up. He darted into the cabin where Tuscaloosa had gone and attempted to drag him out. There was at once an uproar. Moscoso dashed forward to help his foolhardy friend, but seeing how hopeless the odds were against that crowded roomful of picked warriors, he backed to the door shouting, "Baltasar, come out, or I shall have to leave you. I can't wait any longer."

The concealed Indians, hearing the noise, swarmed out. De Soto and all his men were in full flight, making for one of the exits from the town, all of them hard beset. The Governor fell, or was knocked down three times by clubs, and was saved only by the devotion of his men, five of whom were killed. The survivors, fighting desperately, managed to cut their way out, and were reinforced by De Solís and Roderigo Ranjel, the governor's secretary.[4] Before the charge of these two mounted men the Indians drew back a little, giving those on foot time to get away. Ranjel tells us that he had no less than twenty arrows sticking in his quilted doublet; but he and De Solís had saved the life of their General. Baltasar de Gallegos and Moscoso succeeded in escaping through the other gate in the stockade.

The horses left inside were promptly killed; and the carriers who, in the confusion, had been left unguarded, were drawn into the enclosure, where their manacles were struck off, and bows and arrows put into their

---

[4] Who does not minimize his prowess.

hands. They climbed up to the top of the palisade and tauntingly held up some of the articles of the baggage. Included in these were all the spare arms.

Meanwhile the two priests — one of them a friar, probably the same person as the Juan de Gallegos mentioned by one of the chroniclers as afterwards hanging on the outskirts of the battle, and a brother of Captain Gallegos — barricaded themselves in a hut, along with the cook and the women servants. The cook's was the only sword among the three, so he stationed himself on one side of the door, leaving the two priests to guard the other with clubs. This they did so doughtily that the Indians, unable to force an entrance, had begun to take off the roof to get at them, when, with the arrival of the main body of the Spanish force, their attention was called elsewhere. This allowed the trapped Christians to escape to their comrades.

De Soto, upon getting out of the stockade, rallied the men who had escaped and those who had been waiting for him outside. But with so few he could not expect to hold his ground. They were too near the battlements of the enemy, and presented an easy mark to the arrows raining down upon them. He therefore withdrew to the plain in as good order as possible, with the Indians coming on as near as they dared.

Seeing this, the cavaliers who had been covering the retreat pretended flight in order to lure their attackers into the open field. Then, suddenly wheeling their horses round, they charged the savages. One officer let his impetuosity carry him too far. This was Carlos Enríquez, who was married to De Soto's niece. He ventured right up to the stockade, where his horse received an arrow in the breast. Don Carlos leaned forward to draw it out, and at that moment was shot through the neck, "at which, seeking confession, he fell dead." But his feinting movement had at least served the purpose of teaching the savages not to venture again beyond their protecting palisades.

With the arrival of reinforcements, De Soto arranged his men in four divisions of foot, that completely encircled Mabilla, with the cavalry posted at various points behind to cut off any Indians who tried to escape, and to act as supports wherever they were needed. They then settled down systematically to carry the invested town.

Axes were plied against the logs of the stockade, and torches put to them, while the Indians shot their arrows down upon their asasilants. Several times the Spaniards pressed through the gaps that they had made, only to be beaten out by the raging valor of the defenders, or by a change in the wind blowing the smoke in their faces. Again and again the Spaniards banged themselves against the stockade and swung their axes, their physical exertion, like their courage, raised to the highest pitch. Sweat flowed almost as freely as blood, for the excessive labor was performed round a circle of flame. When after several hours of this exhausting fighting they withdrew in order to drink at a pond near by, they could taste the gore with which it was tinged.

It was impossible for the Indians, however numerous and brave, to keep De Soto and his men out forever. Late in the afternoon they succeeded in getting far enough inside to apply their torches to the huts of wood and straw. These flared up at once, driving those who had been shooting from the lofts into the streets. Women and boys of four [5] fought in their frenzy beside the desperate warriors of the tribe, or hanged themselves, or leaped into the blazing huts rather than be taken.

The flames did their work quickly. In less than an hour the whole village was a level mass of smouldering timber. A few minutes later the decisive moment had come. The Indians showed no signs of yielding, and were still firing with deadly effect. So the cavalry was brought up, and after the men at arms had hacked their way through for the last time, the lancers charged. From end to end of the enclosure they went, over and across and back again. And still the bowmen kept on shooting from the height of the stockade, until the halberdiers pierced them. The force of the arrows may be gauged from the fact that Nuño Tobar had his ashen lance pierced as clean as though by an auger without being split, in such a way that the arrow made a cross with it. De Soto himself was hit in the buttock, but having no time to pull out the shaft, continued to ride standing in his stirrups.

It was soon over, lance and sabre and fire all uniting in destruction. Not one Indian escaped. Just before darkness fell, the last three defenders came out with the women who had danced for De Soto that morning. They crossed their wrists, to show that they were ready for the manacles, and made signs that the soldiers should

---

[5] Incredible as this may seem, we are assured that Indian children of a much younger age were carefully trained in ferocity, and were equipped with bows and arrows at which they shot at beetles if no better game was available.

advance to take them prisoners. As some halberdiers went forward to do so, the three warriors jumped on one side and began shooting again. After two of these had been chased and killed, the sole remaining Indian ran back, clambered upon the stockade, whipped the cord from his bow, tied it round his neck, and, leaping forward, hanged himself.

More than twenty of the Spaniards were slain,[6] including Carlos Enríquez and another of the Governor's relatives, Francisco de Soto, his nephew. One hundred and forty-eight men were wounded by Indian arrows, receiving among them a total of six hundred and eighty-eight wounds. Ranjel, who gives these figures, adds that the total loss to the army since its landing in Florida was one hundred and two men. As he was secretary to the Governor, his may be taken as the official list of casualties. But Biedma and Elvas, with their rougher computations, say much the same thing.

Two thousand dead Indians were found in the town, including the tall son of Tuscaloosa, who was run through with a lance.[7] Hundreds of dead and dying were lying outside — those who had succeeded in crawling to the bushes. The victory of the Spaniards was complete. So also was their ruin.

[6] Eighteen, says Elvas; twenty-two, says Ranjel; more than twenty, says Biedma; eighty-two, says Garcilasso.

[7] Two thousand five hundred, says Elvas; three thousand, says Ranjel. But Fiske shrewdly comments that upon the basis of comparative losses between white men and Indians, these figures may safely have a nought taken off. Garcilasso puts the number of Indians slain at ten thousand.

CHAPTER XV

DESPERATION

THE SPANIARDS dressed their wounds that night with the fat of the Indian slain. They were reduced to such ointment because their medical stores had been lost in the fire. Though it was St. Luke's day, the "beloved physician" did not do much to help them. In the absence of bandages, or even spare shirts, they had to strip the dead or make lint from their own clothing.

Not only their medicines, but the whole of their baggage was destroyed, clothing and bedding and tents, so that many a man there had nothing except the clothes in which he stood, now mostly in shreds, and the weapons in his hands. They were as bare as Arabs.

The most disastrous loss was that of the pearls that De Soto had brought from the burial houses of Cutifachiqui. He had intended sending them back to Havana after he had effected a juncture with Maldonado, who was bringing up the ships. They were to be exhibited there and in Spain as a proof of the wealth of Florida. Now they were gone, and with them his credit in the eyes of the world. Bitter at heart, the conqueror contemplated his ruined hopes.

The ironic gall of it all was that the Spaniards had

[214]

themselves started the fires which had eaten everything that they possessed. It had been the only means of victory. But how barren was their valor ! In destroying their enemies they had destroyed themselves.

To the soldiers the loss was serious enough; to their General it was crushing, devastating, final. Some time or other they would buy new shirts. But where could De Soto buy what he had lost ? It was in his power, he reminded himself, to march back and ransack the "mosque" of Talimeco. But he was too ashamed to appear before the princess — especially after the way he had treated her — with this rabble of scarecrows. No, some other means must be found. If only he could locate the land of gold. Oh, it was not that he was a needy adventurer seeking a fortune. He could return to Spain and live a life of opulent ease — the life that had so irked him. But gold would be the measure of success. The conquest of a rich province would cover him with the glory for which he hungered.

His men hobbled about the camp in rags, bowed down and numb to the soul with depression. He went among them now and then trying to cheer them, as was his duty. The poor devils needed him. He was their father, and he pitied them. But he, who needed pity a thousand time more, where was he to find it ? With Isabella ? Her great heart would understand. But he felt that he could never look her in the face again until he had retrieved this disaster. Until the fabulous wealth of Florida had been finally won by his sword.

Gloomily he brooded in his hut, seeing nothing but darkness ahead. When his servants brought him in his food, a mess of sparse pounded corn, he ate listlessly, and pushed the plate away with a sudden spasm of rage. At night he tossed upon the bare ground sleepless, swearing. Then, starting up in a febrile fit of energy, he would go the rounds of the camp to see that the sentries were at their posts. As he stepped over sleeping soldiers, huddled with their feet towards the warmth of the fires, he envied them. As he looked upwards he saw skies bright with stars and empty of all hope. Oh, if he could reach up to those bright points, and have his hands crowded with diamonds !

Muffled in his tattered cloak he stood one night in the shadows and overheard a group talking. Their words were all about ships — Maldonado was coming with the ships; then they would go home. It was useless for them to stay any longer. There was no gold to find. The General was crazed. No one would wish to serve under a better officer, true! but he would go on until they all had starved to death in this wilderness. It was strange that they had not heard of Maldonado and the ships. They could not be very far away.

The listening De Soto felt his heart grow suddenly cold. Then as suddenly it hardened. They should never go home while he was alive. Not until he had found gold.

The next day an Indian came in with news. He told it to Ortiz, who went in great excitement to the General. De Soto heard it with darkening brow, and then snapped at Ortiz, "Does any one else know of this ?"

"No one, my lord."

"Then I command you never to say a word of it to

anyone. Do you understand ? Those are my orders, and they are not to be ignored." The Indian was brought in, and De Soto slowly drew his finger across his throat. "Tell him," he said to Ortiz, "what will happen to him if his tongue wags. The dogs."

The wretch went out trembling. There was little danger from that source. Nobody could understand him except Ortiz, who was safe.

The course of extreme desperation upon which De Soto was now resolved, was one that condemned his army to three years of terrible privation and hopeless wandering, and himself to an unconsoled death. He did not know that; but had he known it, his will would have been unmoved. He developed a fortitude that became appalling, bleak, inhuman.

It is possible to observe in him a great change after the disastrous victory of Mabilla. The old boyish gaiety disappeared, or was seen only in flashes. He was moody, at times almost morose, and grew more and more taciturn. Despair settled upon him, and he was able to sustain himself only by his sterile courage. For moments he would have glimpses of the Conqueror's Star. God would surely work a miracle for them. But no miracle ever came. And the star became hidden behind sullen clouds of lead.

Yet he went on, determined never to give up the quest to which he had dedicated himself. The order to march was given on November 14th, but it was not towards Pensacola Bay, where Maldonado was waiting with the ships, but in the opposite direction, due north.

It is a signal instance of De Soto's power over his men

that the order was obeyed. They and all their officers expected to get in touch with Maldonado. And now their commander without explanation threw all their plans and hopes to the winds and told them to plunge again, without baggage and with their clothes in fantastic rags, into the wilderness. Yet they did it.

It is clear from the chroniclers' accounts that the army had heard a rumor of the three ships being near at hand. News has a way of spreading like wildfire among Indians. And they talked among themselves, pointing towards the coast. Though the soldiers could not understand what was said, they understood at least the gesticulations they saw. To obey their commander's orders meant cutting themselves off from all aid from Cuba, and from all expectation of returning to Spain. They never could forget what had happened to Narváez and his men. Yet they bowed to De Soto's inexorable will, and followed him north. It would be hard to match such devotion. It is impossible to match De Soto's capacity for command.

They had only a few carriers left. But there was not much need for any now. A dozen baskets or so of corn; a little fish from the river. There was no bedding, and no clothing. They had made themselves — taking a hint from the moss aprons of the Indian women of the peninsula — garments of grass and wild ivy. The case of Don Antonio Osorio, who was a brother of the Marquis of Astorga, was typical. This gallant gentleman, who had an income in Spain of two thousand ducats a year, wore, without complaint, as his only covering, an

Indian blanket, torn at the sides where his flesh showed through the rents. Bare-footed and bare-headed, carrying his heavy shield upon his back, he rode through severe frosts and cold. In this, says Ranjel truly, he showed his illustrious lineage.

Even the spiritual comfort of the Mass was now lacking. The chalices and the wine had been destroyed in the fire, and also the whole supply of altar-breads. It might have been possible to have found a few grapes growing wild, and to have crushed out the juice. But the priests agreed that the coarse corn-bread could not be consecrated. Yet every Sunday and Holy Day they did the best they could in the circumstances, erecting a rude altar at which a friar, wearing buckskins roughly shaped like vestments, said the Confiteor, the Kyrie, the Collect, and read the Epistle and Gospel of the day with the Creed; but stopped short at the Canon. It was the *Missa seca,* such as priests in prison for the Faith have often said. Afterwards the celebrant, or one of the other priests, would explain the Gospel, and follow it with a brief exhortation. "Thus," says Garcilasso, "our men consoled themselves a little for not being able to adore Jesus Christ under the sacramental elements of bread and wine."

The advance of the army was in cold weather, colder than that of Burgos, so the chroniclers tell us; and hostile Indians, though they did not venture upon pitched battle, annoyed them by skirmishing. But at Chicaça, reached after a five days' march through a desert, they found food, shelter from the snow, and the dubious friendship of the local chief. From him they obtained what they sorely needed in their nakedness, a supply of blankets and furs. In his village they decided to winter.

The Indians of Chicaça [1] took a great fancy to the Spanish pork, which was being kept for an emergency, and every night would creep in to the pigsties, a crossbowshot away from the camp, to steal what they could. Three of these thieves at last were captured, whereupon De Soto had two of them shot, and the third sent back to the chief with his hands cut off as a warning. The *Cacique* pretended to approve the punishment. He soon had an opportunity for getting even.

Four Spaniards, two of them the Governor's personal attendants, wandered out one day on horseback and stole some clothing. Even before the Indians could lodge a complaint against them, De Soto heard the men boasting of their exploit and laughing about it. He at once had them arrested, and ordered the two leaders of the gang to be beheaded. Loot might be taken when it was necessary for the support of the army; but he always refused to countenance private marauding.

The officers united with the priests in begging for mercy for the condemned men. They had intended no more than a prank. But De Soto, inflexible in his justice, would not yield.

The sentence would have been carried out except for an amiable trick played by Ortiz, the interpreter, who was put up to it by Gallegos. Shortly before the culprits were about to be led out to execution, some Indians ar-

---

[1] Chicaça of course is the same word as Chickasaw. The settlement is placed by Lowery in the present state of Mississippi, near the headwaters of the Yazoo and Mobile rivers. Lewis places it a mile northwest of Redland, Miss.

rived from the chief to demand redress. Ortiz, seeing his chance, twisted their impassioned complaint into a plea for clemency. The chief, so he made them say, was not in the least offended; on the contrary he would take it as a favor if the Governor would let the men go. To the Indians he said that the Governor had already sentenced the thieves, and was about to inflict upon them such condign punishment as should be an example to the rest of the army. The emissaries therefore returned perfectly satisfied; and the Spanish soldiers were overjoyed at seeing their comrades escape De Soto's wrath.

As soon as March came the Governor thought it time to continue his journey in search of that rich kingdom in which no one who had travelled through that desolate country for so many hundreds of miles could any longer believe. But if he was now without a definite aim, he was by no means lacking in energy. Out of the black brooding that possessed his soul came, instead of the nerveless despondency which would have fallen upon nearly all other men in such a situation, a bitter resolution. He possibly already felt death coming; but he would die as he had lived, going forward.

According to his custom he asked the chief of Chicaça for two hundred bearers for his newly collected stores — meagre enough — of blankets, furs, and corn. And the chief, not unnaturally, was dismayed by the demand. But, having thought the matter over, and having seen the determination of the Governor, he considered it wise to agree to furnish what was needed. He said he would give it the following day, which was March 4th.

De Soto, who had now learned from experience, felt

that trouble was brewing. Upon his return from his interview with the chief, he said, so that all could hear, "To-night is an Indian night. I shall sleep armed and with my horse saddled. All of you must do the same."

But the Master of the Camp, the easy-going Luis de Moscoso, though strictly enjoined to take extra precautions that night, which was to be their last in Chicaça, ignored the instructions, or carried them out very imperfectly.[2] The diary of Ranjel does, it is true, say that the Governor himself went to bed undressed and that his horse, like all the others in the camp, was unsaddled. But this would seem to be an interpolation on the part of Oviedo. For on the very next page of his account Ranjel tells us (and in this he is supported by Elvas and Garcilasso) that in the disaster which came upon them, De Soto and a soldier named Tapia out of the whole army were the only men ready instantly to repel the attack. Grace King says of the Governor, "There was one very notable and memorable circumstance always related of him; that in assaults, surprises, and engagements with the enemy by day, he was always the first or second, and never the third, to get into the fight with his arms; and by night, he was never the second, but always the first, so that it seemed to the men that he first armed himself and then ordered the alarm to be sounded."

The attack was made at four in the morning. Two of the three horsemen appointed to watch were "of low degree, the least value of any in the camp." Obviously Moscoso was seriously negligent in putting them on duty. The third was a nephew of the Governor. He had been

[2] For this his position was given to Baltasar de Gallegos.

thought a brave man until then, but showed himself, in that sad emergency, a coward, like the other sentinels.

Just before dawn over three hundred Indians, coming in groups of twos and fours, crept into the camps, eluding the sentries. Each man carried with him a little clay pot containing fire — charcoal smouldering, and, in those vessels, invisible. Each also bore, it is said, three ropes — one for a horse, one for a pig, and one for a Christian.

They were well inside the camp before being discovered, and then the sentinels, seeing their numbers, fled in panic, leaving the Indians free to set the place on fire undisturbed.

The Spaniards awoke to find flames everywhere. Horses were plunging and neighing with terror in their stalls, and, flying sparks having set the sties ablaze, shrill squeals came from the pigs as they were burned alive. Blinded by the smoke, unable to find their arms or to saddle their steeds, the soldiers stumbled out going in all directions, bewildered in their consternation.

The rout might have been complete except for Nuño Tobar, who on this, as on other occasions, showed how excellent a soldier he was. He rounded up the fugitives shouting, "Where are you running ? Do you think that the walls of Córdoba or Seville are here to shelter you ?"

De Soto at the first alarm had mounted, and followed by Tapia, charged the Indians. The savages, had they displayed a little more courage, could easily have exterminated the Christians; but instead of rushing upon the Spaniards they waited for them in the open space outside the burning camp. There was no time for the Governor to attempt to restore order — nor was such a thing possible at that appalling moment. The confusion was so great that the Indians themselves failed to perceive how complete it was. They heard in the darkness such horses as had been able to get loose galloping madly about, and took them to be cavaliers charging. They thought that De Soto and Tapia were only the two foremost of the horsemen, and did not stand to await the onset.

Shouting "Santiago! Santiago!" the General ran through with his lance the first Indian he encountered — the only Indian killed in the affray — and thrust with such furious force that the saddle-girths of his high Moorish saddle, which had loosened during the night, slipped; and he fell to the ground. Had not those Indians shown themselves to be such abject cravens they could have made an end of him and of all their enemies that night.

Eleven Spaniards were burned to death in their huts; another died three days later. Two others for a long time afterwards had to be carried in their pallets on poles upon the shoulders of the porters. One woman — the only Spanish woman who was with the army — Francesca Hinestrosa, also perished. She had left the shelter in which she was lodged with her husband, and then, remembering her pearls, went back to get them. But the flames reached the door before she could get out again, and no one could push through to her. She was with child.

Fifty-seven horses were lost and three hundred pigs. Only such as were young and small enough to squeeze through the wattles of their stye were saved. But of these there were luckily about a hundred.

It was a disaster worse even than that of Mabilla, for now most of the lances were burnt, and "if, by good luck, anyone had been able to save a garment up to that time, it was there destroyed."

The army lay for the rest of the night and the early morning naked in front of the fires made by the soldiers, each man turning first one freezing side and then the other to the blaze in a vain effort to keep warm. Yet miserable as their plight was, they realized that it might have been worse. "God, who chastiseth His own as He pleaseth, and in the greatest wants and perils hath them in His hand, shut the eyes of the Indians, so that they could not discern what they had done." They certainly had the unconquerable *Conquistadores* at their mercy that night, but failed to follow up their advantage.

This was true not only of that night but of the next. The Christians hourly expected to be attacked and knew that, were they attacked, they would be overpowered. The Indians, too, must have had the opportunity of observing their plight. Yet such was the prestige of Spanish prowess that the savages did not dare to strike, even when their enemies were helpless.

It is impossible not to feel the utmost admiration for the determined courage of the Christian army. An equal amount of admiration must be given to the Christians' resource. Juan Vega, one of the soldiers, hit upon the expedient of making mats of dried grass; and since the Indians had abandoned their own huts, those shelters and the mats saved the Spaniards of perishing from the cold.

Arms also and saddles had to be refashioned. At once a forge was set up with bellows made from bear-skins and with musket barrels for nozzles. So they retempered their swords and lance-heads and shaped new shafts from ash trees providentially growing there. Within a week everything reparable had been repaired. When the Indians returned in force on March 15th, at last having mustered enough courage to complete their work, they found the army carefully watching, having been instructed by harsh experience, and equipped with new weapons. This time great valor was displayed, and no one failed to do his duty. As Ranjel grimly remarks, "Unfortunate was he who on that occasion did not well defend his life and prove to the enemy the quality and arms of the Christians."

Upon resuming their march, on April 26, 1541, the Spaniards soon encountered at Alimanu [3] Indians of a very different stamp from those of Chicaça. These, without having any stores or women to defend, put up a stockaded fort right in the road the Spaniards were taking, and challenged them, merely, as it afterwards turned out, for the purpose of measuring savage against Christian manhood. Elvas describes them: "Many were armed, walking upon it, with their bodies, legs, and arms painted and ochred, red, black, white, yellow, and vermilion in stripes, so that they appeared to have on stockings and doublet. Some wore feathers, and others

[3] Supposed to be upon the Tallahatchie River, near New Albany, Miss. See Hodges and Lewis, *Spanish Explorers*, p. 200.

horns on the head, the face blackened, and the eyes encircled with vermilion, to heighten their fierce aspect."

The stockade was stormed, but at a loss De Soto could ill afford, seven or eight of his men being killed and twenty-five being wounded. Only one Indian was killed, the rest escaping across the stream. "Everyone," says Elvas, "thought the governor committed a great fault in not sending to examine the state of the ground on the opposite shore, and discover the crossing-place before making the attack." The criticism is just.

Starting again on the last day in April they marched for nine days through a deserted country. The way was rough, mountains alternating with swamps, until they reached the village of Quizquiz. De Soto must have smiled at the name. It was the same as that borne by the last of the recalcitrant chiefs in Peru, whom he had defeated. Perhaps it would prove to be of good augury now.

They arrived upon the settlement so suddenly as to take its inhabitants quite unprepared, the men being away working in the cornfields. Three hundred women captured were restored when their husbands came home. The Governor thought it prudent at that time to risk no battle with the natives, his men being weary, and weak from lack of food, and their horses lean.

It was here that De Soto learned that he was near the Espíritu Santo river, which we know to-day as the Mississippi. It meant that he was coming to that part of the country most familiar to Cabeza de Vaca. And that meant gold.

CHAPTER XVI

THE FATHER OF WATERS

THE NEXT day, upon which De Soto was hoping to see the chief, a large company of Indians came, fully armed and in war-paint, with the purpose of attacking the Christians. But when they saw that the Governor had drawn up his army in line of battle, they remained a cross-bowshot away for half an hour, discussing the situation. They did not like the look of the men in iron and on horseback.

Then six chiefs came forward saying that they only wished to find out who this strange breed of men were, for they had a tradition from their ancestors that they were to be subdued by a white race. This may have been nothing but an attempt to veil their craft by flamboyant flattery. If they really had such a tradition it offered another curious parallel with Peru.

The Governor, suspecting that they would attack if he gave them the chance, felt it necessary to act with caution. The chief, whom he had particularly wished to meet, had not come to see him; nor did he send any message. The Spaniards saw as they moved forward that this land was thickly settled: therefore, capable of making formidable resistance unless good feeling could be

[228]

established. De Soto wished above everything else to
avoid fight. He had had quite enough of it. The Indians were redoubtable warriors, and always inflicted
severe losses upon them. Already more than a third of
his men had been killed, and a few had deserted. Every
casualty now was serious. For while they had so far always defended themselves with success — in the sense of
beating off their assailants — the time would inevitably
come, if conflict continued, when the army would be so
depleted as to be an easy prey for the first hostile tribe
encountered. He wished to make friends with the Indians. As it seemed difficult to do that, he advanced
slowly, by short stages, turning a little to the north to
avoid the natives, and to find a good approach to the
Great River. They reached it on May 21st, a Saturday.

There has been a good deal of discussion as to the exact
spot at which De Soto looked first with astonished eyes
upon that volume of water. It has been often maintained — so often that it has come to be generally accepted — that the place was the Fourth Chickasaw Bluff,
at the present city of Memphis. But this has been questioned. Indeed a somewhat acrimonious controversy
has raged between those who wish to retain the honor for
Tennessee and those who claim it for the State of
Mississippi. Without going into the matter here, in
what would be tedious detail, it must be said that those
who locate the discovery at a more southern spot seem
to have distinctly the best of the argument.[1]

[1] See for a full discussion of the subject *A Symposium on the Place of the
Discovery of the Mississippi River by Hernando de Soto,* edited by Dr. Dunbar
Rowland. He and Professor T. H. Lewis are vehement for the claims of
Tunica County, but Dr. Rowland's concluding word is, "If it is not certain

DE SOTO AND THE CONQUISTADORES

What is infinitely more important than establishing —
if it can be established — the exact location of the discovery is a vivid realization of the valor and hardihood
of the pioneers who had persisted in advancing through
the wilderness, in the face of furious opposition, and
after having endured, within four months, the successive
disasters of Mabilla and Chicaça. To the loyalty, fortitude and courage of the Spanish army admiration is due;
but there are no words adequate to express what should
be said of its commander, the brain, the heart, and the
unfaltering will of the expedition.

In the halls of the Capitol there hangs a famous paint-
ing, familiar to all visitors to Washington, and often
reproduced for the benefit of American school-children.
It will be seen from what has been recorded in these
pages that it is grossly unhistorical. And by putting De
Soto and his men back into the finery with which they
landed in Florida, a great injustice has been done them.
Sentimentalism has once again killed romance.

---

that De Soto first saw the Father of Waters in the vicinity of Commerce, it is
quite certain that he did not discover it at the Fourth Chickasaw Bluff."
Delisle's beautiful map, the most detailed and accurate work of the early
cartographers, as far as De Soto's expedition is concerned, gives a still lower
mark at Willow Point. D'Anville and others indicate "Point d'Osiers" as
half-way between the St. Francis and White rivers. Ellicott's *Journal* places
it a little above the mouth of the White and below that of the Arkansas. The
map used in the 1851 edition of Theodore Irving's *Conquest of Florida* indicates a point between Norfolk and Commerce. My own inclination is to
locate the place of discovery near the mouth of the St. Francis River. In cor-
respondence with me Dr. Rowland urges that this would have to be ruled
out for topographical reasons. This I concede if what is meant is the *present*
mouth of the St. Francis. But the Mississippi and its confluents are restless
in their beds, and in the course of four hundred years the St. Francis probably has wandered far astray. I hold this opinion lightly, however,
knowing as I do that it is practically impossible to reach certainty on the
subject.

The weather was indeed brilliant,[2] but the Spanish Army presented a most bedraggled appearance. Their armor, rusty and dinted though it was, remained for the most part intact. But the gaily-sashed doublets of taffeta had long ago yielded to shreds of Indian fibre-blankets or the skins of wild animals, bald with wear. Many had not even so much as this, but wore habiliments somewhat similar to those assumed by Adam and Eve after the Fall, cloaks and aprons of pampas grass, Spanish moss, or ivy. Few of them had any horses; those that still remained were scrawny, poorly shod, and distempered. The bloodhounds and the Irish greyhounds, savage from scarcity of food, were held in leashes baying hoarsely. The pigs, like the other animals and their masters, were thin; and they were young, for only the smallest porkers had been able to squeeze through the interstices of their sties in the last fire. These rooted where they could, or greedily snatched at offal. The white habits of the Dominicans and the black cassocks of the priests were lost or torn to tatters. They were as wild and matted of hair and beard as the others, bare-legged, wearing buckskin drawers and, as the only sign of their holy office, the rude skin vestments painted with a cross in which they said their "Dry Mass." These they were perforce often obliged to use as their daily garments. Even to the Indians of the river the Spaniards must have seemed like savages.

These were the men who had discovered the Missis-

---

[2] Lowery in his *Spanish Settlements in the United States* (Vol. I, pp. 238, 239) makes a curious slip in an otherwise excellent book. He speaks of "those bleak March days," whereas it was late May when the Spaniards reached the Mississippi.

sippi. Through the humid air they looked at the enormous mass of water, turbid, tawny, warm. It was a dirty
giant, sprawling out here into bayou and morass, reveal-
ing there little level islands of mud, choked elsewhere
with cane-brakes. The swiftness of its current was shown
by the uprooted trees carried along like broken twigs.
Over its surface and from the swampy banks rose a thin
white mist.

People who speak of De Soto to-day immediately, and
rightly, at once connect his name with the finding of the
Great River. To him it was a stupendous sight, which
might be worth gazing at for ten minutes, but which
was after all primarily only an obstacle to be crossed.
The chroniclers all dismiss it in a line or two. Ranjel
and Elvas both refer to it casually as being about a
league away from a village in which they found some
corn. They did not appreciate their own achievement.

De Soto was now confronted with the task of building
boats. Had the Indians been friendly, the army could
have crossed in canoes; but it was evidently difficult to
conciliate these savages. The Spaniards therefore picked
out a spot suitable for their purpose. It was a low-lying
patch of land by the side of the water, under a bluff upon
which cross-bowmen could be posted to protect the carpenters while they were at work. The locality was well
wooded, and timber was cut for the construction of the
barges and to make houses for the men.

The local chief, a very exalted personage long awaited
by the Governor, at last arrived. He came with about
two hundred large war canoes, that held in all about

seven thousand men. The canoes were made from trees and hollowed out with fire, in much the same way as those already seen at Cutifachiqui.

The Indians were all observed to be tall, well-built warriors, painted with ochre, and with their heads adorned with colored plumes. In their hands they bore shields made of interwoven canes and decorated with feathers. These were so tough that a cross-bow quarrel could hardly pierce them. At the stern of the largest of the canoes, in which the high chief sat, was an awning. This brilliant flotilla, "like a famous armada of galleys," was in strong contrast to the wasted and miserable appearance of the Christians.

But though the chief indulged in the customary Indian eloquence, protesting that it was his intention to serve the Governor, who he had heard was one of the most powerful men upon earth, he declined to land — very possibly because he had heard other things about him. He sent, however, three canoes to the shore full of presents of fish and loaves made of pressed prunes.

Some gesture was made, unfortunately, that revealed, or that seemed to reveal, to the Spaniards, that all this was by way of a ruse. For the cross-bowmen, who had been posted in readiness, and were watching every movement of the savages, began to fire. Elvas records the perfect discipline with which the Indians retired, not a man leaving the paddle, though the one next to him was struck down by one of the Spanish bolts. Every day afterwards, promptly at the same hour, three o'clock in the afternoon, they would come up in their "famous armada of galleys," and pay their respects to the Christians by shooting at them from long range. But they never dared to come close enough to do much damage.

After a month of laborious and harassed work, under blazing skies and enervating humidity, four large barges were completed; and on Tuesday, June 18th [3] the crossing of the Mississippi was effected. Three hours before daybreak — the hour was chosen in order to get the operation finished before the Indians came to contest the passage — they tied the barges one behind the other, putting four picked cavaliers and some cross-bowmen in the hinder three, and the rowers all in the leading vessel of the train.

The strong currents of the river made it impossible for them to cross directly over to the opposite shore; and they landed so far down that the Spaniards standing on the bluff could hardly make out at that distance whether they were human beings or not. In this way all the men were carried over, and everything had been accomplished by noon. Having landed without mishap on firm ground they "gave thanks to God that nothing more difficult could confront them."

They were vastly mistaken. It was well for them that De Soto had the foresight to have the barges knocked to pieces on the western shore in order to keep the nails and the bolts for another emergency. They were needed.

Two weeks later, after having passed through the

---

[3] Ranjel, who gives the date, says the 8th, but from another date given by him we can see that he made a slip of the pen. Or Oviedo did in copying his diary.

DE SOTO AT THE MISSISSIPPI

[From *Voyagie van Don Ferdinand de Soto na Florida*, Leyden 1706]

abandoned villages of the Aquixo territory, and crossing again swamps that reminded them of Florida — for all that day they had to wade waist-deep in water — they reached land, high, dry, and level. It was near the St. Francis river. Walnut and mulberry trees abounded there, and the fields were well cultivated. The villages were so thickly set that from a slight eminence a man might see two or three of them at once.

After a two days' march through this country De Soto reached the settlement that was the headquarters of Casqui, the chief of the district. He received the Governor well and made him a fine — though somewhat quaint — speech. "Very high, powerful, and renowned Master, I greet your coming. As soon as I had notice of you, your power and perfections, although you entered my territory capturing and killing the dwellers upon it, who are my vassals, I determined to conform my wishes to your will, and hold right all that you might do, believing that it should be so for a good reason, providing against some future event, to you perceptible but from me concealed; since an evil may well be permitted to avoid another greater, that good can arise, which I trust will be so; for from so excellent a prince, no bad motive is to be suspected."

From which it may be seen that Casqui was something of a philosopher as well as a discreet politician. He added to his eloquent words presents of skins, shawls, and fish. The villages along the way had done the same thing, for the Indians had recognized in the Spaniards "men from heaven, whom their arrows could not harm."

De Soto, however, knew too much about the wiles of

the Indians to relax his vigilance. He refused to take up his quarters in the village, thinking it safer — after Chicaça — to encamp in a grove of trees, a quarter of a league away.

There the inhabitants would come to entertain him with their songs, and to show their reverence by prostrating themselves on the ground before him. And one day the chief arrived with some blind men whom he asked the Governor to cure. Was he not the Child of the Sun ? A trifle of this sort would be nothing to him. Would he not leave them a sign, since he had to go away, from which they might derive support in their wars, and upon which the people might call when they needed rain ? The chief had been observing the Spanish crucifixes.

The Governor had no objection to Casqui's notion of his divine origin; but he was scandalized at the suggestion that he possessed the power of working miracles. However, he would give them the sign that they needed; and so had a tall cross constructed from the tallest pines procurable. This, he told them, was what they had to adore.

Standing beside it, De Soto remembered his missionary obligations. He had never actually forgotten them, but the business of conquest had given him few opportunities for attempting the conversion of the heathen. The army had moved rapidly from place to place; and had generally had too much fighting to do. But now he preached a sermon to the natives, saying that there was One who could make their blind whole. "This was He who had created the sky and the earth and man in His own image. Upon the tree of the cross He had suffered to save

[236]

the human race, and had risen from the grave on the third day — what of man there was in Him dying; what of deity being immortal — and, having ascended into heaven, was there with open arms to receive all that would be converted to Him." Really, none of the friars could have put it better! And it carried more weight with the Indians coming from the redoubtable Governor's own lips.

De Soto and his men knelt before the rough cross, telling the natives that Christians venerated it in memory of that other cross upon which Christ had died. And Casqui and his people imitated the example of the Spaniards. "Their faith," says Ranjel,[4] "would have surpassed that of the conquerors if they had been taught;" and, adds Oviedo tartly, "would have brought forth more fruit than those conquerors did."

They left Casqui's village on Sunday, the 26th of June. On the same day, far off in Peru, there was given by Francisco Pizarro, a signal example of Christian faith and devotion, *Conquistador* style. Young Almagro, the son of the old Marshall executed by Hernando Pizarro, and his friends forced their way into the house of the man they most hated, shouting "Where is the Marquis? Death to the tyrant!" There was a scuffle in the passage in which several men on both sides were slain, and Pizarro, having no time to don his armor, fought with a cloak round his arm until a sword point caught him in the throat. Stretched upon the floor, he had just sufficient strength left to make the sign of the cross

[4] The *Jesuit Relations* abound in most touching instances of the piety exhibited by the northern Indians after their conversion.

in his own blood. He dragged himself forward and kissed it; then with the name of Jesus upon his lips the Lion of Peru died.

In this he was like his cousin, Cortés — strong in faith, though not always showing the conduct of a good Christian. The same thing may be said of the apostolic De Soto. After having preached to the heathen, he accepted from Casqui — who expressed a desire to unite his own blood to that of so illustrious a man — a daughter to be his wife. He did not think it necessary to carry his exposition of Christian doctrine far enough to explain that, already having one wife, a second was forbidden by his religion.

He did even worse. From Pacaha, the next chief whom he visited, he accepted two sisters, and in the sight of all men set up a harem.[5] Elvas gives their names; Maconoche was one, Mochila the other. "They were symmetrical, tall, and full: Maconoche bore a pleasant expression; in her manners and features appeared the lady; the other was robust."

Meanwhile Doña Isabella went up every day to a tower in the harbor in Havana to scan the horizon for her husband's sails.

---

[5] Ranjel says De Soto was given three women, one of Pacaha's sisters, one of his wives, "blooming and very worthy," and another Indian woman of rank. Garcilasso says that both were the wives of Pacaha, who gave them to his guest because he suspected that they had been violated when captured by other Indians. He adds that De Soto accepted them only because he did not wish to give offence.

CHAPTER XVII

FURTHER EXPLORATION

WHEN DE SOTO left the settlement of Casqui on the 26th of June, it was to march north in the direction of the territory of Pacaha,[1] Casqui went along with the army because he and Pacaha were mortal enemies. With the aid of the Spaniards he fully expected to conquer him. He did not do that, but he managed to rob his village, and then, fearing that the Christians would take his spoils from him, decamped with all his warriors.

De Soto had no serious intention of wantonly attacking Pacaha for the benefit of a rival tribe; and, deserted by his ally, he at once made peace with the enemy. The Spaniards found the settlement surrounded, or partly surrounded, by a moat, connected with a lake which, in its turn, was connected with the Mississippi. This gave the inhabitants a steady supply of fish, which they scooped out of their moat in nets. It was a more satisfactory method than those commonly employed elsewhere, that

---

[1] Garcilasso renders it more correctly as Capaha, obviously the same word as Quapaw, for it was this tribe that De Soto was now visiting. But because Elvas renders it Pacaha, this name, has been used here for the sake of uniformity.

of shooting or spearing the fish when they came near the surface.[2]

We hear something about these fish, nearly all of them belonging to varieties that were strange to the Spaniards. Elvas describes some of them for us. There was the *bagre* "the third part of which was head, with gills from end to end, and along the sides were great spines, like very sharp awls." These were as big as a pike and some of them weighed a hundred and fifty pounds.[3] There was another fish "like bream, with the head of a hake;" but the most curious fish of all was one with a long shovel-shaped upper lip. This was the paddle-fish or *Polydon spatula.*

While the Spanish soldiers were looking into the ways of the fish in those waters, De Soto had been engaged in winning over Pacaha. He did so too successfully for Casqui, who quickly came back with tearful reproaches.

"How is it possible, my lord," he exclaimed when he had come into the Governor's presence, "that after having pledged your friendship to me, and without my having done you any harm, you desire to destroy me, your friend and brother ?"

The thing that most alarmed the newly baptized chief was that Pacaha and his followers had also become Christians, and were proudly displaying crosses upon their heads. Casqui no doubt felt that a large part of the value of his conversion would be lost if, instead of his being allowed to enjoy the unique advantage of it, bap-

---

[2] Another method was that of intoxicating the fish, and taking them when they floated to the top of the water.

[3] The cat-fish.

tism should be indiscriminately administered to the other tribes, including that of his enemies.

He continued with, "Now, my lord, when God has heard us by means of the cross, and has given us water in great abundance and refreshed our cornfields and plantations; now when we had the most faith in it and your friendship, you have turned against us. Why did you desire to destroy the confidence we had in you ? Why did you desire to offend your God and us, when for Him and in His name, you received us as friends ? With what object were you actuated even to think of such a thing against us, the friends of the cross, and your friends ?"

The sign had conquered, and rain had fallen in answer to his prayers. The note of naïve conviction in his voice was irresistible. And he could not have chosen a better ground — how confidently he stands upon it ! — for appealing to De Soto than that of their common Christianity. His theology was still extremely shadowy; but in what he had grasped he had faith. That was enough for those who heard him.

De Soto was greatly moved, and his eyes filled with tears at "the goodness and faith of the man" as he replied, "Look, Casqui, we do not want to do you any harm. What your belief in the cross has done for you is a small thing in comparison with what it will yet do, if you continue to love and believe in it. But when you ran away from me, I supposed that you held the teaching that we had given you as of small account. I thought that it was in pride you went off. Now I want you to know that pride is the thing which our God most abhors, and for which He punishes us most. But as you have come back in humility, you may be sure that I wish you more good than you think. If you need any-thing from me, tell me and I will do it for you. Of this you may be certain, because to speak a lie is a very great sin amongst us. Have no more fear. God, our Lord, commands that we love you like a brother. You and yours are our brothers. Such is the injunction of God."

This speech is a complete exposition of the spirit of the *Conquistadores* — pitiless to those who opposed their mission; generous to those who accepted the faith they had come to bring.

De Soto had another Christian duty to perform, and one that was not an easy one. He had to reconcile the two enemies, Casqui and Pacaha. It was with difficulty that he prevented Pacaha from springing upon his rival with a knife; and the chief begged the Governor to let him give Casqui at least a slash in the face. Which would indicate that the Christian charity of the new con-verts had not yet become very well developed.

New trouble started when dinner-time came; for each chief wanted to sit at De Soto's right hand and began making a speech setting forth his claim. Neither yield-ing to his opponent's logic, they commenced to fight for the place of honor. The Spaniards were amused by the scene, which Biedma says was well worth witnessing. But De Soto thought that the atmosphere was getting a little too heated, and tactfully solved the problem of precedence upon the basis of making both seats equal in dignity.

Still there was no sign of gold, and the Indians could tell them of none though they vaguely suggested that towards the south, which they said was thickly settled, some might be found. But upon hearing of a mountainous district to the northwest, De Soto decided to travel in that direction, thinking that possibly the mountains would make a difference to the soil, and that silver and gold might be found there. He was not confident about it any more; so he kept in reserve a second object of his journey, the discovery of the passage to the South Sea, or Pacific. This mythical strait haunted the imagination of explorers then and for some time afterwards. Leaving Pacaha on the 29th of July, he retraced his steps, for the first and last time on this expedition, to the village of Casqui. From there he set out towards the west. His men were paddled across the St. Francis River by Casqui's Indians.

After travelling a hundred and ten leagues they reached Quiguate towards the end of August.[4] It was the largest town the Spaniards had discovered up to that time, and was situated upon an arm of the Rio Grande, which was most probably the Arkansas. Fearing treachery, De Soto had half the huts burned, so that no cover might be offered in the event of a night attack and that he might have a free space for the use of his cavalry. The chief was kept under guard in the Governor's quarters along with his two wives, but for some reason, was

---

[4] There is a difficult discrepancy here. Ranjel says they left Quiguate on the 26th of August; he seems to indicate that they arrived there on the 5th. But as Elvas gives the distance travelled as a hundred and ten leagues, and says that they reached mountains forty leagues farther on, I am obliged to believe that they arrived at Quiguate much later than the 5th.

not taken along as a hostage. He furnished guides and porters, however, to the army.

Already, De Soto had gone through the present states of Florida, Georgia, parts of South and North Carolina, Alabama, and Mississippi. He had come from the southeastern corner of Tennessee, where the settlement of Pacaha was. He was about to ride as far as the confines of Indian Territory, from where he went into Louisiana. After his death, his army marched into Texas. This constitutes the most considerable feat of exploration ever performed upon the American continent. Yet if it is difficult to plot the route he took from the time he landed at Charlotte Harbor to his crossing of the Mississippi, it is impossible to write with much assurance about where he went east of the river. Most of the writers who have drawn maps to illustrate his movements have given up the task as hopeless at that point. Up to June 1541 we grope in a thick forest, through which, however, we do find some trails; afterwards we wander blindly in a mist.

The six days' ride to the mountains proved to be over bad ground. For four days on end they had to go through one swamp after another, "through an immense pathless thicket of desert." They even had to sleep in puddles of water. But they found plenty of fish for food. These were so plentiful that the Spaniards killed them with blows from cudgels, which was made all the easier by the fact that the Indian carriers from Quiguate, who were travelling in chains, disturbed the muddy bottom with their dragging manacles, whereupon the fish, becoming stupefied, would swim to the surface.

Coligua was situated in the gorge of the Arkansas

River.[5] The soil there was rich, so rich that the old grain
was thrown out to make room for the storage of new.
And beans and pumpkins abounded. But still there was
neither any sign of gold nor news as to where it might
be found. And the Indians of the interior had never
heard of the sea, so the South Sea passage was clearly
not to be discovered by journeying farther in that direction.

At Coligua, however, happened something of which
we should like to have been told a great deal more: bison
were encountered. But the chroniclers are as disappointing here as in their curt references to the Mississippi.
Elvas alone mentions it, and even he very casually:
"From there, at mid-day, they went to kill some cows, of
which there are many wild ones." That is all.

The skins of the animals had often been seen, and
had served as bed-coverings. Several times they had also
seen the horns, and once, over the doorway of Casqui's
hut, a mounted head of a very fierce-looking bull. But
now they not only saw herds of the huge beasts, but
had what must have been the thrill of hunting them.
Yet we are told nothing about it. Perhaps it was because the Spaniards, having never had any experience in
this form of the chase, were not very successful in making
a kill. They had never found it possible to learn the
knack of bending an Indian bow; and arquebus and
cross-bow were clumsy weapons to use on horseback.

As the mountains gave no indications of containing
veins of gold, De Soto took the advice of the chief of

---

[5] Or perhaps one of the tributaries of the Washita. Lewis puts it in the
valley of Little Red River.

Coligua and turned towards the southeast, where he was assured there were many settlements, and where there might be gold. The fact that the Spaniards were far west is indicated that at Palisema, reached on September 8th, two days after they left Coligua, they found Indians living in wigwams of deer-skins, with designs drawn upon them. The chief was careful to keep out of their clutches, and, because of the broken character of the country, they were able to capture few men for porters. Skins and blankets, however, were found lying in their path, left there as propitiatory gifts.

Following the course of the Washita, and entering what is now the State of Louisiana, the Spaniards reached the settlement of Tunico. There De Soto stayed a month, partly because of the excellent fodder he found in the place, but partly because he was at a loss to know what to do. Winter was approaching, and still there was no news of treasure.

But he found salt, of which the army stood in great need. Elvas describes the process by which the Indians obtain it. "The salt is made along by a river, which, when the water goes down, leaves it upon the sand. As they cannot gather the salt without a large mixture of sand, it is thrown together in certain baskets they have for the purpose, made large at the mouth and small at the bottom. These are set in the air upon a ridge-pole; and, water being thrown on, vessels are placed under them wherein it may fall; then, being strained and placed on the fire, it is boiled away, leaving salt at the bottom."

It was now necessary to find a suitable spot for winter quarters. So, hearing of Tula, a thickly populated district a day's march and a half down the river, De Soto moved forward with a body of cavalry and fifty foot-soldiers to reconnoitre.

Tula, however, proved to have a very serious draw-back. The Indians of the locality were the fiercest the invaders had ever seen. All the other natives had been handsome, well-formed people; these were hideously ugly. They deliberately tried to heighten their ferocious aspect by artificially deforming their heads with bandages which were put on at birth and kept on until the desired result had been achieved. They further disfigured their faces with flint knives, and blackened their lips after having pierced them. "Thus," says Garcilasso, "they render themselves so frightful that one can hardly look upon them without dread. In addition to this, their minds are even worse formed than their bodies."

The ferocity even of the women may be measured by a story the same chronicler relates. A soldier of the name of Reinoso was in a loft of one of the huts when he was attacked by five of these viragos. They sprang upon him with the intention of strangling him, and he, being ashamed either to draw his sword against women or to call for help, would have been killed if the cane floor had not broken. Another Spaniard in the room below, seeing a leg sticking through the hole, was on the point of slashing it off with his sword when he noticed the color of the skin. But upon coming upstairs to see what was the cause of the scuffle, he found it impossible to make the women let his comrade go, and was obliged to kill all five.

The warriors of the tribe came out to meet their visitors and furiously attacked them all along the way. "They came at us," says Biedma, "in packs of eights and tens, like worried dogs," armed with long spears whose points were hardened with fire. As they wounded seven or eight of the Spaniards and eight or nine of their horses, De Soto thought it well to attempt no further advance until he had brought up the rest of his forces.

Even with these they had difficulty in crushing a tribe so outrageously savage. His men had a bitter struggle in the village, a house to house battle, with the Indians climbing upon the huts and shooting their arrows at them. When they had been beaten off one roof they would get upon another and shoot again. The battle went on for so long that the horses got too tired to run, and no Indian who could draw a bow had his life spared him,[6] except six men who were sent back, with their right hands and their noses cut off, with De Soto's compliments to the chief.

This had the desired effect. The chief at once sent messengers bearing loads of "cow-skins" as presents, which they offered in obeisance, weeping. Three days later the chief himself came before De Soto, he also weeping — "the token of obedience and the repentance of a past error, according to the usage of the country."

The Governor raised him up, and told him that he was forgiven for all that had happened, thanking him for his gifts and for the interpreter he had brought.[7] And in

[6] But Elvas, who records this, says fifteen Indians were killed. It was not a massacre, but only a fight without quarter.

[7] Juan Ortiz was still with him, but the difficulties of translation had greatly increased, for Ortiz knew only the language used by the Indians to the south, and was far from that district now. Consequently he often had

reply the chief made a speech offering De Soto his person, his vassals, and his country. This speech, and all those the Spaniards had listened to, as Elvas notes, were so elegantly phrased that no orator could do any better.

Taking with them the bison hides, which they found extremely useful in the cold weather, the soldiers proceeded farther toward the southeast, still following the Washita, under the direction of guides from Tula, until, eighty leagues away, they reached Autiamque.

De Soto had been told that it was a district well stocked with grain, which had been scarce in Tula, and was, moreover, near a great water, "which, from their account, appeared to him to be an arm of the sea." It was his intention to winter there and, upon the arrival of warm weather, to go to the shore of the Gulf of Mexico, where he would build two brigantines, one of which should be sent to New Spain and the other to Cuba for the military supplies so badly needed. He hoped also to secure reinforcements. Two hundred and fifty of his men were dead, and he had lost a hundred and fifty horses. Three years had gone by since he had been heard of by Doña Isabella, or by any person living in a civilized community.

It should be noted that De Soto was as far as ever from entertaining the thought of abandoning his sterile enterprise; but he had become sufficiently chastened to do what he had refused to do a year before, when he avoided contact with Maldonado and the ships. He still had nothing to show that could entice prospective recruits to

to line up natives brought from different territories, one of each locality; and the questions, being passed down the line, had the answers brought back in the same way — through a series of interpreters.

join him. But he retained a large part of his fortune intact. By some means or other — though these could not have been clear to his mind — he would gather reinforcements, found a colony upon the banks of the Great River, refit his expedition, and go on to find and conquer the rich district which must be somewhere in that immense country.

CHAPTER XVIII

THE DEATH OF THE CONQUEROR

IT WAS on the second of December that De Soto took up his winter quarters at Autiamque — not too soon, for the weather grew bitterly cold almost at once, and there was a heavy fall of snow. For one whole month out of the three that the army remained there it was snowbound; the men could go only to a wood a couple of bowshots away, along a road banked higher than their heads. From this they brought in fuel; and there the Indians, who were now allowed to go at large without shackles, shot rabbits and hares for them. In the village itself there were ample stores of corn and beans and walnuts and prunes.

The Governor strongly stockaded the encampment, but, for fear of the local Indians setting this on fire, he had an open space left between it and the houses it surrounded. So vigorously was the work prosecuted that it was finished in three days.

Even with this protection, De Soto was disinclined to take any chances. The disasters of Mabilla and Chicaça had been due to a lack of adequate precautions. A warning of what might happen came one night when a soldier on guard at the entrance to the fortifications

[251]

caught a prowling Indian peering in. The sentinel pressed himself back against the wall, waiting to see what would happen, and, upon the savage crossing the threshold, slashed at him with his sabre and cut his hand off. The man was taken before the Governor to be examined about his intentions in trying to creep in; "but fell dead without utterance," such was his terror.

The next night, therefore, and every now and then at intervals, De Soto ordered a drummer out to beat the alarm, so as to test his men's promptitude in answering it. Any laggard was severely reprimanded. In this way a high degree of disciplined watchfulness was maintained. The old gay mood of jaunty recklessness had long ago disappeared.

One irreplaceable loss was sustained at Autiamque. Juan Ortiz, who had been of such value to his comrades since they had found him living as a savage amid the swamps of Florida, sickened and died. One of the lads captured at Cutifachiqui had learned in the eighteen months he had been with the Spaniards a little of their language; but it was, after all, very little Castilian that he knew. What Ortiz used to get out of the Indians in a few minutes took nearly a whole day now for its unravelling. And then more often than not the exact opposite of what was said would be understood. As a consequence the Christians in their subsequent journeys would often march for two or three days, wandering up and down, lost in thickets, without any idea of where they were, only in the end to be obliged to return to the point from which they had set out.

This convinced De Soto that it would be folly to make

any attempt to push westwards, lest he and his army should get into an impassable wilderness where they would perish for lack of food and water. That door being closed, and only because it was closed, the Governor decided to carry out the plan he had been turning over in his mind since the beginning of the winter: that of reaching the sea and of building ships on the coast with which he could put himself again in communication with civilization.

So as to carry this out the more speedily, he would not wait for settled fine weather, but marched south from Autiamque on March 6, 1542, in search for Nilco, which the Indians said was near the Great River. He had now barely three hundred effective men, and, of the forty horses left, many were lame. For the Spaniards, having been short of iron, had allowed them to go for a whole year unshod. The main value of the mounts now was in putting up a show of cavalry.

The Governor and his men crossed the Washita River by means of a piragua, and encountered at once heavy snow, which held them upon the farther bank for four days. But when the weather improved they set out again, passing Tutelpinco, a deserted town, and arriving at Nilco on the 29th of the month.

Here De Soto found the most thickly settled district so far reached by the expedition, and supplies of food. The local chief — or rather a man who came as a spy, pretending he was the chief — presented him with a magnificent marten-skin cape, and a string of pearls, receiving from the Governor in return a few cheap beads, which were presented with great ceremony. Pressing on from that spot, in order to reach the sea, which he believed was not far away, De Soto reached at last, on Sunday April 15th, the settlement of Guachoya, where the Red River enters the Mississippi.[1]

It was a good town, excellently built and stockaded, just what they wanted; but its chief, though apparently well disposed, could tell De Soto nothing about how he might reach the sea. The Governor distrusted the answer, which he suspected was made to get rid of him — since he was thinking of making his brigantines there, if he could not get to the gulf — and sent Juan Añasco out to explore.

Eight days later Añasco and his little troop of horsemen came back. They had not in all that time been able to advance more than about fourteen leagues down the river: the Mississippi mud and the cane-brakes had been too much for them. And in those dismal reaches they had found no sign of a settlement. It had been worse, far worse, than the bogs of the Floridian peninsula; for no headway whatever had been possible.

Hearing this, the great spirit of De Soto gave way to profound despondency. It had long suffered an inhuman strain; but, being human, the breaking point had been reached. His men and horses were continually diminishing, and he despaired of supporting himself in that dreadful region without the succor which seemed to

---

[1] It may, however, have been the Washita, which in those days probably emptied directly into the Mississippi. The accounts of the chroniclers, taken as a whole, fairly clearly indicate this or the Red River, but an expression in Elvas would seem to point to the Arkansas, at the mouth of which Professor Herbert E. Bolton places Guachoya. Theodore Lewis does the same. That would be too far north for the Spaniards to have got any rumors of the sea, and would leave no room to account satisfactorily for De Soto's travels west of the Mississippi.

be beyond his grasp. Clear-eyed at last, he saw how vain was his dream. The country could not be conquered or even explored by this handful of destitute men.

Gold might be there; gold was there, could he but find it. But the disasters suffered by the expedition made certain that no recruits would be secured. How difficult Pizarro had found it to induce men to join him, and yet he, almost from the beginning, had come across some gold — enough to offer the necessary encouragement. But, worst of all, he had led these six hundred poor devils to their death. Half of them were already in their graves. The others had death waiting for them. Unending mud-flats stretched between them and the sea, which was — who knew where ? Even if they could reach it, there was little chance of building boats stout enough to make the shores of Cuba and Mexico.

His heart, hitherto strong to endure all things, broke with disappointment and grief. He still preserved his stoical silence. No word passed his lips of railing against fortune or complaint about man; but every member of the army knew from what disease De Soto was dying.

They called it fever; and he did have fever. But it was not fever that killed him. His robust constitution could have shaken that off, had he wanted to live. But there was nothing to live for. Was he to go home to be laughed at, to practise parsimonies in order to keep up a hollow pretence at grandeur, to grow into a disappointed querulous old man ? No, anything was better than that. *Finis coronat opus* — well, work of this sort had only one fitting end, that of death.

It was the way out. He had sworn that he would

never leave Florida before he had found the gold of which Cabeza de Vaca had spoken. He would keep his vow. But these fine fellows who had followed him so loyally, why should they suffer for his sake ? Life surely held much for them. Perhaps after he was gone they would find a method of leaving the country which he, while life was in him, would never permit them to use. His death was for them as well the way out.

Yet even in such a state of mind and body he sent a message to a powerful Natchez chief named Quigaltam, whose settlement was upon the eastern bank of the Mississippi, calling upon him to render homage and, in token of his submission, to bring with him something that he held in esteem. Lacking other means of overawing him, he announced himself as the Child of the Sun.

Quigaltam sent back by De Soto's own messenger a haughty reply: "As to what you say of your being the Child of the Sun, I will believe you as soon as you make him dry up the Great River. As to the rest, it is not my custom to visit anyone. On the contrary all of whom I have ever heard serve and obey me, and pay me tribute, either of their own free will or because I make them. If you want to see me, come to me. If you want peace, I will receive you in peace; if you want war, you shall have it. But neither for you nor for any man will I set back one foot."

By the time the messenger returned De Soto was very ill. But the anger of the *Conquistador* flamed up. "Oh, if I were only well enough," he cried passionately, "I

[256]

would cross the river and humble that arrogance !" To have done so would have been a difficult undertaking at any time — for the river was a mile and a half wide and strong in current. It was obviously impossible just then. The lion was chained, and chafed against his fetters. His fury did not help to diminish the fever consuming him.

The chief of Guachoya then came in to tell him that he had heard that Quigaltam intended to come over himself — not at all for the purpose of offering his submission, but to attack the Spaniards. De Soto suspected that this was said treacherously, that it was Guachoya who was intending to make the attack, that he had said this merely in order to observe whether it frightened the Governor. So he returned the reply that he would punish Quigaltam as soon as he got well; and followed it with a characteristic gesture. To let the Indians see that he was not afraid of anything they could do, he ordered the gates of the stockades to be left open. But as a counter-balance to the apparent rashness of this defiant challenge, he ordered the sentries to be redoubled.

The last act of De Soto was one at which we must shudder. In order to strike terror into the Indians of Nilco, who were being refractory, and at the same time to placate those of Guachoya, who were their traditional enemies, he consented to send some of his men to attack the village. For what happened Garcilasso lays upon the Indians all the blame, but Elvas explicitly says that the order was given by Nuño Tobar and Juan Guzman, the officers in command. It was that every man in the place should be massacred. And for this De Soto must be held ultimately responsible.[2]

The settlement was one of six thousand people. There must therefore have been about fifteen hundred men in it capable of bearing arms. As only a hundred men were killed, either the massacre was only partial, or all but these few managed to escape.

This is the greatest blot upon De Soto's fame — for we must reluctantly believe Elvas. The Governor may have been persuaded that it was necessary to strike terror among the Indians at such a time, when he was himself incapacitated from leading his army which was in so perilous a position. But he had never behaved like this before, and the army had been in dangers as great.

The only way of accounting for it is that it was the act of a man whose mind was partially unhinged by fever. But if that fact condemns his judgment of the massacre as a military necessity, it releases him at the same time from a large part of the moral responsibility of such an atrocity. The Gentleman of Elvas had his stomach quite turned by this incident. There is no doubt that his sentence expresses the horror felt by all except the group of butchers involved in the affair: "To the ferocious and the bloodthirsty, God permitted that their sin should rise up against them in the presence of all — when there was occasion for fighting showing extreme cowardice, and in the end paying for it with their lives." [3]

[2] Garcilasso says, and let us hope that what he says is correct, that De Soto, when he heard of what had taken place, was extremely indignant. But Elvas distinctly says that De Soto wished to make an example of Nilco, so that neither that town nor Guachoya would dare to attack him afterwards.

[3] Being a Portuguese he had no brief for the Spaniards, and often criticized De Soto. His comment here is obviously not intended to apply to

Now De Soto knew that his end was near. He therefore confessed his sins (let us hope including the enormity just perpetrated); but he could be neither anointed nor receive the Viaticum — the Blessed Sacrament having been absent from this group of Christian men for more than a year. But we are told that he made his will; and he appointed his successor.

If any will was made at Guachoya it was lost. But we may examine instead the document drawn up in Cuba on May 10, 1539. It is of the highest value and interest, and reveals a great deal about De Soto's character.

It begins with an affirmation of his faith.

"Know ye who shall see this testamentary letter, that I, the Adelantado, Don Hernando de Soto, being of sound body and free mind, such as my Redeemer Jesus Christ has been pleased to bestow upon me, believing firmly in what the Holy Mother Church believes and holds, in the Most Holy Trinity, Father, Son, and Holy Ghost, three persons and one only true God, promising as

the Governor, but to the men who took part in the massacre. His account leaves room for the supposition that, though De Soto had ordered an example to be made of Nilco, Tobar and Guzman exceeded their instructions. As for De Soto himself we have this lucky shot from Las Casas: "Of the fourth Tyrant that came well instructed lately in the year 1538, we have had no news these three years. This we are sure of, that at the beginning he carried himself very cruelly; and if he be alive most assuredly he hath destroyed an infinite number of people; for he among all those who have done most mischeife in ruining both Provinces and Kingdoms, is famous for his savage fury: wherefore I am apt to believe that God hath put the same end to his life as to the others." (From *The Tears of the Indians*, London 1656.) The good bishop refers here, of course, to Ponce de Leon, Ayllon, and Narváez as the other three tyrants. Putting the number of Indians killed in Florida at the highest reasonable estimate, they would not amount to more than five thousand — not "an infinite number." But it must be admitted that, according to the Las Casas system of arithmetic, they would have been put down as at least two millions. That is the lowest figure he ever condescends to deal in.

a faithful Christian to live and die in His Holy Catholic faith, mindful of the blood that Jesus Christ shed for me as the price of my redemption, and endeavouring to repay and satisfy so great a benefit, knowing that death is a natural thing, and the more I shall be prepared for it the better He will be pleased, I declare that I commend my soul to God, who created it of nothing, and redeemed it with His most holy passion, that He place it among the number of the elect in His glory, and I order the body to the earth, of which it was made."

He then gave instructions that he was to be buried at his birthplace Xerez, in the sepulchre where his mother lay, in the church of San Miguel. He left money for the building of a chapel in honor of our Lady of the Immaculate Conception, and for supplying it with the necessary chalice and vestments. There every week five masses were to be said for the repose of his own soul and the souls of his wife and parents.

A tomb was next provided for, which was to be covered with palls on which were to be placed the red cross of a Commander of the Order of the Knights of Santiago, and his own coat of arms.

A list followed of masses that were to be said. Among these were twenty for the repose of the soul of his old friend Compañón, and sixty for the souls in Purgatory.

The bequests were numerous and elaborately detailed. The most interesting are those of four hundred ducats to a boy "who they say is my son, called Andres de Soto," and one thousand ducats to his illegitimate daughter María, married in Nicaragua to Hernán Nieto — the larger amount in her case probably accounted for on the ground of a higher degree of certainty concerning her parentage.

Leonora de Bobadilla (Nuño Tobar's wife) and her husband, and the maids were remembered suitably. The bulk of the remaining property was divided between Doña Isabella and a fund for bestowing marriage portions every year on three girls of Xerez. Preference was to be given to those of his own line to the fifth degree, and afterwards to the orphans of impoverished nobles, "of the poorest there may be." A most charming provision.

One clause of the will referred to the instrument of partnership drawn at Cuzco on June 27, 1535, between De Soto and Hernán Ponce de León. It reaffirmed that one-half of the estate he then possessed or should come to possess belonged to his friend.

De Soto, having set his other affairs, spiritual and temporal, in order, now summoned all the officers into his presence. They came in gloomily, for no one knew what was before them. All that they could see was that extreme danger was staring them in the face, the danger of perishing in Florida without leaving a trace behind. Each man there thought that he needed sympathy as one doomed to death. They entered the hut feeling that they had little sympathy to spare for the man who had brought them to this pass.

But their hearts were touched when they saw that handsome face wasted to the bones. The thin parched lips smiled a little at them, as did the sunken eyes bright with fever. He made a slight courteous gesture with his hand — now impotent, that had once held lance and sabre so firmly.

Speaking in a voice weak but level, he told them that, as they already knew, he was about to go into the presence of God to give an account of his life; and that since the Almighty had been pleased to allow him to know beforehand of his approaching death, he returned thanks. He confessed his deep obligations to all his men. Their love and loyalty, he honored and had intended to reward. For their part, would they pray for him that he might be pardoned for his sins, and his soul be received in glory. And he hoped that they would release him for any indebtedness he might be under to them, and forgive him for any wrongs he might have inflicted.

But it was now necessary, he went on, to appoint a successor. So he asked them to elect a commander with whom they would be satisfied, and all swear to obey him. He assured them that if he knew that this had been done it would abate somewhat the pain he suffered, and moderate the anxiety he felt in leaving them like this, no one knew where.

Baltasar de Gallegos, the second in command, replied for the assembled officers. Deeply moved by so greathearted an address, he said eagerly that De Soto might rest his mind; he was under no indebtedness to any one of them. As for prayers, he could count on them in life and after death. The Governor was to remember that those whom God called earliest out of this world, so full of toil and affliction, were those most favored by Him. Despite the keen sorrow they all felt at losing him, it was necessary for him and for them to conform to the Divine Will. As for electing a new governor, he was sure that he spoke for all present when he said that they would prefer De Soto to appoint one himself.

All nodded their assent. It was an extraordinary mark of their love, and their confidence in the dying man. They had often criticized him for his rashness, but they admired him as the best soldier they had ever known, and had found him as a commander invariably just. No one that they could elect would have the same authority as a man nominated by him. They understood that it would be an extension of his will — the will that had been their support in so many dismaying situations — even beyond the grave.

At this De Soto appointed Luis de Moscoso. He had been deposed after the disaster of Chicaça, since when his position had been held by Gallegos; but the dying man divined that Moscoso was the commander his officers really preferred. And he knew that, while Gallegos might be the better man for attack, Moscoso was better fitted to lead a retreat. The men round the bed swore faithfully to obey the new governor in everything.

"The next day, the 21st of May," says the Gentleman of Elvas, "departed from this life the magnanimous, the virtuous, the intrepid Captain, Don Hernando de Soto." It was just a year to a day since he had discovered the Mississippi.

All the officers thought it necessary to conceal what had happened from the Indians. The Governor had told them that Christians were immortal. If Guachoya or Quigaltam found out that De Soto was dead, they might venture to attack. The natives held him in the greatest veneration, and many more than half believed him when he told them that he was the Child of the Sun. Besides the dead man on several occasions, when he had been given information by his spies, had shown them that he knew many things the Indians supposed hidden from him. They could not understand how this could be. So he had obligingly explained. Holding up a mirror he showed them their own countenances reflected in it. "In this," he said, "I can see all that you think or intend to do."

Now he was gone. Secretly and at midnight his body was buried between the posts of the gates of the encampment. At that place horsemen had continually to ride in and out, so the loosened soil of the grave would not be noticed there.

But it soon became clear that savage cunning had guessed at the truth. Indians were seen pointing significantly at the spot. And Moscoso, fearing that the body would be dug up and mutilated, had it removed the following night.

They weighted the shroud, consisting of a pair of marten-skin cloaks, with sand, and, taking it in a canoe out to the middle of the Mississippi, dropped it into the depth of the stream.[4]

When Guachoya a few days later slyly enquired, "What has become of my brother, the Governor?" Mos-

[4] Garcilasso says that De Soto was buried in a hollow oak weighted with sand. Both statements may be correct. Though if one is to be rejected, it must be his. The Governor may have been put, in his skin shroud, into the hollow oak. But such a coffin would have taken some time to prepare and would not have helped in the keeping of the secret. A klavern of the Ku-Klux Klan claims the possession of this coffin — which is marked with Masonic emblems!

coso lightly answered that he had ascended into the skies — a common practice with the Child of the Sun. But he would be back before very long.

This was too much even for a superstitious savage to swallow. He had observed the loose earth over the newly dug grave. So he came bringing with him two young men, whom he proposed killing that they might serve the Governor on his way through the regions of the shades. It was the custom of the country, the chief said, to do this when any great lord died.[5] The new General was aghast at the suggestion. Reproving Guachoya for so evil a practice, he again assured him that De Soto was not dead, but would soon return. He and all the Span·iards feared that a massed attack would be made upon them if it was known that a man so dreaded for his prowess would never strike another blow.

Moscoso's words were belied, as the Indians must have noticed, by his actions. For the Governor's property was sold at public auction. This consisted of three horses and seven hundred pigs and two male and three female slaves. Were these the two sisters of Pacaha and the daughter of Casqui ?

The pigs had been kept by De Soto for an emergency. Moscoso was not proposing to practise so rigid an economy; so the men bought freely. Each slave or horse brought from two to three thousand *cruzados,* each hog two hundred. But as nobody had any money promis-

[5] This fact strongly supports the location of the place of De Soto's death near the mouth of the Red River. Because it was in that district that the Natchez tribe was settled; and the Natchez and the Taënsa were the only tribes to have this custom, which was unheard of among the Quapaws who were settled around the juncture of the Arkansas and the Mississippi rivers.

sory notes were accepted. It was observed that those who had any property in Spain that could be attached, bought much more sparingly than those who had nothing.

The sale of the pigs gave the men plenty of pork; and now having a regular supply of meat, they kept the fasts of the Church, which had been neglected for a long time past. They had their excuse: during a period when they often went two or three months without tasting flesh, they felt free to eat it on any day that it chanced to come their way — even if that day happened to be a Friday.

Well might Elvas say of De Soto: "He was advanced by fortune, in the way she is wont to lead others, that he might fall the greater depth." His career is the perfect stuff of tragedy. And the most ironical note in it all is the fact that he actually did find, without knowing it, the rich land of which he came in search. He was buried in furs, and the river that he discovered became the main artery of the fur-trade which was subsequently developed — a fabulous source of wealth which he ignored.

He had provided for himself a splendid tomb in the church of San Miguel in Xerez. In the Mississippi he obtained a more famous memorial than he had ever imagined.

CHAPTER XIX

THOSE WHO SURVIVED

IT WAS not altogether surprising that, though the army loved De Soto, many among both officers and men felt relieved by his death. They knew that retreat was foreign to his nature. Had he got well some small piece of luck coming his way would have sent him on again upon his hopeless quest. Even without that, they understood perfectly well that he would never have abandoned what he had begun. Luis de Moscoso, on the other hand, was, as all were aware, a gay cavalier who had long been sick of hardship. His one idea was to get out of Florida as speedily as possible. De Soto's perception of this had been his motive in appointing him, with a contemptuous pity for those so lacking in hardihood, to lead the Christians home. They were destined, however, to endure further wanderings and privations and dangers for another fifteen months.

The idea of building brigantines had been abandoned following upon Juan Añasco's failure to locate the sea anywhere near. That was at best only a counsel of despair, for they had no facilities for ship-building, or any experience in it; and they shuddered when they recalled how Narváez, after all his epic expenditure of resource and energy, had perished miserably upon the same waters where they would have to venture. A storm would overset any vessel they could construct; they had no compass or chart; the river in all likelihood was full of hostile canoes lower down; or it might even reach a fall — their distraught imaginations pictured something like the stupendous volume and height of Niagara. They determined, therefore, to march westwards. If they went far enough they would be sure to come to Mexico and settlements of their own countrymen. On the 5th of June they set out, with a guide from Guachoya. As Miss King says, "It was not a march, but in truth a flight."

On the 20th of the month, after a six days' journey through desert, they reached Chaguate, whose chief had previously brought presents to De Soto at Autiamque. Here, Francisco Guzman deserted his comrades, rather than surrender his native mistress, a beautiful girl of eighteen, to the man to whom he had lost her as a gambling debt.

The incident throws a light upon the character of a type of soldier not uncommon in the army. Guzman loved the girl enough to give up for her sake all hope of seeing Spain again. But he could not resist gaming, and, having nothing else to wager, he used her as his stake.

Through Aguacay the march continued, which was reached on July 5th, and then through Amaye, reached on July 22d to Naguatex. Here they were fiercely attacked, but beat off their assailants; and Moscoso sent one of the captured Indians, with his hands and nose cut off, to the chief, who decided it would be advisable to sue for peace.

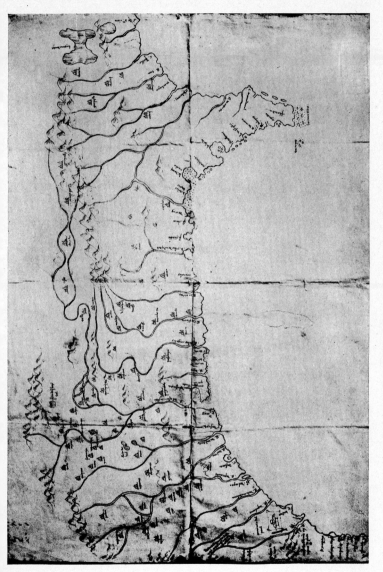

THE CONTEMPORARY MAP OF THE EXPEDITION

[This is now at the Archivo de Indias at Madrid, and is conjectured to have been made by Moscoso.
It is much more likely to have been made by Añasco.]

A wide river was now found (probably the Sabine), so swollen that all were astonished: it was midsummer and no rain had fallen for a month. The Spaniards supposed at first that this was caused by the sea flowing in; but upon their tasting the water they found it was fresh, and that it came with a strong current from the north. None of the Indians had so much as heard of the sea.

Continuing west, the guide furnished at Naguatex deliberately took the Spaniards in the wrong direction, and was hanged. Another guide secured at Nondacao tried the same trick. The chief had ordered him to lead the Christians into the desert where they would perish of hunger. He was cast to the dogs — the punishment most dreaded by the Indians.

At Guasco and Naquiscoça the General inquired if any Spaniards had been seen in the district; and under torture the Indians made up a tale of their being at Naçacahoz, two days' march farther west. At that place a woman was found who professed that she had once been captured by white men and had escaped from them. But later this was discovered to be a lie, like nearly everything the Indians said. No sign of Europeans or horses having been there was found.[1]

It was now the beginning of October and food was already scarce. Moreover Cabeza de Vaca, who had gone through the country before, had said that farther on the deserts began. The Indians of those districts, according to his account, wandered like Arabs, living on roots and prickly pears and game. The prospect of wintering

---

[1] Yet it may have had some foundation in fact. A little while before Coronado had struck north in his search for "the seven cities."

there did not appeal to the easy-going, indolent Moscoso, "who longed to be again where he could get his full measure of sleep, rather than govern and go conquering a country so beset with hardships." He determined to retrace his steps to the Mississippi.

The decision disgusted many of the men, who were hardier in soul and body than their commander. For they were now finding turquoises and "shawls of cotton" that came from the Pueblos of the Rocky Mountains; and Cabeza de Vaca had distinctly said that "after seeing cotton cloth, would be found gold, silver, and stones of much value." A little further, and the wealth they had endured so much for would be in their grasp to repay their toils. "Many," says Elvas, "far preferred peril to their lives than to leave the country poor." Moscoso was fiercely cursed for his cowardice, and one officer declared that he would gladly pluck out an eye if by doing so he might pluck out one of the General's at the same time.[2] Apart from the question of abandoning the wealth for which they had come to Florida, it seemed a hopeless business to attempt building ships.

The Spaniards on their return march took a road slightly to the left of that by which they had come — a longer road, but through a less desolate country. This passed, however, through some of the points it had passed through on the outward journey. The Indians of Chaguate again came out to meet the Spaniards, but without

[2] According to Garcilasso there were a great many complaints on this score after the army had reached Mexico. Feeling ran so high that Moscoso and the officers who had advised returning to the Mississippi could not leave their houses with safety.

Guzman who, they said, refused to accompany them. Upon hearing this Moscoso wrote to him, sending pen and ink for a reply, reminding him that he was a Christian, and that they were all going to leave Florida. But the Indian who took the letter, brought back only the signature of the deserter. And when twelve mounted men were sent after Guzman to bring him back by force, he hid himself. He preferred a quiet life with his native wife.

Probably some of his comrades envied him. Hardly a man now ventured to hope to get out of the country. Food was running short. And all that was before them, even did they live to reach the Mississippi, was the fate of Narváez. In their extremity they threw themselves upon the mercy of God.

Their prayers were answered. The people of Nilco — either forgiving the massacre of May, or, more probably, fearing another — came forward peaceably, and told them that two days' journey to the south there was a town named Aminoya in a fertile district that skirted the Great River. It was welcome news, for December had come with a sharp north wind and heavy sullen rains. Many of the native porters were dead, as were several Christians; and sickness broke out in the army, one marked with "inclination to lethargy" — malarial fever. But there was food in Aminoya, and the protection of a well-stockaded town, and an abundance of better timber for ship-building than they knew of elsewhere. This, then, was the miracle for which they had prayed.

Other miracles were still needed. Some of these were sent from heaven: others they performed themselves.

One of the Portuguese, who had once been a slave with the Moors, had learned while in Fez to saw lumber. He luckily had his tools with him, and was able to prepare the timber. A native of Genoa, "whom God had been pleased to spare (as without him we could not have got away, there being not another person who knew how to construct vessels)" built the ships with the help of four or five Biscayan carpenters. Two calkers, one from Genoa, the other from Sardinia, closed up the seams of the planks with a little flax, and to this was added the ravelled threads of the Indian blankets and the bark of mulberry trees. And the cooper, though sick to the point of death, worked manfully in his weakness to make two half-hogsheads to carry water for each of the brigantines. It was fortunately a mixed cosmopolitan company: the Spanish hidalgos knew nothing of any craft or trade except that of war.

The nails that had been used in the building of the barges by which the army crossed the Mississippi had been saved. But there were not enough of them; moreover, they were not long enough to hold thick planks together securely. The fittings of the cross-bows and the chains of the Indians were therefore fashioned into bolts; but, in order to eke out the meagre supply of iron, these, like the nails, were skimpily made, and were hardly stout enough to stand the strain put upon them. The timbers had, accordingly, to be accommodated to their fastenings; and were cut much too thin for safety.

Anchors were hammered out of stirrups, for which others made of wood were substituted. Ropes were obtained by twisting the fibre of the mulberry-tree bark;

and sails were patched together from the skins which the Indians brought in.

To add to the disheartening difficulties attending the work of ship-building, with the melting of the snows in March the river flooded its banks, until it actually reached Nilco, nine leagues away. And Indians brought in reports that on the opposite shore it extended an equal distance. The town of Aminoya was flooded. The horses therefore had to be placed upon rafts, and the same contrivance was used in the huts, until even this proved insufficient; whereupon the Spaniards retreated to the open lofts of their shelters. This was the condition of affairs for two months, during which time no work could be done upon the boats.

The Indians were planning to muster their forces and wipe out the Spanish force. Three days before the day settled upon they sent presents of fish, the better to veil their treachery. But Moscoso, suspecting their designs, secretly seized one of the men who had brought in these presents, and, putting him to torture, they discovered the details of the whole plot.

Three days later, thirty men came, as the captive had said they would, bringing other presents, but with the intention of setting fire to the encampment, which was to be the signal for the attack. They were all arrested, and sent back to the chiefs with their hands cut off, and a message. It was this: the Indians might come as soon as they liked; Moscoso desired nothing better. But they should understand that they were incapable of thinking a thought which he did not know beforehand.

The fearful punishment, and Moscoso's bluff, had the

desired effect; the chiefs came in terrified to make excuses, and to beg for pardon.

At last, towards the end of June, the seven brigantines were launched, and somewhat to the surprise of their builders floated sufficiently well. The surrounding districts were scoured for grain, so thoroughly that the Indian population began to suffer from famine. It is pleasant to record that though Moscoso gave strict orders that none of the food stored for the use of the army should be given to the hungry natives, his soldiers had pity upon them and shared their rations with the Indians. With the grain and the water put into the boats went stores of dried pork and horse-flesh — all the mounts except twenty-two of the best being slaughtered. On the 2d of July 1543 the seven brigantines, accompanied by large war canoes, fastened together in couples side by side, sailed for the sea.

With the Spaniards had been five hundred Indian servants. These were left behind in Aminoya, much to their consternation. They had all become Christians, and many of the boys and girls had learned some Spanish. According to the Gentleman of Elvas, who always shows himself to be truthful as well as just and kind-hearted, most of those who were abandoned wept at the parting, "which caused great compassion." Those who treasure the legend of Spanish ferocity will scoff. But the fact is that the conquerors, though severe to stubborn enemies and dealing drastically with treachery, treated all the natives who accepted baptism with paternal indulgence. The Christian Indians had grown attached to their masters. To leave them like this to the vengeance of the pagan tribes seemed to Elvas a most hard-hearted thing.

Moscoso did not shine in the matter. For, though he did take a hundred of these people with him, it was not out of regard for their welfare. He gave out that their services were to be used only as far as the mouth of the river, where they were to be put on shore because of the necessity of husbanding food and water. But he quietly passed the word round among his own friends that they might make up the permitted hundred with their own slaves, and take them to New Spain — a proceeding, it should be noted, expressly forbidden by the commission given to De Soto.[3]

The troubles of the Spaniards were still far from over. Quigaltam, who had long been threatening attack, now saw his chance and came out with a flotilla of a hundred canoes,[4] each holding sixty or seventy men, to attack the departing brigantines. It was difficult to repel them from the ships which, in inexpert hands, manœuvred clumsily. And when the Spaniards attempted a foray in the canoes, Juan de Guzman[5] and eleven others capsized and, under the weight of their breastplates, were drowned before help could be sent.

Few men now possessed armor — most of this having gone to the making of bolts and nails for the ship-building; and there was but one cross-bow to each brigantine, and no arquebuses at all; so that the incessant harassing on the part of the pursuing Indians was exceedingly

---

[3] De Soto had set him the bad example, however, by sending twenty women as slaves to Doña Isabella.

[4] So says Elvas; Biedma cuts the number in half.

[5] He had been in command of the infantry at the massacre at Nilco. His death seemed to Elvas a judgment of God.

trying. Even the mats which the Spaniards used for bedding, and which they hung by day round the sides of their boats for protection, were not wholly effective. For though these stopped arrows, the Indians took to shooting their shafts in the air and letting them fall on the heads of the soldiers. And on one occasion a party of savages ventured to board one of the boats that had dropped behind.

Crawling slowly along in this way, the sea was reached in seventeen days. The journey had taken so long because of the steady skirmishing which, at least once, necessitated a landing in order to disperse the savages. On this occasion some more horses were killed, and the meat cured. The last four or five mounts left were set free — and from these may have sprung the race of mustangs which throve so amazingly upon the northern continent.

Upon reaching the gulf, Juan de Añasco, who prided himself on his knowledge of navigation — in that company the amateur sailor was ranked as an expert — advised striking directly across the open sea for Mexico. But he was overborne, for the men were afraid of what might happen to their frail vessels. So they hugged the circuitous shore, going slowly from headland to headland. They had just cause for alarm. Their equipment may be gauged by the fact that at the mouth of the river one rope broke and an anchor was in consequence lost, its place being taken by a makeshift of a large stone and the remaining bridles fastened together. Another of the little anchors bent under the strain put upon it.

A storm coming up, they took refuge on the shore; but it was with the utmost difficulty that the fragile ships

were kept from breaking up. They had to be held off
the beach by men rowing all night to keep taut the ropes
to which the feeble anchors were fastened. To make
this work harder, swarms of mosquitos gave them "intolerable torment." The sails when daylight came were
black with these insects, and the visages of the Spaniards
were swollen and bloody. But, the storm having passed,
they were able to laugh at one another for the condition
of their faces.

At last, on September 10th, the brigantines reached the
mouth of the river Panuco. "Many, leaping on shore,
kissed the ground; and all, on bended knees, with hands
raised above them, and their eyes to heaven, remained
untiring in giving thanks to God." In this mood of
gratitude, they had a hunger for hearing mass again —
of which they had been deprived for nearly three years.
So without waiting to unload the ships, they hurried to
the Christian settlement fifteen leagues inland, and,
dressed as they still were in their clothing of black-dyed
deer-skins, went immediately to the church to return
thanks for their miraculous preservation. Three hundred
and eleven men out of the original six hundred were
left.⁶ The pious Elvas prays: "Those whom He saw fit
should escape, coming out of Florida to tread the soil
of Christians, be He pleased that they live to serve Him;⁷
and to the dead, and to all who believe in Him, and con-

---

⁶ There is a document, the origin of which is unknown, in the *Archivo
General de Indias,* which gives a detailed list of the names of those who
reached Panuco. It contains two hundred and twenty names; but it may
be incomplete. The figures given above are those mentioned by Elvas.

⁷ Garcilasso says that many of the survivors entered religious orders, "after
the example of Quadrado Charamillo, who chose the order of St. Francis,
in which he died, illustrious by his acts of piety."

fess that in Him is their faith, grant, through His compassion, the glory of Paradise, Amen." As a survivor of the disastrous conquest of Florida, he does well to end his book with the words *Deo Gratias*.

The following month arrived Maldonado, whom De Soto had avoided meeting at the end of 1540, and who, if we may believe Garcilasso, had searched the coast as far north as Canada looking for the lost army. He took to Havana the news that Hernando de Soto was dead. The heart of Doña Isabella broke with grief upon hearing it, and a few days later she died.

BIBLIOGRAPHY *

Abbott, John S. C., *Ferdinand de Soto*. New York, 1873.

Acosta, José de, *The Natural and Moral History of the Indies*, reprinted from the translation by Edward Grimston (1604) and edited by Sir Clements R. Markham. 2 vols. London, 1880. *H. S.*

Andagoya, Pascual de, *Narratives of the Proceedings against Pedrarias Davila*, translated and edited by Sir Clements R. Markham. London, 1865. *H. S.*

Anghera, Peter Martyr de, *De Orbe Novo, the Eight Decades of Peter Martyr d' Anghera*, translated by Francis Augustus MacNutt. 2 vols. New York, 1912.

——, *Decades of the Ocean*, translated by Richard Eden and Michael Lok. London, 1555 and 1577.

Balboa, Miguel Cabello, *Histoire de Pérou*, edited by H. Ternaux-Compans. Paris, 1840.

Bancroft, George, *History of the United States*, Vol. I. New York, 1895.

Bancroft, Hubert Howe, *History of Central America*, Vol. I. San Francisco, 1886.

Bandelier, Adolphe F., *The Gilded Man*. New York, 1893.

Bartram, William, *Travels through North & South Carolina, Georgia, East & West Florida, the Cherokee Country, etc.* Philadelphia, 1791.

——, *The Travels of William Bartram*, (edited by Mark Van Doren). New York, 1928.

Biedma, Luys Hernandez de, *Narratives of the career of Hernando de Soto*, translated and edited by Buckingham Smith. New York, 1866.

——, *Narratives of the career of Hernando de Soto*, translated by

* H. S. = Hakluyt Society Publication.

[279]

Buckingham Smith and Edward Gaylord Bourne, Vol. II. New York, 1922.

Bingham, Hiram, *Inca Land*. Boston and New York, 1922.

Bolton, Herbert E., *The Spanish Borderlands*. New Haven, 1921.

Bourne, Edward Gaylord, *Spain in America*. New York, 1904.

Brinton, Daniel G., *Notes on the Floridian Peninsula*. Philadelphia, 1859.

Brion, Marcel, *Bartolomé de las Casas*, translated by Coley B. Taylor. New York, 1929.

Brownell, Charles De Wolf, *The Indian races of North and South America*. New York, 1853.

Cabeza de Vaca, Alvar Nuñez, *The Journey of Alvar Nuñez Cabeza de Vaca*, translated by Fanny Bandelier. New York, 1905.

——, *Relation*, translated by Buckingham Smith. New York, 1871.

Casas, Bartolomé de las, *The Tears of the Indians*, translated by F. P. London, 1656.

——, *Kurtze Erklärung der Fürnembsten Thaten*. 1599.

——, *Brevissima Relación*. (Included in Francis Augustus MacNutt's *Bartholomew de las Casas*.) New York, 1909.

——, *Historia de las Indias*. 5 vols. Madrid, 1878.

Castañeda de Nagera, Pedro, *The Journey of Coronado*, translated and edited, with an introduction, by George Parker Winship. New York, 1904.

——, *The Narrative of Castañeda* (Spanish text) in the *Fourteenth Annual Report* of the Bureau of Ethnology. Washington, 1896.

Catlin, George, *The North American Indians*. 2 vols. London, 1848.

Cieza de León, Pedro de, *The Travels of Pedro Cieza de León*, translated and edited by Sir Clements R. Markham. London, 1864. *H. S.*

——, *The Second Part of the Chronicles of Peru*, translated and edited by Sir Clements R. Markham. London, 1883. *H. S.*

Claiborne, J. H., *Mississippi as a Province, Territory, and State*. Jackson, Miss., 1880.

De Bry, Theodor, *Peregrinations in America* (Latin text). Frankfort, 1590–1634.

Doering, Heinrich (with Walter Lehman), *Kunstgeschichte des Alten Peru*. Berlin, 1924.

BIBLIOGRAPHY

Donaldson, Thomas, *The George Catlin Indian Gallery*. Washington, 1887.

Du Pratz, Le Page, *History of Louisiana*. 2 vols. London, 1763.

Elvas, A Knight of, *Virginia Richly Valued*, by a Portugall gentleman of Elvas, translated by Richard Hakluyt. London, 1609.

——, *Narratives of the career of Hernando de Soto*, translated and edited by Buckingham Smith, New York, 1866.

——, *Narratives of the career of Hernando de Soto*, translated by Buckingham Smith and Edward Gaylord Bourne, Vol. I. New York, 1922.

Estete, Miguel de, *Report on the expedition to Pachamac*, translated and edited by Sir Clements R. Markham. London, 1872. H. S.

Fairbanks, George R., *History of Florida from Its Discovery by Ponce de León, in 1512, to the Close of the Florida War in 1842*. Philadelphia and Jacksonville, 1871.

Falconer, Thomas, *On the Discovery of the Mississippi*, with a translation of the original MS. of Memoirs, etc., relating to the Discovery of the Mississippi, by Robert Cavalier de la Salle and the Chevalier Tonty. London, 1844.

Fiske, John, *The Discovery of America*. 2 vols. Cambridge, 1892.

Flint, Timothy, *The History and Geography of the Mississippi Valley*. Cincinnati, 1832.

Frank, Waldo, *Virgin Spain*. New York, 1926.

French, F. B., *Historical Collection of Louisiana*, Vol II. (containing translations of Biedma and Elvas). Philadelphia, 1850.

——, *Historical Collections of Louisiana and Florida, Second Series* (containing Memoir of La Salle addressed to Monseigneur de Seignelay, the official account of La Salle's exploration of the Mississippi River, D'Iberville's Journal, Proclamation of Pamfilo de Narváez to the Inhabitants of Florida, Fontanedo's Memoir on Florida, etc.). New York, 1875.

Garcia, Genaro, *Carácter de la Conquista Española*. Madrid, 1901.

Garcilasso de la Vega, el Inca, *The Royal Commentaries of Peru*, translated by Sir Paul Rycaut. London, 1688.

——, *First Part of the Royal Commentaries of the Yncas*, translated and edited by Sir Clements R. Markham. 2 vols. London, 1869–71. H. S.

——, *Histoire de la Conquête de la Florida, traduit en François par*. P. Richelet. Paris, 1711.

——, *History of the Conquest of Florida,* translated by Bernard Shipp and incorporated in his *History of Hernando de Soto and Florida.* Philadelphia, 1881.

——, *La Florida del Ynca.* Lisbon, 1605.

——, *Histoire des Yncas, rois du Pérou, on a joint à cette Édition L'Histoire de la Conquete de la Floride.* Amsterdam, 1737.

Gatschet, Albert Samuel, *A Migration Legend of the Creek Indians.* 2 vols. Philadelphia, 1844–88.

Graham, R. B. Cunninghame, *Hernando de Soto.* London, 1903.

Harrisse, Henry, *The Discovery of North America.* London and Paris, 1892.

Helps, Sir Arthur, *The Spanish Conquest in America.* 2 vols. New York, 1856.

——, *The Life of Pizarro.* London, 1896.

——, *The Life of Las Casas.* London, 1896.

Hennepin, Louis, *A Description of Louisiana,* translated by John Gilmary Shea. New York, 1880.

——, *A New Discovery of a Vast Country in America,* reprinted from the second London edition of 1698 and edited by Reuben Gold Thwaites. 2 vols. Chicago, 1903.

Herrera y Tordesillas, Antonio de, *The General History of the Vast Continent and Islands of America, commonly call'd the West Indies.* 6 vols. London, 1726.

——, *Historia General de los Hechos de los Castellanos.* 4 vols. Amsterdam, 1728.

Hodge, Frederick Webb, *Handbook of the American Indians.* 2 vols. Washington, 1907.

——, (with Theodore H. Lewis), *Spanish Explorers in the Southern United States, 1528–1543.* New York, 1907.

Hume, Martin A. S., *Spain: Its Greatness and Decay.* Cambridge, 1898.

——, *Queens of Old Spain.* London, 1906.

——, *The Spanish People.* London, 1901.

Huntingdon, Henry E., *From Panama to Peru: an Epitome of the Original Signed Documents to and from the Conquistadores, Francisco, Gonzalo, Pedro, and Hernando Pizarro, Diego de Almagro and Pacificator la Gasca.* London, 1925.

BIBLIOGRAPHY

Iberville, Pierre Lemoyne, Sieur d', *Voyage d'Iberville*. Montreal, 1871.

Irving, Theodore, *The Conquest of Florida*. New York, 1851.

Irving, Washington, *Voyages and Discoveries of the Companions of Columbus*. Philadelphia, 1831.

Johnson, William Henry, *Pioneer Spaniards in North America*. Boston, 1903.

Jones, Charles C., *Hernando de Soto*. Savannah, Ga., 1880.

——, *Antiquities of the Southern Indians*. New York, 1873.

——, *History of Georgia*. 2 vols. Boston and New York, 1883.

Joutel, Henri, *Joutel's Journal of La Salle's Last Voyage 1684–87*. Albany, 1906.

King, Grace, *De Soto and His Men in the Land of Florida*. New York, 1898.

Kroeber, A. L., *Archæological Explorations in Peru, Part I: Ancient Pottery from Trujillo*. Chicago, 1926.

La Salle, Nicholas de, *Relation of the Discovery of the Mississippi River,* translated by Melville B. Anderson. Chicago, 1898.

Laudonnière, René Goulaine de, *A notable history containing four voyages into Florida,* translated out of French into English by M. Richard Hakluyt. London, 1810.

Lehman, Walter (with Heinrich Doering), *Kunstgeschichte des Alten Peru*. Berlin, 1924.

Lewis, Theodore Hayes (with Frederick W. Hodge), *Spanish Explorers in the Southern United States 1528–1543*. New York, 1907.

López de Gómara, Francisco, *Historia de las Indias*. Madrid, 1852.

Lowery, Woodbury, *The Spanish Settlements within the Present Limits of the United States,* Vol. I. New York, 1911.

Lowry, Robert (with William H. McCardle), *A History of Mississippi*. Jackson, 1891.

Lummis, Charles F., *The Spanish Pioneers*. Chicago, 1893.

MacNutt, Francis Augustus, *Bartholomew de las Casas*. New York, 1909.

McCardle, William H. (with Robert Lowry), *A History of Mississippi*. Jackson, 1891.

Madariaga, Salvador de, *Englishmen, Frenchmen, Spaniards*. London, 1928.

——, *The Genius of Spain*. Oxford, 1923.

Marcy, Randolph Barnes, *Exploration of the Red River of Louisiana.* Washington, 1853.

Margry, Pierre, *Découvertes et établissements des français dans l'ouest et dans le sud de l'Amérique Septentrionale* (1614–1754). 5 vols. Paris, 1876–86.

Markham, Sir Clements R., *A History of Peru.* Chicago, 1892.

——, *The Incas of Peru.* London, 1912.

——, *The Inca Civilization in Peru,* Chapter IV in Vol. I of Winsor's *Narrative and Critical History of America.* Boston and New York, 1889.

——, *Pizarro, and the Conquest and Settlement of Peru and Chili,* Chapter VIII in Vol. II of Winsor's *Narrative and Critical History of America.* Boston and New York, 1886.

Mason, Otis Tufton, *Indian Basketry.* 2 vols. London, 1905.

——, *North American Bows, Arrows, and Quivers.* Washington, 1894.

Means, Philip Ainsworth, *A Survey of Ancient Peruvian Art.* New Haven, 1917.

——, *Indian Legislation in Peru,* in *Hispanic American Historical Review,* Vol. III, No. 4, November, 1920.

——, *A Footnote to the History of the Conquest of Peru.* New York, 1918.

Menéndez de Avilés, Pedro, *La Florida, sa conquista y colonización.* 2 vols. Madrid, 1893.

Merriman, Roger Bigelow, *The Rise of the Spanish Empire.* 3 vols. New York, 1918.

Monette, John W., *History of the Discovery and Settlement of the Valley of the Mississippi.* 2 vols. New York, 1846.

Montesinos, Fernando, *Memorias antiguas Historiales del Peru,* translated and edited by Philip Ainsworth Means. London, 1920. *H. S.*

Mooney, James, *The aboriginal population of America north of Mexico.* Washington, 1928.

Moses, Bernard, *The Spanish Dependencies in South America.* 2 vols. New York, 1914.

Navarrette, Martin Fernandez de, *Colleción de los Viages y Descubrimientos.* 5 vols. Madrid, 1825–37.

Ober, Frederick A., *Ferdinand de Soto.* New York, 1906.

Oviedo y Valdés, Gonzalo Fernandez de, *Historia General y Natural de las Indias.* 4 vols. Madrid, 1851–55.

BIBLIOGRAPHY

——, *Histoire du Nicaragua,* edited by H. Ternaux-Compans. Paris, 1840.

Parkman, Francis, *La Salle and the Discovery of the Great West.* Boston, 1907.

Phillips, Philip Lee (editor), *The Lowery Collection.* Washington, 1912.

Pickett, Albert J., *Invasion of the Territory of Alabama.* Montgomery, Ala., 1849.

——, *History of Alabama.* Charleston, 1851.

Pizarro, Hernando, *Letter to the Royal Audience of San Domingo,* translated and edited by Sir Clements R. Markham. London, 1872. *H. S.*

Pizarro, Pedro, *Relation of the Discovery and Conquest of the Kingdoms of Peru,* translated and annotated by Philip Ainsworth Means. 2 vols. New York, 1921.

Prescott, William H., *The History of the Conquest of Peru.* 2 vols. New York, 1847.

——, *The History of the Conquest of Mexico.* 2 vols. New York, 1843.

——, *The History of Ferdinand and Isabella.* 3 vols. New York, 1849–50.

Priestley, Herbert Ingram, *The Coming of the White Man.* New York, 1929.

——, *The Luna Papers.* 2 vols. Deland, Fla., 1928.

Quintana, Manuel Josef, *Lives of Vasco Nuñez de Balboa and Francisco Pizarro,* translated by Margaret Hodson. London, 1832.

Radin, Paul, *The Story of the American Indian.* New York, 1927.

Ranjel, Roderigo, *Narratives of the career of Hernando de Soto,* translated by Buckingham Smith and Edward Gaylord Bourne, Vol. II. New York, 1922.

Richman, Irving Berdine, *The Spanish Conquerors.* New Haven, 1919.

Rowland, Dunbar, *History of Mississippi, the Heart of the South.* 2 vols. Chicago and Jackson, 1925.

——, (editor), *A Symposium on the Place of the Discovery of the Mississippi River.* Jackson, Miss., 1927.

Sancho, Pedro, *The Conquest of Peru,* translated and annotated by Philip Ainsworth Means. New York, 1917.

Sarmiento de Gamboa, Pedro, *History of the Incas,* translated and edited by Sir Clements R. Markham. London, 1908. *H. S.*

Scott, James Brown, *The Spanish Origin of International Law.* Washington, 1928.

Shea, John Gilmary, *Ancient Florida,* Chap. IV. in Vol. II of Justin Winsor's *Narrative and Critical History of America.* Boston and New York, 1886.

——, *Discovery and Exploration of the Mississippi Valley, with the Original Narratives of Marquette, Allouez, Membri, Hennepin, and Anastase Donay.* Albany, 1903.

Shipp, Bernard, *The History of Hernando de Soto and Florida.* Philadelphia, 1881.

Skinner, Constance Lindsay (with Clark Wissler and William Wood), *Adventures in the Wilderness.* New Haven, 1925.

Soto, Hernando de, *Letter of Hernando de Soto and Memoir of Hernandez de Escalante Fontaneda,* translated and edited by Buckingham Smith. Wasington, 1854.

Squier, E. G., *Peru: Incidents of Travel and Exploration in the Land of the Incas.* New York, 1877.

Strawn, Arthur, *Sails and Swords.* New York, 1929.

Swanton, John R., *Indian Tribes of the Lower Mississippi Valley.* Washington, 1911.

Vedia, Enrique de, *Historiadores Primitivos de Indias.* 2 vols. Madrid, 1877.

Velasco, Juan de, *Histoire du Royaume de Quito,* edited by H. Ternaux-Compans. 2 vols. Paris, 1840.

Wilmer, Lambert A., *The Life, Travels, and Adventures of Ferdinand de Soto.* Philadelphia, 1858.

Winship, George Parker, *The Journey of Coronado, 1540–1542.* New York, 1904.

Winsor, Justin, *The Mississippi Basin.* Boston and New York, 1895.

Wissler, Clark, *The American Indian.* New York, 1922.

——, (with Constance Lindsay Skinner and William Wood), *Adventures in the Wilderness.* New York, 1925.

Wood, William (with Constance Lindsay Skinner and Clark Wissler), *Adventures in the Wilderness.* New York, 1925.

Xerez, Francisco de, *Report,* translated and edited by Sir Clements R. Markham. London, 1872. *H. S.*

——, *Relation véridique de la conquête du Pérou et de la*

province du Quito, edited by H. Ternaux-Compans. Paris, 1837.

Yoakum, Henderson K., *History of Texas.* 2 vols. New York, 1856.

Zarate, Augustin de, *History of the Discovery and Conquest of Peru,* Vol. IV of Kerr's *Voyages and Travels.* Edinburgh, 1812.

INDEX

Abbott, John S. C., viii, 81, 119
Acla, 29
Aguacay, 268
Alabama, present State of, 202, 244
Alabama River, 203
Alexander VI's Division of the New World, 11, 67, 81-2
Alimanu, 226
Almagro, Diego de, 15, 42, 45; enters into partnership with Pizarro, 47; tries for recruits, 49; quarrels with the Pizarros, 54; arrives at Caxamarca with reinforcements, 95; gets small share of Inca's ransom, 96; insists Atahualpa be tried, 98; hangs Felipillo, 101; reinforces De Soto, 108-9; goes north to turn Alvarado aside, 111; quarrels with Pizarros, 113-4; effects reconciliation, 115; final breach with the Pizarros, 121; defeated by Hernando Pizarro, 130; executed, 237.
Alvarado, Pedro de, 18, 57, 116, 138
Amaye, 268
Amherst, Lord, 12
Aminoya, 271-3, 274
Amritzar Massacre, 12
Añasco, Juan de, 116, 137, 142, 145, 156, 172, 173, 183, 184, 185, 191, 254, 267, 276
Andagoya, Pascual de, 15
Andes, 61, 70, 119
Anhaica, 172, 174
Appalachee Bay, 123
Appalachian Indians, 171, 174-5, 176, 177
Aquinas, St. Thomas, 10, 67
Aquixo, 235
Arkansas River, 243, 245, 254
Astorga, Marquis de, 127, 218
Atahualpa, 24, 44; engaged in civil war, 58; sends messenger to Spaniards, 66-7; musters his army, 70, 71; receives De Soto and Hernando Pizarro, 72-7; his appearance, 74;

his impassivity, 76; advances towards Caxamarca, 79; enters the city square, 80; is addressed by Valverde, 81-3; insults Valverde, 84; is taken captive by the Spaniards, 85-6; his opinion of the invaders, 87; his cheerful disposition, 88; friendliness towards De Soto and Hernando Pizarro, 89; offers ransom, 90; plays for time, 91; released from further obligations, 96; still kept a prisoner, *ibid.*; has his brother Huascar murdered, 97-8; his trial suggested, 98-9; tried and sentenced to death, 100-1; baptized by Valverde, 102; stangled, *ibid.*; mourned by Pizarro, 103; given Christian burial, 103-4, 118, 187, 194
Autiamque, 249, 251-3.
Ayllon, Vasquez de, 123, 192
Aymay, 185

Badajoz, British atrocities at, 12
Balboa, Vasco Nuñez de, superseded by Pedrarias, 28; betrothed to daughter of the Governor, 29; infatuated with his Indian mistress, *Ibid.*; arrested by Pizarro, *ibid.*; tried for treason and beheaded, 30; comparison with De Soto, *ibid.*; his fate predicted by Codro, 31, 33, 45
Balboa, Miguel Cabello, 65, 112
Bancroft, Hubert Howe, 5, 17, 34
Bartram, William, 163
Belloc, Hilaire, 5
Benalcazar, Sebastian de, 78
Biedma, Luys Hernandez de, 141, 194, 213, 242, 248, 275
Bison, 125, 180, 245
Bloodhounds, 25, 135-6, 161, 181, 231
Blue Ridge Mountains, 196

INDEX

INDEX

30; expects to be replaced by De Sosa, 32; annoyed by the activities of González, 33; has trouble with his lieutenant Córdoba, 37; executes summary justice upon him, 40; sells out his share in the Peruvian expedition, 47; Oviedo's criticism, 118, 119, 120, 121, 138
Pedro (Indian guide), 175, 181, 188
Pensacola Bay, 173, 174, 176, 217
Peru, 22, 44; Pizarro sails in search of, 45-6; Panama colonists sceptical about Peruvian wealth, 47; description of sea-coast of, 48, 49, 52; local chieftains, 56; civil war, 58; roads, 61; fortresses, *ibid.*; lack of wheel and arch, *ibid.*; llamas, *ibid.*; osier-bridges, 61-2; architecture, 62; levier of taxes, 63; Virgins of the Sun, 63-4; Inca domination, 64-5; religion, 65; the veneration of the Inca as the Child of the Sun, 66; his marriage to his sister, *ibid.*; Inca superiority to other tribes, 80; a Peruvian temple, 91-2; a Peruvian feast, 110-11.
Persecution, religious, 6-7
Peter Martyr (Peter Martyr de Anghera), 16, 33-4, 172
Piache, 205
Pickett, A. J., 190
Pigs, 136, 159, 183, 220, 223-4, 231
Pineda, Alonzo Alvarez de, 123
Pizarro, Francisco, a *ranchero*, 15; leads army against Urraca, 25-7; arrests Balboa, 29; birth and early life, 44; migrates to La Española, *ibid.*; goes to Darien with Balboa, *ibid.*; plans conquest of Peru, *ibid.*; gains backers, *ibid.*; first adventures, 46; makes new contract, 47; secures services of Ruiz, *ibid.*; sails again for Peru, 48; on Gallo Island, 49; is ordered by Rios to return, *ibid.*; refuses to leave Gallo, 50; crosses with his companions to Gorgona Island, *ibid.*; sustains spirits of his men, 51; reaches Tumbez, 52; goes to Spain, *ibid.*; interviews Charles V, *ibid.*; returns to Panama with his brothers, 53; is deserted by Almagro, *ibid.*; is joined by De Soto, *ibid.*; lands at

Coaque, 55; crosses to Puna, 56; and goes to mainland, 57; hears of Peruvian civil war, 58; and of Cuzco's wealth, *ibid.*; disappoints De Soto, 59-60; prepares to march inland, 60; enters Caxamarca, 71; disposes his forces, 77-8; sends message to Atahualpa, 79; orders attack, 83; captures the Inca, 85; shows humanity to prisoners, 88; closes with Atahualpa's offer of ransom, 90; distributes the spoils, 96; hears of Huascar's murder, 97-8; has Atahualpa executed, 102; mourns him, 103; bitterly reproached by De Soto, *ibid.*; appoints Toparca Inca, 105; reproves De Soto's rashness, 109; makes Manco Inca, 110-11; quarrels again with Almagro, 113; reconciliation effected, 114-15; final breach with Almagro, 121; his difficulty in obtaining recruits, 128; De Soto expected to eclipse his exploits, 129; his possession of interpreters, 145; his example followed by De Soto, 155; his assassination, 237-8
Pizarro Gonzalo (Father of the *Conquistadores*), 44
Pizarro, Gonzalo, 53, 60
Pizarro, Hernando, 53, 59, 60, 71-6, 78, 79, 85, 89, 90-2, 93, 95, 96, 99, 118, 131, 237
Pizarro, Juan, 53, 60, 114
Pizarro, Martín, 53, 56
Pizarro, Pedro, 42, 53, 56, 68, 78, 83, 109, 111, 114
Pocahontas, 149
Ponce de León, Hernán, 23, 42, 59, 114-15, 121, 137-8, 261
Ponce de León, Juan, 122, 136
Porcallo de Figueroa, Vasco, 134-5, 140, 142, 156-8
Portuguese contingent, The, 129, 130, 272
Prescott, William H., viii, 1
Priestley, Herbert I., viii
Protector of the Indians, The, 9
Puna, Island of, 56, 69, 100

Quechua language, 101
Quevedo, Juan de (Bishop of Darien), 29
Quigaltam, 256-7, 275-6

INDEX